THE
WORLD
IN OUR
HEARTS

The Life Story of
YWAM Missionaries
Alan & Fay Williams

ISBN: 0-9645458-0-2
Library of Congress Catalog Card Number: 95-90115

THE WORLD IN OUR HEARTS

The Life Story of YWAM Missionaries Alan & Fay Williams

By Fay Williams

with Meredith Puff Hofmann

Foreword by Don Stephens

Williams Publishing Co.
Kailua-Kona, Hawaii

*Dedicated to the memory of my husband, Alan Williams,
who loved and served God with
all his heart, mind, soul and strength,
and to our daughter Joy, sons Samuel and Stephen,
and their families.*

*To you we pass on an inheritance — one of making an impact on
the nations for Jesus Christ. You may carry the torch differently than
Dad and I, but we pass it with confidence into your hands.
Run the race and run well.*

Foreword

Having wealth and acclaim is the common definition of greatness, but I would define it as following the example of Jesus, by whom all other greatness is measured. Few are the occasions in life when we associate with those bordering on that kind of greatness, and I've had that privilege more than most. Alan and Fay Williams are in that category.

I worked closely with Alan and Fay in the development of YWAM's flagship, the M/V Anastasis. Alan was, and Fay continues to be, key contributors in the founding of what is now the Mercy Ships ministry of Youth With A Mission.

A ministry is born primarily in prayer and intercession, and more than once we discovered Alan down in a lower hold in the bowels of the ship, calling on God for the founding of this vital ministry. Fay also, through intercession, writing, music, and worship, was a key contributor.

This book weaves the launching of the ship ministry into their own personal life story. As I read it, many memories came back to me. I wept with them, rejoiced with them, and felt even closer to them. You may be tempted to think it's a story prematurely interrupted by what many of us would call an early home-going. However, I'm certain God views it from another perspective.

I highly recommend this book to all who are interested in the life of a prophet/evangelist, which I considered Alan to be. It's hard for me to ascertain whether he was more one or the other, and I think that's a good indication he was a blend of both.

As you read it, I believe you will be challenged to a radical expression of your faith. You will admire Alan for his relentless commitment to follow Jesus at any cost. You will admire Fay for her perseverance, prayer, and for hanging onto the word of the Lord for the change and wholeness she sought for the man she loved and the family they led.

Many stories of the beginning days of the M/V Anastasis are still untold, but if the story were recounted by each of the 350 or so involved, we would have at least 350 perspectives of the critical first five years of the ship. This book tells the story through the eyes of Alan and Fay. It's a good perspective, and it's accurate.

People who visit one or more of YWAM's Mercy Ships now will quickly see the development and maturity of the ministry. Evangelism is still center-stage, but we have added many styles of evangelism that are aptly suited for this unique hospital ship that pulls into the neediest ports of the world.

These are our roots. I hope you enjoy them.

Don Stephens
President/Chief Executive Officer
Mercy Ships
A Ministry of Youth With A Mission

Acknowledgments

With love and appreciation:

• To the godly men and women who molded, encouraged and believed in Alan and me in the early days of our walk with God, particularly George Brenner, former director of Open Air Campaigners of New Zealand; the late Alfred Greenway, principal of the Bible Training Center in New Zealand; and Jim and Joy Dawson, beloved friends, mentors and co-workers in the Gospel.

• To the leaders of Youth With A Mission with whom we have worked so closely over the years, notably YWAM Founder and President Loren Cunningham and his wife Darlene; Don Stephens, president of YWAM Mercy Ships, and his wife Deyon; Wally and Norma Wenge of YWAM's Gleanings for the Hungry; and the rest of the founding leadership team of Mercy Ships, including Captain Ben and Helen Applegate, David and Linda Cowie, Mark and Eva Spengler, and Jack and Myrna Hill.

• To the thousands of YWAMers who worked alongside us as we pioneered ventures on the Maori, the M/V Anastasis, the M/V Good Samaritan, and what is now the Kona campus of the University of the Nations.

• To the many who over the years supported Alan's and my ministry through prayer and giving. This too is your story.

• To Alan's family and mine, who never stood in the way of our radical lifestyle, even though it meant years of separation.

• To Meredith Puff Hofmann, who helped to rewrite the initial manuscript and co-labored with me on this project for many months, and to Scott and Sandi Tompkins, who edited the book into its final form and gave much insight and encouragement. To Chris Cook for the typesetting and photos; and to the staff of Art Lab (Media Plus) for designing the cover.

• To Bob Fitts and the University of the Nations' Worship Department staff, who believed in this project and stood with me during times of discouragement.

• And finally and most significantly, I thank my God, whose awesome love, exhibited in the death of His son Jesus, brought Alan and me out of darkness and into the light, producing a quality and purpose of life we never dreamed possible.

The Athens Three – Alan Williams, Costas Macris, Don Stephens.

1

On Trial

The overcrowded Athens courtroom was stifling hot, with no movement in the stale air. With every seat taken, spectators pushed and shoved to keep hard-won pieces of standing room. The air buzzed with indistinguishable Greek words, fluctuating between loud whispers and excited shouting, and the chaos pressed in on my raw nerves.

At least tonight I had a seat near the front. A few nights before, I couldn't even get near the front to view the proceedings, and I was the wife of one of the accused. The appeals trial was front-page news all across Greece and had attracted media attention worldwide. The good thing about this notoriety was that it had prompted thousands of Christians to rally behind my husband, Alan Williams, and his friends, Don Stephens and Costas Macris.

I still couldn't understand how these dedicated Christian leaders could be on trial like common criminals. Yet just 18 months earlier, a Greek court had convicted them on charges of proselytizing a minor. They now faced a three-and-a-half-year prison sentence for the "crime" of giving a New Testament to a 16-year-old boy who was eager to hear about Jesus Christ.

Their appeal trial was now in its fourth day, and growing more tense by the hour. Because Alan and I had lived in Greece for three years, we were used to their customs, but the courtroom activity was pushing me to the brink emotionally. Just yesterday Alan had used all the strength of his five-foot-seven frame to push through the crush of people so we could visit the restroom. To our dismay, returning into the courtroom looked even more impossible. But Alan responded with characteristic humor.

"Hey! Excuse me!" he yelled with his street preacher's voice, motioning our need to get through for those who didn't speak English. "I am on trial – could you let me through?"

The nearest people laughed heartily, but we still had no pathway. At last Alan grabbed my hand and bulldozed through, pulling me after him.

Even with all the difficulties it presented for us, it was hard to be upset with this disorderly crowd. Most of them were born-again believers belonging to various denominations, minority groups in a country where Greek Orthodoxy had dominated the culture for centuries. Their eyes were full of misgivings. Would the long-awaited verdict give them new freedom to evangelize in their country without fear of persecution? Or would they be even more limited in their expression of the Gospel?

Nearly three tension-packed hours had passed since the three judges secluded themselves in chambers to arrive at a verdict. There was no jury in this system. Time seemed to be on hold while we waited for their decision.

Questions nagged at my mind. Would Alan be taken to prison in a few more hours? How could a government known for centuries as the birthplace of democracy now limit such a basic right as religious freedom? It was hard to fathom – but our Greek lawyers were interpreting the long recess as ominous to our cause.

Don Stephens, leader of the Mercy Ships ministry, now stood

near the front speaking to some Greek pastors. The trial had brought together church leaders who otherwise would never have met or even spoken, and Don was taking advantage of that to exhort them to greater unity. His wife, Deyon, sat near me in a pensive mood. If Don went to prison, for her it meant raising four children alone, including one mentally and physically disabled child. But Deyon was as strong in spirit as anyone I've ever known, and she was obviously willing to pay the price. She and Don together led the Mercy Ships ministry of Youth With A Mission (YWAM, pronounced why-wam), an international, interdenominational missions organization. Over the years, Alan and I had worked closely with Don and Deyon and the rest of the team, together seeking to launch a new ministry where ships would serve the nations by giving practical relief as well as the message of the Gospel. We now had two ships, the M/V Anastasis and the M/V Good Samaritan, which were regularly carrying food, medicines, building supplies and the good news of Jesus to needy nations. As we had worked together to see this dream come to pass, Don and Deyon had not only earned our highest respect, but had become like family to us.

I looked over to the dark, dynamic Greek evangelist Costas Macris, the head of the Hellenic Missionary Society who was once a missionary in Irian Jaya. Because of his relationship with us, Costas was now also accused in the trial. I watched as he vigorously moved about the front of the courtroom, talking excitedly and loving every minute of the challenge. In contrast, his attractive wife, Alky, sat quietly composed in the seat in front of me as she tended to the two youngest of their six children. Her dark brown eyes radiated an inner strength and I imagined she was praying constantly. What a close family they were! I loved and respected them.

Though it was only my husband Alan, the ship's evangelist, who had actually given young Kostas Kotopoulos a New Testament, both Don and Costas willingly stood trial with him. Don was held responsible for the ship being in Greece and Costas was charged because he was the leader of the evangelical youth group the boy attended. Despite the seriousness of their situation, jokes abounded among the three about which one was the real culprit.

All three expected to go to jail, but we all prayed for a lighter sentence from this appeal. Thousands of letters and signed petitions had come in to support the so-called "Athens Three" and they were piled desk high at the front of the courtroom.

I wrapped myself again in the comfort of Jesus' words in John 19:11 (NIV) that became like scaffolding to my emotions: "You would have no power over me if it were not given to you from above," Jesus had said to Pilate at His own trial. In the same way, I had to believe our three men were not victims of the Greek judicial system but that God, the Highest Judge of all, was in control. If He deemed a time in prison to be fruitful, perhaps providing a catalyst for greater religious freedom in Greece, then we had counted the cost and were ready.

The painting hanging on the dingy wall behind the judges' bench caught my attention. It portrayed Christ with a crown of thorns on his head. As I viewed the agony on his face, my own resolve grew stronger. The prospect of imprisonment, separation and further persecution were harsh realities, but Jesus had suffered so much more than we ever would.

Joy, our 24-year-old daughter, stood nearby talking to an old friend, and I thought again how like Alan she was. Joy and her husband, Rob, served on staff for Youth With A Mission in Hong Kong, and I was so thankful she could be with us now.

Stephen, our youngest, was 19, and had that morning boarded a bus to return to England. None of us thought the trial would last this long, and when Stephen was obligated to return to work, he wept in Alan's arms.

"I don't want you to go to prison Dad," he said through tears. "But if it's God's will, I accept it."

Samuel, 21, had been unable to leave his responsibilities in Hong Kong, where he also served on YWAM staff, but he anxiously awaited news of the trial.

No matter what happened in the next few hours, I knew I didn't have to worry about our three grown children. I was so thankful that all three had a firm faith in God, and were very supportive of their dad. Growing up with the belief that God always came first now helped them accept God's hand on our lives.

Alan, removing himself from a lengthy conversation with a Greek pastor, now pushed his way over and claimed the recently vacated seat beside me.

"If we think this is tense, imagine what it must feel like to wait for the verdict at a murder trial," he said with a sigh. His small blue eyes looked weary and I noticed the chiseled tension lines etched in his deeply tanned face. Twenty hours on trial in this heat had taken its toll, and tonight he looked every bit his 52 years. Being forced to sit so long on those straight wooden chairs at the defendants' table was trial enough for this human dynamo I had married 24 years ago.

What a life we'd had! Certainly this was the most difficult obstacle in our lives, but it was by no means the first. As I looked into Alan's eyes, my heart was warmed with love.

"How did we get 'ere?" I said, dropping my "h" to mimic his Liverpool accent. It was an old family joke we used in unexpected or difficult situations. Alan rolled his eyes and held his hands upturned, copying a Greek gesture that amused him.

"Don't ask me!" he said.

I chuckled and shook my head when I thought how familiar that joke had become. We were no strangers to adversity, not at all – and we had come so far...

Alan preaching on OAC platform as Fay looks on.

2

Then Jesus Came

Only someone who knew his dark past could understand the divine irony of Alan being on trial for his Christian witness. Alan grew up in the tough industrial city of Liverpool, England, and he became as rough as his environment there. He lived recklessly and his lifestyle often triggered conflicts with his Father. By age 17, Alan eagerly left home – first to join the army, then to immigrate to New Zealand, then off to sea on a merchant ship.

His life away from Liverpool grew even worse as he plunged into a life of drunkenness, brawling and immorality. I was thankful I never saw that side of Alan's life. The first time I saw him was on a brisk fall evening in 1959. I had just hurried from my nurse's trainee job at St. Helen's Hospital in Auckland, New Zealand, so I could join in a Sunday night evangelistic street meeting. Our group from the interdenominational Open Air Campaigners (OAC) went to parks, beaches, factories or anyplace else we could share the Gospel with a crowd.

These Sunday night meetings were the highlight of my week. I thoroughly enjoyed sharing the Gospel with people who never darkened the doorway of a church. Most of all, I loved sharing the Gospel through singing Gospel songs and playing my accordion.

As I joined the back of the crowd, I saw the singing was over. Our leader began announcing that a young English seaman named Alan Williams was to share his testimony. I stretched up on my toes to catch a glimpse of this newcomer, and could just see his head bobbing above the crowd.

Taking his place on the platform, he looked to me like a typical English seaman, dressed in a leather jacket and jeans and sporting the slightly longer sideburns most merchant seaman wore. Although he wasn't very tall, his olive complexion, chiseled jaw and mischievous blue eyes quickly drew my attention. I was also charmed by his thick Liverpool accent.

"My life was radically changed by an experience I 'ad in my 'otel room six months ago," he proclaimed. "I came out to this country seeking a new life, an escape from the 'urts of my past – but after a short time I found I was in a downward spiral, both spiritually and morally. I was drinking so much, I would black out and not know what I'd done or 'ow I got back to my ship."

The sizable crowd seemed glued to the pavement…and so was I! This man was magnetic, a powerful communicator. He was so intense, every part of him was caught up in what he was saying.

"One morning I was in a 'otel room when my ship was laid up for repair," he continued. "I 'ad a shocking 'angover, you know – champagne at night and real pain in the morning!"

He laughed and we all joined in. I could tell the crowd liked him because he spoke their language without Christian cliches.

"I was often violent when drunk," he went on. "Sometimes I couldn't remember what I'd done the night before and it frightened me. I wondered if I'd 'urt anyone. Just then I 'eard church bells nearby, and I began asking myself some questions: Where 'ave I come from? Why am I 'ere? And where am I going? I wondered if I went to church, maybe I could turn over a new leaf!"

Alan's eyes swept over the crowd as he looked boldly into our faces. "I got dressed and walked to the nearest church, but finding no service, I just entered the empty church and knelt down to pray. I thought the church would fall in on a sinner as bad as me." Laughter rippled through the crowd.

"I prayed, 'Lord, if you're real, please 'elp me find the right way to go in life. Please show me the truth to all these religions in the world.' " He went on to explain that exactly one week later he entered a small cafe where he took the only available seat – next to an elderly New Zealand Maori gentleman.

The man had a large, black Bible on his lap and he used it to explain the Gospel to Alan. Then only moments after the two parted, another man stepped out of the shadows to press a tract into his hand. Tears formed in Alan's eyes as he recounted how he read the tract later in bed.

"I want you to know, friends – God answered the prayer I prayed in that church a week before," he said tenderly. "As I was reading, my eyes fell on these words: 'I am the way, the truth, and the life; no man comes to the Father but by me.' I couldn't believe it! 'ere was God telling me the truth wasn't in a religion – 'e was the truth. There wasn't a right way – 'e was the way!

"I threw myself down at the side of my bed and told God I was sorry for leaving 'im out of my life all these years. For the first time, I realized that Jesus died for me."

Now the young seaman stretched out his hand to the crowd. "Did you know 'e died for you?" he said soberly. "Come and receive Christ for yourself! Your life can be transformed like mine!"

People began to move up toward the front to answer the invitation, and my mouth fell open. It had been a while since more than one or two had responded at our meetings.

Deeply stirred, I offered a spontaneous prayer from deep down inside me. "Lord, I want to marry a man like that – a man with fire and zeal, so we can serve you together all of our days!"

My life had been as much a miracle as Alan's. For most of my early life I had been paralyzed by feelings of inferiority and fear. Those feelings were no doubt rooted in my parents' troubled marriage and in the ugly incident that so shook my life as a small child.

I will never forget being awakened by foul, alcoholic breathing hovering over me in the dark. I was petrified as I felt rough lips slobbering on my mouth, and hands touching me where by instinct I knew they shouldn't.

"Don't tell anyone or you'll be in real trouble!" came a deep raspy voice I didn't recognize. Even after he was gone I was too terrified to move. I buried this dark secret down deep inside me, telling no one. It wasn't until a few years later, when I was about seven, that I heard that raspy voice again.

"How about if I take Fay on a vacation to meet my nieces?" the man said to my parents. The terror of that night resurfaced as I realized the phantom from the dark was a friend of my father. A few days later I huddled next to the bus window in fear as we rode out to the country to visit his relatives. The next evenings were filled with the same fearful violations and threats, although he never caused me physical pain. It was then I concluded that there must be something very bad about me for these things to happen.

After that trip, the man completely disappeared from my world, but fearful nightmares took his place. I would sometimes awaken on the floor with my heart racing and a stark terror that there was some dark, ugly thing out to get me.

That same year, my parents' marriage broke up, and I began escaping into a private fantasy world. One of my favorite pastimes was to spin my wiry body around and around on the lawn by the hedge of pink roses, until I could spin no more. Finally throwing myself down flat on my back, I panted as I watched the sky spin until all was still again. Then as I stared at those white fluffy clouds, they became people, animals, and far-away cities. I daydreamed of going where everything was peaceful, safe and happy.

The reality was that my life was anything but peaceful and

happy. When my parents separated and Mom moved out of our suburban Auckland home with me and my two sisters, it did end some of our domestic strife, but I was totally unprepared for the other struggles that would follow. My insecurities mounted while my grades at school plunged. I soon began to hate school, but more than that, I hated my life.

We moved back in with Dad a few months later, but their marriage only grew worse. By the time I turned 11, it was over for good. My mother left us with Dad this time and moved out alone.

My father turned to alcohol as an escape, and rowdy parties in our house often kept us up late at night. Dad was a good singer, and when he wanted to entertain people, he would drag me out of bed in the early hours of the morning to sleepily accompany him at the piano in my play-by-ear fashion. Next we would put on our ape skit routine, making everyone laugh. In spite of the inner numbing pain I now carried with me continually, those times with my dad were special and I loved him dearly.

Sometimes he came home in the wee hours of the morning, drunk and depressed. Coming into my room, he sobbed beside my bed and poured out all the pain he felt when our mother left us. Feeling helpless, I tried to comfort him, but it only added to my own hurt and confusion. It seemed he should be comforting me – but he couldn't.

As soon as I could – at the age of 15 – I dropped out of school, glad to be free from the place of such heartache. I still lived at home with my father, and soon found a job as a seamstress in a large workroom. But my real desire was to become a nurse – I wanted to have a job helping people.

In a way that dream seemed impossible because of my fears and excessive shyness. My only real social outlet was in trips to the local swimming club. It was there that I met a tall, kind-eyed blond fellow who seemed almost as shy as me. He began trying to make friends with me, and one day he mustered the courage to say, "Would you like to go to a beach party with my church youth group?"

The word "church" had always conjured up images of people who were boring and strict, but my new friend was none of these. "All right," I agreed.

I looked forward to the evening in anticipation, and I wasn't disappointed. The night was filled with fun and laughter as the large group sat around a big bonfire. They sang songs and some of them told how God had helped them. Looking around the circle, I thought how kind and pleasant these people seemed. They were obviously different from my co-workers, who told coarse jokes, stayed in cliques, and competed with each other for favor with the boss.

Afterward, several of the girls came over to me. "Would you like to attend the upcoming Youth Camp at Easter?" they said. After such a fun evening I thought I would enjoy it, so I agreed.

When I asked my father for permission, he laughed, and said, "Watch out, you might get saved." I had only heard that word used in a derogatory way, but I figured that whatever it meant, it was worth the risk.

Again I was welcomed by the girls the moment I stepped on the bus. The campground was located near an Auckland beach called Block House Bay. That evening, we all crowded into a large tent to sing songs and listen to someone talk about God. I noticed a smaller tent nearby which everyone called "the place of prayer," and it sounded kind of spooky to me. Only later would I learn that the small tent contained some dedicated people who were praying, among other requests, for the new teenage girl who wasn't yet a Christian.

Meetings were held each evening and games and sports events during the day. The songs they sang were so different from any I had heard before. The words played over and over in my head.

By Easter Sunday, I began to experience strange, powerful emotions which I didn't understand. I became desperate for the kind of happiness these church people had. That afternoon, I passed by the large tent where two of my newfound girlfriends were practicing a duet for our special evening service. Suddenly I began to choke with tears, as the words of their song pierced my heart:

> It was His love for me,
> That nailed Him to the tree,
> To die in agony, for all my sin,
> For my own guilt and blame,
> The great Redeemer came,
> Willing to bear the shame,
> Of all my sin…

Embarrassed, I ran to a secluded place among the trees and let the sobs come. What was happening? I didn't understand it. After spending a troubled afternoon, I dragged myself to the evening meeting with confused thoughts swirling in my head. I was so different from the people here. What if they knew my past, the times I'd been molested? I was sure that if they knew I came from a broken home, they probably wouldn't want to be my friend anymore.

As the singing started, I began to settle down. Then a film of the Easter story was shown, and I watched in awe as the story of Jesus Christ was portrayed before me. He was so kind and loving. When cruel men began mistreating him and nailing him onto a wooden cross, I was deeply moved. I suddenly realized the film was portraying the same subject as the song that had so moved me a few hours earlier, that Jesus gave His life so people wouldn't have to die for their own sins.

Afterward my friends began singing the sweet melody again up on the platform, and I could hardly bear it. All my life I had looked for secure love, for someone who really cared. Was this Jesus the one?

"If you want to give your life to Jesus, the one who died on the cross for you," a man was now saying, "I invite you now to make a public confession of it by standing to your feet."

Suddenly the old familiar fear gripped my pounding heart. Oh, I wanted to know this Jesus so badly – but to stand in front of all these people? I just couldn't!

All at once I felt a force stronger than my fear pulling me to my feet. I felt as if Jesus were calling me, holding out His nail-pierced hands to me. Leaving my seat, I walked down the grassy aisle to the front, as if Jesus were right there in front of me. The people forgotten, I knew then that I wanted to serve Jesus and follow Him the rest of my life. I basked in His love, aware that something special was happening.

After the meeting a kind lady shared several Bible verses with me about my new salvation, and instructed me to read the Bible myself every day and pray. "And don't forget, go home and tell your parents what you've done," she said.

"Oh no!" I thought, dreading my father's reaction, but I knew she was right. I had to tell him. Most of all, I didn't want to lose the joy that I felt flooding into my heart.

When I got home, Dad was hungover and bleary eyed, but he asked me right away how the weekend had gone.

"I...got saved," I blurted out awkwardly, not at all what I planned to say. After a moment of surprise, he burst into as much of a laugh as his aching head would allow. When he saw the expression on my face as I stood beside the bed, he stopped and stared at me in a strange silence.

"Good night, Dad," I said as I kissed him on his forehead.

"Good night," he answered thoughtfully, and I turned and went to my room.

Flopping down on my bed, I felt the courage of a moment ago drain out of me. I wasn't afraid of Dad, it just seemed that what had happened to me was so foreign to his world. I didn't want my new faith to put a wedge between us, but at least I had told him!

Now my eyes traced the walls of my room, this place where fearful nightmares had plagued me as long as I could remember. Even though I was now 16, I still feared someone might come through the large window beside my bed. As I began to unpack my bag from camp, I couldn't help wishing for the safety and comfort I'd felt at camp. Why couldn't it have lasted forever?

I thought of all the fun I'd had and the new friends I'd made, and an overwhelming loneliness engulfed me. Wasn't it supposed to be different now? Suddenly, the words of the lady at camp came back to me.

"Fay, Jesus is in your heart now," she had told me. "He will never leave you, and He'll be with you everywhere you go."

Wow! If that were true, then Jesus was here now, right in this room. A peaceful feeling settled over me and somehow everything seemed brighter. As I turned off the light, the loneliness gradually subsided, and my heart was warmed with a soft glow.

"Thank you, Lord Jesus, thank you for being with me," I whispered. My life would never be the same again.

Fay and Alan in the 1950s.

3
BOY MEETS GIRL

A few months later I heard that Alan Williams was giving up his sea life to be a full-time worker in Open Air Campaigners. I was still a volunteer worker, and soon I was working beside Alan in the street meetings. We noticed our singing voices blended well, and began singing duets for the crowds.

I was deeply attracted to Alan's intensity of love for Christ, which was evident in everything he did. I learned from his friend that Alan rose at 4:30 each morning to pray, and while the rest of our team sang, joked, or talked trivia on our way to meetings in our van, Alan always spent the time learning Bible verses on little cards. He once told me he'd wasted so much time reading trashy books as a seaman that he now wanted to fill his mind with God's Word. I was impressed, and as time went on, I found myself developing strong feelings for this young Englishman.

At the same time, I was torn with guilt because I was already engaged to another man. For the first time I understood I was not really in love with my fiance. Because I'd come from a broken home, I desperately wanted to marry to belong and have my own family. Alan's life now challenged me with a greater desire for God, and I realized my whole motivation for marriage was to seek security.

With this surprising revelation came the realization that I had to break my engagement. Although I tried to put it off, after a few weeks I knew God required it of me. My fiance lived in another town, so I wrote him a letter, explaining why I thought I needed to break the engagement. He was shocked and soon came to try to change my mind. Friends from church were also upset by my decision, and warned that I was making a big mistake. I was so afraid of hurting these people and couldn't bear their rejection – yet deep inside I knew I had to make the break. The tug-of-war raged inside me for weeks. I was so nervous I couldn't eat. Would I follow God or man?

At last I sat down to write him again, this time making it final. I knew he was deeply hurt, and I was still afraid of the reaction of our church friends. So many people had been excited for us and had shown their generous support – but I knew God wanted me to go a different way.

I continued to pour out my heart to God and wanted desperately for Him to speak a word of confirmation to me. One evening as I was reading my Bible, a verse seemed to leap out at me in Jeremiah 1:8 : "Be not afraid of their faces; for I am with thee to deliver thee, saith the Lord." All at once I was aware of God's presence in the room, and I knew it was a word from Him. Over the next days, as I stood my ground against those who disagreed with my decision, this verse was a constant comfort. Then, a few nights later when I walked back to the nurses' dorm in the dark, another verse I had recently read in Isaiah 41:13 popped into my mind: "For I, the Lord thy God, will hold thy right hand, saying unto thee, fear not; I will help thee."

Making sure no one was behind me, I looked up at the starry sky. In a childlike way, I reached out my hand to grasp the hand of this God who was becoming so intimate with me.

"God, if I can better serve you by being single, I am willing never to marry," I prayed out loud as I walked. That night, I dedicated myself afresh to be a missionary. Letting my active imagination run wild, I pictured myself wading through African rivers with leeches sucking at my legs — but even if that were to happen I knew inside it all would be worth it to serve this great God.

I still mistakenly thought God liked people to suffer so they would be holy, and only had an inkling about the goodness of God's character — but despite my fears, I'd prayed the prayer now, and I really was willing to do what God had for me.

For me the next step was going to Bible School in nearby Hamilton, New Zealand. Even though I was almost 21, I knew now that I wasn't ready for marriage yet. I still found myself attracted to Alan, but I had given up the idea of anything happening between us. I thought God had simply used the situation to lead me to break off my engagement and go to Bible School.

But one day as I was packing my belongings, a friend stopped by my dorm room with some shocking news — Alan had been told of my affection for him. More embarrassing was his reaction.

"Not Fay," he had said. "She's just a really good friend, that's all." I was so upset! How could I ever face him again? I had only confided in one person of my feelings for Alan and would never have wanted him to find out.

The next time we were part of a street meeting together, I tried to avoid him, but afterward he called me aside.

"I think we need to talk," he said quietly, motioning for us to take a walk up Queen Street. He asked about my plans for Bible School, and seemed genuinely happy for me. We stopped to sit on a park bench and after a nervous moment he said, "Look, I 'eard about 'ow you feel about me, and I want to tell you I think you're such a nice person, but...I just don't feel anything romantically toward you. I mean, you're like a special sister, and I love working with you, but..."

I fiddled with my fingers in agony. "I know that," I almost

snapped. "I'm really sorry you were told – it wasn't my idea." Now my cheeks were burning and I broke my eyes from his intense gaze. After a moment I looked up again to see him grinning at me. He turned serious again as he swept his hand out toward the stars.

"Listen Fay, I'll tell you one thing – if God meant you for me, and me for you, nothing will keep us apart, nothing!" He was emphatic now. "And I know whatever the future 'olds, God's got big things for both of us!"

I could barely see his silhouette now in the darkness, but he swung round to face me. "If God ever does anything, I'll let you know!" he said. "I mean…if 'e changes my feelings for you."

Now I was mad! This wasn't how it happened in the movies! "If God ever did anything" – that was really unique! If and when I did marry, I surely didn't want someone to tell me God had made them love me! My thoughts were racing, but I said nothing.

Then, into the silence, Alan began to commit our future to the Lord in prayer. Then his baritone voice pierced the night in song with the words of a familiar hymn:

> God holds the key of all unknown, and I am glad,
> What if some other should hold the key,
> Or if He trusted it to me,
> I might be sad – I might be sad.

I looked at his silhouette in surprise. I hadn't thought of hymns as romantic, but now my heart swelled with emotion. I would be going to Bible School soon, and I felt sad to think I wouldn't be singing with this Liverpool seaman anymore.

He went on:

> What if tomorrow's cares were here, without its rest,
> I'd rather He unlock the day,
> And as the hours roll open say,
> Thy will is best – Thy will is best.

As the final strains ended, I had to agree — God's will was exactly what I wanted. We said a friendly goodbye with a handshake, and that was that.

A week later, just before I was about to leave for Bible School, I went to say goodbye to the OAC team at the Auckland train station where they were departing for New Zealand's South Island for an outreach campaign. Alan had decided to go with the team at the last minute, and I was surprised to see him.

"Well, I may never see you again," I said. I held out my hand to shake his, and his gaze met mine.

"It's been great working with you," he said with a quick smile. "God bless you Fay. I just know God's got great things for you."

As their train pulled out, he turned to wave, his eyes revealing that cheeky, mischievous twinkle. When I could no longer see him, I turned to go, and wondered if I ever would see him again.

On the way back, I stopped off at a lovely mountain spot called Mount Eden. It was a prominent landmark in Auckland and was the place I often went as a child when I needed to get away and think. I climbed a short distance and found a secluded place under a bushy oak tree.

"Lord," I prayed, "I put my feelings for Alan Williams on the altar. I trust you to take them away from me so I can now concentrate on what You have for me."

As Abraham had done with Isaac, I made a plunging movement with my hands, as if to knife all my feelings lying there on the altar. I meant it with all my heart, and I felt a heaviness lift off me. As I began walking back down the mountain road, I had a new march in my step. I was free!

But by the time I reached to the bottom, I couldn't help wondering how successful God would be at getting Alan Williams out of my mind and heart.

Fay and Alan at Bible Training Center, Hamilton, N.Z. 1950s.

4

I Think God is Doing Something!

I could scarcely take it in – here I was, sitting at my own desk as a student at the Bible Training Center in the beautiful Waikato River area! Although I'd already been here three months, I was still in awe.

I had dreamed of going to Bible school almost ever since I'd found the Lord at 16, but I knew my limited education disqualified me from attending the one in Auckland. It wasn't until January, 1960, when I attended a retreat where Dr. Alfred Greenway was the guest speaker that my dream was rekindled.

In his 50s, with thinning gray hair and blue eyes, Dr. Greenway was every inch the scholarly gentleman. Dressed plainly in a gray pinstriped suit and minister's collar, his round figure and rosy cheeks accompanied a loving and pleasant manner. During the retreat, I hung on every word as, in a marvelous Welsh accent, he presented eloquent messages on the empowerment of the Holy Spirit, going verse by verse through each Bible passage. As I listened, I was astounded by his wisdom. Rising deep within me came an insatiable thirst for God's Word and a desire to be empowered by His Holy Spirit. How I longed to sit and learn from this man!

When Dr. Greenway announced he was beginning his own Bible School the very next month, my heart did a flip. I was just finishing my nurses' training, and was wondering what my next step toward the mission field would be.

Plucking up enough courage to speak with this man who was known as "Scholarship on Fire," I approached him and began pouring out my heart.

"I…I'm really interested in your Bible School," I stammered. Smiling, he put his hand on my shoulder and looked at me intently.

"From the first day I saw you here," he said gently, "the Lord whispered that I should ask you to be a student."

I was so overcome, tears sprang to my eyes. God had shown him that?

"Well…there is one big problem," I said through the tears. "I'm not very clever and I left school at 15."

"Well, my dear," he said reassuringly, handing me a large white handkerchief from his suit pocket, "for my school, you only have to be able to read and write and have a call from God! I felt the Lord tell me to run a school for young people just like you, who for whatever reason don't have as much education as others."

I pulled myself upright, mopping my eyes dry. "Oh, I can read and write well," I assured him.

"Well, then, why don't we pray together about it?"

As we bowed our heads and he began to pray, peace flooded my heart. Deep inside, I already knew God was guiding me to attend. Suddenly the love of God was brought home to me in a new way as I saw that God had created such a college for me. Even with my insecurities, I saw that the mission field wasn't only for the well-educated after all!

"We'll see you in February then," he said kindly. I felt so comfortable with him and my heart swelled with gratitude. I knew I had found a true spiritual father. When I tried to return the handkerchief, he motioned for me to keep it.

"I always carry one, just in case," he said with a twinkle in his eye.

Now that the Bible College was underway, we students had begun affectionately calling him "Doc." Each day, it was such a joy to feast from his great storehouse of wisdom. He made us work hard, with lectures each morning and working in the local community each afternoon to pay our rent and minimal school fees. Evenings were filled with study and assignments.

Besides the solid Bible knowledge Doc daily imparted to us, one of his greatest gifts was his belief in us. He and his sweet wife had no children of their own, and because she suffered with ill health, we didn't see her much – so it was as if we were Doc's kids. He affirmed us in all we did and I loved the school.

As the weeks went by, I continued throwing myself into classes and study. But even in my busy life, thoughts of Alan went around and around in my mind. How I missed the old days of our street work together!

My eyes often fell longingly on the scrappy old card propped on my bedside table which bore two Bible verses Alan had once written out for me: "I will instruct thee and teach thee in the way which thou shalt go; I will guide thee with mine eye. Be ye not like the horse, or like the mule, that have no understanding, whose mouth must be held in with bit and bridle, lest they come near unto thee." (Psalm 32:8-9)

The verse was such a reminder of Alan – I often laughed to myself that he was more like a horse raring to go than anyone else I knew. But I had to admit, Alan's barely legible left-handed scrawl was just as important to me as the verse, since it was a little bit of him I had left to keep.

I had been in Bible School about four months when the entire student body went to a little country town nearby for a church conference. One night at a prayer meeting in the church, I remembered Doc's teaching about the filling of the Holy Spirit. As I knelt before the Lord, once more I told Him I was so tired of the chains of fear and inferiority that still governed so much of my life.

"Lord, I want that power Doc told me about," I prayed. "I want to be free. Please, please fill me with your Holy Spirit!"

All around me people were singing softly, and in faith I raised my arms as if to receive this gift from God's hand. Suddenly, what felt like pins and needles rushed up my arms. I quickly lowered them only to find the feeling wouldn't leave. My head felt giddy and I felt like laughing.

"Jesus!" I murmured over and over, feeling a fresh love for Him inside my heart. All at once I began praising God in a loud voice, and for once I didn't care who heard. I just felt so good all over!

Then, all at once, the strangest language I had ever heard began coming out of my own mouth. Was I making it up? For a moment I stopped and tried to form the words with my mind, but nothing came out. Once I began praising Jesus again, the strange language poured from my lips. I was filled with overflowing joy!

"Hallelujah!" I shouted again, lost in His love and full of gratitude to the Lord. I felt so fresh and clean inside – the Holy Spirit had come to me as I asked.

Twenty minutes later, I walked out of the church with weak knees. As we stopped on the walkway, I joyfully told a friend what had happened to me as people began streaming past us. All at once I thought I overheard a bit of conversation that startled me. I tapped the nearby student on the arm.

"Excuse me, but what was that you said?" I interrupted.

"A new student arrived today," he repeated. "Seems he's an English seaman. Doc told him he could join if he caught up on the classes he's missed."

Only one English seaman could be at a Bible college at a small place like this! "Where is he now?" I asked eagerly.

"He just went into the meeting over in the church hall – it's about to start any minute," he shrugged. "If you hurry you may catch him. Do you know him?"

"I think so!" I called over my shoulder, already heading with my friend toward the hall. How could this be? I thought I'd never see him again. I was doing so well in my life, and now this! Even harder to deal with was the knowledge that only one empty seat remained in our classroom – the one next to me! How would I concentrate with Alan Williams sitting next to me in class?

As we went to the meeting hall, the intense joy I had felt at the church seemed to vanish. My friend and I took a seat near the middle, and my eyes began scanning the auditorium.

There was Alan sitting in the front row, already soaking in what the speaker had to say. I tried to put him out of my mind and listen, but it wasn't easy. After it was over, he spotted me and came up where I was standing outside.

"Hello, Fay, 'ow are you?" he said with a hint of humor in his eyes. My heart was thumping double time.

"Great," I said acting calm. "How did your outreach in the South Island go?"

As he went on to tell me with animated gestures about the harvest of lives newly converted to Christ, I stared at his angular jaw and expressive blue eyes. It was so good to see him again! Finally curiosity got the best of me.

"How did you get here?" I asked.

He smiled. "Well, I'd 'eard of Dr. Greenway from you and others, and when I prayed about the future, the Lord showed me I was to come under Doc's teaching for a year. Some friends in Auckland told me about this conference, so I thought I'd come here to see 'im," he ended with a shrug.

I stared at him, carefully hiding disappointment. So that was it? Nothing about us? Quickly excusing myself, I joined a friend nearby, but had trouble listening to the conversation. After the weekend when we assembled back in school, sure enough, there was Alan seated right next to me. I did my best to focus on the lectures, but as the weeks sped on, I decided God had brought

Alan there to build my character and deal with hidden sin as my personal thorn in the flesh! I handled the situation by teasing Alan unmercifully, to the point he began to call me his own thorn in the flesh – it was mutual.

"Pity the man who marries you," he teased me one day, and my heart skipped a beat, thorn or not.

But even with the difficulty of it, I was thriving in the Lord more than ever. I felt like blotting paper as Doc taught us, and sometimes wished his lectures would never stop. But I didn't realize how much God was setting me free until another church conference that our class attended in June.

The conference was held in my home city of Auckland, so I arranged to stay with my mother in Remuera, only a 20-minute drive away. The students were helping serve the other conference participants, and were also asked to give their testimonies to the crowd.

The third night, I was walking out onto the big stage in front of the largest attended meeting, when it suddenly hit me – I wasn't afraid! God had actually broken the chains that bound me for so many years! As I adjusted the microphone on the podium, I knew what I had to share.

"For as long as I can remember, I've been bound by the chains of fear," I proclaimed, feeling God's power helping me with the words. "I was so afraid as a child, I would sit in the dressing room for hours at the swimming pool, afraid to face the other children. Even as an adult, I shook with fear when I had to meet new people.

"But now tonight, I stand here as a testimony of God's miraculous power," I continued. "Even a few months ago, I could never have stood before you. God has truly set me free!

As I went on to explain how I'd come to the Lord and subsequently been empowered by the Holy Spirit, I could tell the people were listening intently. When at last I sat down, I was so elated I shook with delight. I thanked God for His precious Holy Spirit and His work in my life.

Being back in Auckland, I knew I needed to visit my elderly grandmother. It appeared my only chance would be the next night, when our class was doing street evangelism. Alan was asked to lead that night's street meeting, and of course I didn't want to miss it, but family loyalties were calling.

The next morning Alan came striding toward me with a strangely troubled look.

"Why weren't you at the street meeting last night?" he demanded. I had never seen him in this mood, and wasn't sure why I needed to report my whereabouts to him.

"I was visiting my Grandmother," I explained with a shrug. When I started to walk away, he grabbed my arm and stared at me intently.

"The meeting just didn't seem the same without you there," he said. Then his voice softened. "I missed you."

My stomach jumped. Alan Williams missed me? Speechless, I swallowed hard.

"Look, I think I'd better take you 'ome after tonight's meeting," he told me. "I need to share some things with you."

I nodded nervously, reminding him it was about a 20-minute drive to where I was staying with my mother. As we walked into the morning session together my mind was racing. What was he going to tell me? After that, it was a long day indeed!

Finally after the evening meeting ended, I climbed into the seat next to Alan in the small borrowed car. We drove in silence for most of the journey, and I didn't dare look sideways for fear the dream would end. Was this really happening?

At last we parked outside my mother's house and Alan turned off the lights. Only a distant street light illuminated us in the shadows. After long moments, Alan spoke.

"I think God is doing something," he said in the darkness. "I mean…I really did miss you at the meeting, and that's the first time I noticed it before.

"When I was away on outreach I even wrote to tell you I didn't think there would ever be anything between us, but somehow I couldn't remember your address, even though I knew it well. I don't know what to say – except I think God is doing something!"

My heart began beating faster. Wasn't this the part where the knight sweeps you up on his horse and tells you you're the only one for him? This English seaman sure was different! But, I had noticed that before!

Gingerly, Alan put his arm around me and drew me close. But rather than giving me the kiss I expected, he said, "Let's pray." I let out a deep sigh as he began. What else could I expect? Alan was always praying.

"Lord, I don't know what you've got in mind for us, but you know we are willing to do anything, anything at all," he prayed. We then committed our relationship to God. After Alan finished, we sat in silence for a few moments, enjoying the warmth of the moment. Could it be that this wonderful man was falling in love with me?

When it came time to say our goodbyes, I was amazed to find that it was almost midnight. I went into the house in such a daze. Sleep came with difficulty that night, and the next morning I awoke as if still dreaming. Rolling out of bed, I got down on my knees and turned to the One who was Master of my life.

"Oh, God, if you give me Alan Williams for a husband," I prayed in ridiculous abandon, "I'll praise you every day of my life for him!"

Jim Dawson, the late, well-known Maori evangelist Muri Thompson, Fay, Alan, Joy Dawson.(l. to r., back row). John Dawson and Gillian Dawson (front row).

5
Divine Surgery

The next morning I arrived for the final session of the confer–ence full of excitement. Alan would be speaking today! I found a seat in the large meeting hall and searched the platform to see Alan's small, sturdy frame sitting erect in anticipation. When my eyes found his, Alan raised his eyebrows in response. How handsome he looked! All eyes and ears were riveted on him as he rose and gave the crowd a penetrating challenge for missions.

During school, Alan had been working hard to shed his Liverpool accent so his preaching would be more effective, and in this sermon his diction was as clear as his message.

Soon after the closing prayer, Alan strode to my side. "Look what the Lord gave me this morning," he said with a smile. Flipping through his Bible to Proverbs 31, he pointed to verse 10 and handed it to me.

"Who can find a virtuous woman? For her price is far above ru-bies. The heart of her husband doth safely trust in her, so that he shall have no need of spoil." As I continued to read down to the end of the chapter, a soft glow warmed my heart. When I stopped and looked up at him, our eyes met.

"I believe God is saying you are the one for me," he said tenderly.

My heart leapt with joy at his words, but I also trembled with apprehension. The woman in Proverbs 31 sounded perfect — I could never be like that! My self esteem was still so low, I could hardly believe God had given Alan this passage to speak about me.

I knew I had to hear from the Lord myself. Later that night, while reading the Bible alone in my room, Jeremiah 32:39 leapt off the page: "And I will give them one heart, and one way, that they may fear me forever, for the good of them, and of their children after them."

"One heart and one way," I repeated aloud. The Lord was truly leading us together!

I could hardly believe this was happening to me. But it was no dream. Later that night Alan wrapped his arms around me, and kissed me tenderly. At his gentle touch, my skin tingled with excitement and my heart nearly burst with joy. In spite of my insecurities, I determined to be the best wife I could be for this special man.

From then on, Alan and I began studying together in the evenings, and he taught me new discipline in my study habits. Much to his chagrin, I often got the better marks on exams, but I knew that was largely due to my ability to express myself on paper. At last, life seemed to be truly wonderful and the future bright.

Then one frosty winter morning, after parking my bike outside the school, I rushed inside and greeted Alan warmly. To my surprise, his response was as cold as the frost. Sitting in class all morning, we didn't even speak. Finally by lunchtime, I had to know what was up.

"Alan," I began at last, "what have I done wrong?" "Nothing," he mumbled without looking up, until finally I walked away. I couldn't understand what was going on.

The next day I came to school in apprehension, only to discover he was his usual cheery self. Watching him joke and laugh with the other students, I was relieved — but there was a knot in my stomach. I was no stranger to rejection and a warning bell was ringing: more pain…more pain. How could I endure more pain, especially from this one with whom I was now so vulnerable?

As I suspected, that was only the start. One day Alan would act as if he hated me, and the next he'd be warm and loving. Although he was always full of nervous energy, his dark moods caused him to be edgy and uptight. I never knew which mood he would be in, and the recurring cycle began to tear me apart. What was left of my security was now raw and bleeding, and I knew I had to confront him.

When I could bear it no longer, I led Alan to a private spot by the Waikato River. As we settled into the shade of a willow tree, I tried to plan what I'd say. But my anguish came out in a torrent.

"What are these moods you get into?" I cried. "I can't go on living like this!" Tears welled up in my eyes and I began to sob. How I longed for him to put his arms around me and tell me it would be all right! Instead, he sat as though transfixed, staring at the river with eyes I couldn't read.

Only after my sobs died down and we again sat in silence did he speak, shaking his head.

"I don't know what to say, Luv," he began. "I know I'm hurting you, and I cry out to God for answers, but nothing changes. I know God has called us together, but…but sometimes I just want to run away. I feel scared. I…I guess I don't know what love is, or how to love a person properly." His quivering voice trailed off.

"I feel so ashamed!" he said after a moment. "Here I am, an evangelist, wanting to serve God, and yet behaving like this!"

The reality of his words hung in the air as we sat in silence together. I knew Alan had suffered a traumatic childhood because of his father's neurotic fears. Once Alan told me he grew up feeling so inferior and angry he used his fists to bluff his way around, proving he was in control of various situations. Later, when Alan gave his life to the Lord and quit his immoral lifestyle, he made a pact not to date again until God brought the right one. I deeply respected him for that, but could all these events be part of the reason for his present behavior?

Looking into my eyes, he pulled me into his arms. "I'm sorry Luv, I really am," he murmured.

"You know…before I was a Christian, having a girlfriend was purely selfish. I just used her, and if she tried to get too close, I would drop the relationship like that." He snapped his fingers, and I shuddered.

"Now that I know you're the one God has given me, I can't do that. I have to let you come close…and I'm really, really, scared!"

Alan Williams scared? He usually had such an air of self confidence, I would never have thought him capable of it! But as I looked at this man whom I so deeply loved, I realized he lived inside a thick-walled castle, complete with draw bridge and moat. On nice days, the bridge went down and we could take a pleasant walk around the courtyard – but when that bridge was up, only God could help me climb over the wall to get in.

I had always wanted someone to be strong for me, and I knew my own emotional strength was no match for what I faced. Insecurity was still a constant companion and I knew only the Lord could give the strength and security I needed.

Once again, that strength came through His Word. In my room that evening, my eyes fell on a passage that rang so true: "He hath made every thing beautiful in its time: Also he hath set the world in their heart, so that no man can find out the work that God maketh from the beginning to the end." Ecclesiastes 3:11

I dropped to my knees. Even with all our problems, I knew God had called us together and He could make something beautiful out of our lives. "Lord, I trust you to take our broken lives and make them beautiful in Your time," I whispered.

I began to see light at the end of the tunnel when our good friends, Jim and Joy Dawson, agreed to pray with Alan about it. Alan and I had often worked together with them in evangelism and attended prayer meetings in their Auckland home, so it was natural to bring this difficulty before the Lord with them.

Joy said God could not only heal physical sickness, but could perform a type of divine surgery to heal hearts and minds wounded by emotionally damaging experiences from the past. When Alan boarded the bus to spend a weekend alone with them in Auckland, I was filled with hope.

Upon his return, I was dying to find out what had happened. I met him at the bus station and his normally intense face was unusually peaceful. He greeted me with a big grin.

"Tell me what happened!" I said excitedly.

"Hey, take it easy, there's plenty of time!" he teased. For once, he was the one calming ME down. Alan took the driver's seat, and drove me home. Once we parked outside, Alan put his arm around me and I leaned close to share what had happened.

"As soon as Jim and Joy began to pray, God started to reveal wounds and negative experiences from my childhood that they couldn't have possibly known."

One of the most remarkable revelations was his confusion between love and hate.

"Those I looked to for love, I saw fighting each other," he said. He recalled that once when he ran away from home for a week, his father, who owned and operated a men's hairdressing salon, responded by threatening Alan with a razor to his throat.

"My dad was so worried, his reaction was to turn on me," Alan explained. "He probably wouldn't have used the razor, but I was scared out of my wits."

Joy had explained that this experience and others had left scars that now needed to be taken to the Lord for healing. Relationships with those outside the home had also left wounds.

"Once when I was 18," Alan continued, "I came home from the army and found my first serious girlfriend was pregnant by another fellow.

"I guess with one thing after another, I shut the door and decided love could stay away."

Alan said Jim and Joy had prayed through all the hurts that came to mind, asking the Lord to heal each one.

"When they prayed, I knew the presence of the Lord was right there in the room," he said. "Now I'm trusting the Lord to bring about the needed change."

Sure enough, over the next weeks subtle changes began to occur. For the first time in his life Alan was able to relax, and although he still fell into occasional depressions and started to withdraw, now we knew the cause and could talk about it. As he began to let me go deeper into his life, his moods didn't affect me as they had before. God was making us beautiful in His time!

We set our wedding for Nov. 11, 1961, almost a year away so I could complete my final year's commitment to Bible college. Alan's one-year commitment to Bible School was almost up, so we decided it was best for him to work at sea again to save money for the wedding and our future.

The separation would be difficult for me, but I knew it would give Alan some space to prepare himself for marriage. Even with all the healing in his life so far, Alan was still a loner by temperament. The separation could give him a chance to let the walls of protection down slowly. When we kissed and said goodbye at the bus station, his wistful eyes told me this would be hard for him too.

At first, the days seemed to drag by. But as I set myself to studying and absorbing Doc's teaching, the loneliness of our separation eased. Alan's letters, written in his left-handed scrawl, were now full of stories about his trips to the South Pacific, the spiritual needs of the island people, and his desire to get married. Sometimes he would draw little stick figures of a man pushing his ship home faster. I so looked forward to the day we would be together for good.

As I set about preparing for the wedding, I learned new lessons about trusting the Lord to provide for our needs. Long ago my father told my sisters and me that he wouldn't pay for our weddings or even attend if my mother brought the man she remarried.

There was no way I could expect my mother to come without her husband, so I could only commit it to the Lord.

To my delight, a friend who was an excellent seamstress and designer offered to make my dress at cost. Someone else rented us a beach house north of Auckland for the honeymoon, and another loaned us his car and gave us gas money. Our hearts overflowed with appreciation for the generosity of our friends, knowing it was a sign of God's goodness and blessing on our marriage.

But one of the greatest blessings was when my father changed his mind at the last minute and not only paid for the reception, but decided to come to the wedding. God was faithful to us in the midst of every obstacle.

Now standing at the front of the church next to Alan, I knew God had great things ahead. I really was marrying Alan Williams! Dear Doc, who had recently laid his own sweet wife to rest, officiated at the ceremony. His powerful sermon was from Luke 24, portraying the story of the two walking the road to Emmaus.

"Jesus drew near and went with them, and that my dears," he said looking right into our eyes, "is the wonder of Life's Greatest Companion. Who knows where He will lead you – but remember, He will always be with you!"

Campbell McAlpine, Bob Sands, Fay, Alan's brother Ronald. Whangerei, N.Z.

6

Jehovah Jireh

E ven in all the excitement of starting our new life together, we
had no idea what God had planned for us. We felt a growing
certainty that He was calling us to full-time ministry, but no clear
direction on what that ministry would be. As we began to ask
God to guide us, one of the hardest tests was trusting Him to provide financially.

Our first little love nest was in Whangerei, a city north of
Auckland, where we were offered a cottage rent-free for several
months if we would paint and redecorate it for future sale. The
cottage was named May Shan (or Beautiful Mountain) by the
previous owners, a former missionary couple who had retired
there after years in China.

Walking in the door for the first time, we were met with an atmosphere of peace. Prayer cards adorned the walls of the tiny
kitchen, and we knew this dear couple – now at home with
Jesus – had spent their last days praying for those still on the mission field. Seeing the cards only fanned the fire in our hearts to go

into missions ourselves, and we praised God for His obvious provision.

Alan and I began painting and decorating the cottage together until Alan took a temporary job as a hairdresser, a skill he had learned well working for his dad as a youth. I filled my days by painting and soon began a children's Bible club in our newly spruced up living room. Then to our great delight, we discovered we'd soon have a child of our own.

We weren't there long when the Lord sent another resident to May Shan. Well-known Bible teacher Campbell McAlpine, a Scotsman called to live and work in New Zealand, was beginning a new ministry, the Tell New Zealand Crusade. He temporarily moved in with us and used our cottage as a base of operations. The goal of the crusade was to saturate the North Island with God's Word and to place the Gospel of John in every home in the nation.

Campbell's presence began making a deep impact on our lives. I knew he had a prophetic ministry, so at first I feared he would point out all my weaknesses – but this sweet-natured man, with his tender blue eyes, put me at ease immediately. He lavished me with gratitude for even the smallest task I did for him.

I was mostly impressed by Campbell's disciplined prayer life. Whenever I passed his bedroom door, I was likely to hear him weeping and crying out to God for men, women and children to find Jesus Christ as their Savior. God deeply convicted me that I also needed to be willing to pay the price in disciplined prayer to effectively minister into others' lives.

Alan and I both began helping Campbell in the ministry whenever we could. First going door to door to distribute the Gospel of John to each home in a designated area, we would then end each week or so by sponsoring a large, evangelistic crusade with several of the local churches. Before long, Campbell needed so much help, Alan felt God directing him to give up his temporary job in order to minister with Campbell full time.

As I continued the children's ministry and redecorating work in

May Shan, Alan and Campbell began traveling farther north to minister. I loved listening to their exciting stories about each day's witnessing activities, and Alan and I praised God together for bringing this wonderful ministry right to our doorstep.

But as the months rolled on, and more and more decorating was completed, we knew May Shan would soon be sold. Our daily prayers were filled with asking God to show us the next move we were to take.

One morning as I was making our bed, Alan came in and made a stunning announcement.

"I believe the Lord is saying I'm to go back to England," he said. "You know my dad's been so sick – I'm afraid if I don't go soon, he may die before I get there."

He now looked at me with a clearly hopeful expression. Alan had left for New Zealand when he was 21, and though he had fully adopted New Zealand as his new homeland, he longed to see his family again. He had tried many times to go home for a visit, but something always stopped him. The only one in his family I had even met was his older brother, Ronald, a merchant seaman who had worked on ships in and out of New Zealand.

"How did God speak to you?" I asked eagerly. We sat down on the bed together as he flipped through his Bible and showed me the story of Jacob fleeing Laban in Genesis 31:3 : "Return unto the land of thy fathers, and to your kindred; and I will be with thee," he read aloud. "It just stood out to me like 3-D!"

In those days, a trip to England meant an expensive six-week trip on a passenger ship, since the price of airplane tickets was exorbitant. We had so little money, the thought of even one ticket was far beyond our means.

"I don't know where we'll get the money, but the Lord will provide if it's His timing," I responded. I leaned over to plant a kiss on his cheek. "I will really miss you, Darl," using the abbreviated form of my pet name for him, Darling.

We didn't know God had something else in mind. A few days later in my own Bible reading, God's word to Abraham in Genesis

12:1 leapt off the page: "Get thee out of thy country, and from thy kindred, and from thy father's house, unto a land that I will show thee."

In amazement, I realized God was telling me to go along with Alan – and certainly that meant we would be there longer than a short visit! I saw afresh how intimately God guides His children – while he told Alan to go back to his homeland of England, He was now telling me to leave my homeland of New Zealand.

When I later told Alan the news, he also praised God – but it boggled his mind to think what it would cost not only to move us and all our belongings to Liverpool, but also to provide for the baby now on the way.

Over the next days, Alan was unusually quiet, and I could tell he was brooding about the financial challenge before us. Even with all the obstacles Alan had already overcome in faith, it was obvious he was now fighting off a growing inner fear. Alan had often told me he always believed God would provide, but only as he worked hard with his own two hands. The amount of money we would now need to obey God would require nothing short of a miracle! Even so, I knew God had directed Alan to leave his paid job and go to England, so I had no doubt God would take care of us.

Campbell of course was disappointed we wouldn't continue serving in the crusade, but we knew we had his blessing when he gave us a financial gift toward our journey. It was hard for Alan to receive monetary gifts, and once he even tried to refuse a donation to his ministry – but God clearly showed Alan that he needed to humble himself to receive God's provision, however it came. It was all part of learning how to walk in God's ways, not our own.

As our departure time drew near, I found Alan in the newly painted kitchen of May Shan, nailing shut some wooden boxes filled with our belongings. I walked in to see Alan sit back on his heels in exasperation.

"This is crazy!" he moaned. "This stuff has to be down on the wharf hundreds of miles away in Wellington by Wednesday, and we only have half the fare!"

Sweat ran down his red face, and his brows were knit in anxiety. I knew that he as the traditional breadwinner felt keenly responsible for our welfare, but the best I could offer to lift his sagging spirits was to say, "Looks like you need a 'cuppa cha' (the Liverpool term for tea)."

Coming back with the steaming mug, I found Alan bending forward on his elbows on one of the boxes, apparently praying. He looked up and smiled slightly as I put the tray down.

"It's okay, Luv," he said. "The Lord just seemed to be asking me if I believed He was sending us, and I had to answer yes – I mean, there's no way I would do this if it weren't God's idea! Then the Lord assured me He would provide all our needs. Remember what Doc used to say? 'If faith is not tested, it has no testimony!'"

How thankful I was again for all the godly principles Doc had invested in our lives!

"So God is giving us the chance for a greater testimony," I reflected. "We just have to step out in faith."

He nodded his head in agreement. "You know, I'll never forget when I was a young Christian, how God dealt with me about trusting Him."

I could hear a long story would be coming, so I poured us each another cup of tea and settled down on a kitchen chair to listen. "Tell me," I said eagerly.

"I was working as a ship's Silver King," he recalled. "That meant I had to clean all the silverware for the tables and keep stock of the equipment. I was just swabbing the deck and about to finish for the day, when I heard this voice say, 'Give all your money away!' It was so real I looked around to see who was there.

"I was so shocked, I rebuked the devil." His face puckered with a smile. "I continued on with my work, and again I heard it: 'Give all your money away!'"

His eyes widened as he explained he had saved a sizable amount to return to England and start his own hairdressing salon." I really loved the security of that money. Of course, I'd become a Christian now, but I couldn't bear to think of giving that money away.

Still, the voice wouldn't go away. I knew it had to be the Lord."

Finally willing, Alan said he went to his cabin and got out his bank book, planning to give some money to a good shipmate from Wales who wanted to bring his wife out to New Zealand.

"I thought surely that was what the Lord meant," he said. "I began making a list, giving so much for him and then so much for me to stock up on various kinds of new clothes. When I tallied it all up, I felt so pleased with myself. I still had a big amount left to give God." He laughed and shook his head. "Did I have a surprise coming!"

That night, Alan said he tossed and turned in his bunk until he finally climbed out onto the floor.

"Lord, what is it?" he said in desperation.

"Forget your list. I want every penny!" came the reply. Alan now grinned mischievously. "I wish the Lord would always speak as clearly as He did that day! At last I gave in and told the Lord I would."

A certain ministry among lepers came into Alan's mind, and only after he told the Lord he would give all his money to that work could he finally crawl back into bed and sleep.

"But that wasn't the end of it. The next day when I was praying, the Lord said, 'You've given your money – now what about you? Are you willing to give your life to work among the lepers?'

"Whoa, I really struggled over that, arguing with God about how young I was and how I might die – but as before, there was no peace until I surrendered to God's prompting."

Alan said he realized the latter had been a test, and not a true calling to work among lepers.

"From that time on, I understood the principle in Christianity, that you throw your life away to save it," he said. "If you hoard your life, you'll lose it!"

He locked his gaze on mine, and I knew we were both thinking the same thing.

"And that's what God is asking us to do now," I said after a moment. "We can trust Him.

The next Monday, we left the security of our little cottage with only our hand luggage. We would take the bus to Auckland to say goodbye to relatives and friends and then go on to Wellington by train. Everything we owned was stored in a warehouse on a wharf in Wellington, waiting to be loaded onto the Southern Cross ocean liner that would take us halfway round the world.

Yes, we were all set – but we still had only half the fare. The tickets and final payment were due the following Wednesday.

Once in Auckland, we stayed on for a few days with our good friends Jim and Joy Dawson. We knew they had no extra money to help us, so we freely told them how we were stepping out in faith and obedience to God. They joined us in prayer and watching in faith to see how it would work out.

The second evening we were there, Jim came home from work with a strange look on his face. Before long, both he and Joy went off to a room to pray together. After 15 minutes or so, Joy came out and asked us to pray they would have God's wisdom for a decision they were making. We didn't know what it was, but asked God to speak to them.

Soon Jim and Joy came out and sat us down.

"For six months we've been waiting for a bonus check from work," Jim began. "It just so happened that it arrived today."

Joy explained they were in the middle of a faith project themselves, and although they really needed the money, the Lord had shown them to give a certain amount to us. Although we hadn't told them how much we needed, the amount on their hearts was to the penny what we needed for our ship tickets!

Together we praised God in amazement. Alan and I especially prayed that Jim and Joy would see God's blessing result from their act of sacrifice and obedience.

The next day we went downtown with great joy to pay for the tickets right on the deadline. Before we ever got to Wellington, several other friends pressed money into our hands and we were filled with gratitude. We knew we would need it when we stopped at various ports during the six-week trip to Southampton, England.

Another blessing was that Alan's older brother, Ronald, had decided to return with us on the trip to England. Ronald was fairer skinned than Alan, with light brown hair and a square-shaped face, but the likeness was easily seen. With only a 13-month age difference between them, he and Alan were very close, and the two of them teased me endlessly.

At last, the three of us boarded the Southern Cross and we set out to sea. All I'd heard about Liverpool made it sound a dreary place, but I so looked forward to meeting the rest of Alan's family that now my heart was filled with anticipation. As the shore of my homeland grew smaller and smaller in the distance, even the waves of seasickness that quickly washed over me couldn't dampen my spirits.

However, the next day, my seasickness grew more and more violent, intensified by my pregnancy. At first I tried to attend the meals, but soon the only thing I could do to stop the retching was to lie flat on my bunk. Often I poured out my heart to God and wondered how could I endure this misery for six weeks.

The only good thing about missing the meals was that I didn't have to face our fellow travelers. Many of them were so wealthy they wore a different outfit to every meal, while I had only my one best dress. Of course, this didn't keep Alan from reaching out to the passengers. He even conducted a regular Bible study while on board.

During those days in my bunk, I often tried to understand why God was sending us to England when our hearts burned with the desire to serve Him in missions. If God hadn't spoken so clearly to us that we were to go, this might have seemed like a detour.

One night as we neared the end of the voyage, I tried to lie still next to Alan, but sleep escaped me. Ironically, the gentle rocking of the ship now gave me a strange sense of comfort as I felt the early fluttering movements of our baby in my womb. Once again I was struck by the oddity of our situation. The baby was due in just four months, yet we didn't know where we would live or get money to feed and clothe it, let alone ourselves.

I rolled over in the darkness and put my arm around my sleeping husband. Despite all the apparent insecurities of our future, in that moment I felt a supernatural peace wrap around me like a blanket.

*Arrival in Southhampton, England. Ronald, Alan's mother Eleanor,
Alan's Aunt Betty, Alan.*

7

Chasing The Shadows

Alan, Ronald and I lined the rail on a cool but sunny Spring day as the Southern Cross neared the Southampton docks in southern England. At last it was almost over! After six long weeks at sea, I had had enough seasickness to last the rest of my life. It was fine with me if I never went to sea again.

Of course the trip was not without its blessings — Alan loved conducting the Bible studies in the ship's lounge, we had lots of time to talk and pray, and two Christian couples who attended the Bible study had given us financial gifts. Still I couldn't wait to feel good, solid earth under my feet.

Now looking out to the crowd gathered at the pier, my eyes fell on a tiny auburn-haired woman ducking under a policeman's arm as he and others tried to control the waiting crowd.

"Alan, is that your mother?"

I began to point her out, but by now Alan and Ronald were

waving to their radiant mother and laughing at her highly animated signs to them. She was obviously acting out some inside family joke.

"So that's where you get your personality!" I joked. I could see Mom Williams was attractive even from a distance, and I could tell I was going to enjoy this new mother-in-law of mine.

After clearing immigration, we rushed to greet Mom Williams and her smiling sister, Alan's Aunt Betty. After giving my new mother a hug, I pushed Alan toward her.

"Here's your son! I've had him to myself for a long time – now it's your turn," I said with a broad grin.

She looked at me thoughtfully with the same small eyes that Alan had, and thanked me genuinely before giving him a big hug.

That night, we all stayed in a rooming house and awoke to a filling English breakfast of bacon and eggs, tomatoes and mushrooms, toast and marmalade, and of course, the traditional "cuppa cha." Alan and his mom had so much to catch up that I wondered if they'd be able to stop talking long enough to eat. Their rapid-fire conversation continued non-stop on the 250-mile trip to Liverpool, and with their thick Liverpool accent, it was sometimes like listening to a foreign language.

Alan's father was waiting to pick us up at the big Liverpool train station. He was just home from the hospital, recovering from his long illness, and although thin and gaunt, he greeted us warmly. He was well-groomed and smartly dressed, and I could see he must have been quite handsome in his youth. My heart warmed to see that same chiseled jaw of Alan's.

Dad Williams seemed anxious to get home, so as we moved along to the family car, I was introduced to Alan's youngest brother, Keith, and his only sister, 14-year-old Gwen. She had only been five when Alan left for New Zealand, so they barely knew each other now. Once back at the family house, which was one of many in rows of two-story double-brick houses, I was introduced to another brother named Tommy.

Walking into the comfortably furnished living room, I looked in fascination at the family photos lining the mantlepiece and the pretty lace curtains on the windows. Alan's mother served the another "cuppa cha" for everyone, and we sat down to discuss our situation with the family.

Alan's brother Keith, we were told, had been temporarily managing his father's hairdressing salon because Dad Williams was not yet fully well. Now Keith wanted to work in London, so it was decided Alan would begin managing the hair salon, located just a few blocks away from the Williams' home.

Alan and I thanked God again for His provision, but that was only the first answer to our prayers. Situated in a block of red brick shops, the salon had one set of stairs leading up to the hairdressing salon and to a tiny kitchen, bathroom and living room, while a second flight of stairs led up to two bedrooms on the top story. In exchange for our renovation of the salon and living quarters, it was agreed that Alan and I could live there rent-free, just as we had at May Shan. God was again proving Himself faithful!

Ronald, Alan and I stayed at the family home for a few weeks while the three of us began renovations. Then after Ronald went to work on the isle of Jersey, Alan and I moved into the half-renovated apartment.

Before this I had only lived in New Zealand suburbs with green fields and wide open spaces, so it wasn't easy for me to adjust to life on top of a block of shops. Even looking out the windows presented a tedious view of TV antennas, tar-covered yards, and brick walls with glass set in them to defeat would-be thieves. A dismal view indeed! I continued to spruce up the inside of our apartment instead.

But the warm-hearted people of Liverpool made up for it, and I quickly fell in love with them. Liverpudlians all seemed to possess a unique sense of humor, and Alan told me many successful comedians had come out of Liverpool. A sense of humor, he explained, was probably the way they learned to survive in the depressing conditions in the industrial north of England.

Although Alan disliked the cold, rainy Liverpool weather, he loved being back home with his family. I thoroughly enjoyed getting to know them too, and as Dad Williams' health improved, we visited them as much as we could. We were saddened to find, however, that Dad and Mom Williams had become Jehovah's Witnesses about the same time Alan gave his life to the Lord. At first some disagreements arose about doctrine, but soon Alan and I decided to show Christianity to them by serving rather than preaching.

We had been in Liverpool about a month when one Sunday afternoon, Alan grabbed my hand.

"Let's go for a walk," he suggested. "I want to show you my old stomping ground as a boy."

Glad for the chance to walk about the tree-lined streets, I eagerly followed him out the door into the chilly spring air. While we walked through the back streets of Huyton, Alan gabbed nonstop about what he used to do in each place. Soon it began to sound like confession time.

"This is where I used to rob the orchards," he said making a face. "And look here, see this room?" He pointed to a small room attached to the old stone church.

"This is where I broke in to steal the orange juice they stored for the weekly baby clinic. And that cemetery is where I snatched freshly placed flowers from graves and sold them 'round peoples' houses."

"Alan, I'm shocked!" I teased with a grimace. "You never told me these things before. I sincerely hope this baby of yours won't follow in your footsteps!"

"I agree," he said soberly as we rounded a corner. "I was absolutely wild, and must have driven my parents crazy."

As Alan went on and on with story after story, I could only listen in wonder.

"Well, I'm sure glad you became a Christian!" I said at last.

Yes, I was very glad that Alan's dynamic energy and strong will were now harnessed for God's purposes. But even as these memories long forgotten were now being stirred, darker shadows of

Alan's past also began to surface. As Alan and I set about the daily renovations, sandwiched in between salon customers, Alan began to fall back into depression. It was as if his past were coming back to life in these familiar surroundings. Did God have another purpose for bringing him back to Liverpool?

Especially as we renovated the actual salon, Alan's moods grew as bleak as the gray English sky. One day, I got alone and cried out the Lord. Soon I heard that still small voice I was starting to recognize as God's: "He makes all things beautiful in His time." Over and over it echoed in my mind.

"Lord, I stand on this verse!" I prayed. "I trust you to use the memory of even these painful experiences to bring a deeper healing work than Alan has ever known!"

A few days later when business was slow, I brought Alan some tea where he sat brooding. As I placed it down on the counter, he almost leapt off the salon chair and looked me in the eyes.

"This is the place, right here, where my Dad held the razor to my throat," he said.

I was strangely pleased to hear the story again. Was this how God would bring a new level of healing? Then he grabbed my hand and pulled me to the windows.

"This is where I was going to jump out of the window," he said gravely, apparently reliving it again. "I was terrified." A huge lorry passed the main Liverpool trunk road below, rattling the windows as it went. I tried to imagine the terror Alan must have felt back then.

"But I never hated him you know. Somehow I knew he couldn't help his depressions or the way he was. Sometimes he used to sit in front of the fire here on slow business days in the winter and worry. He would tell me he could see himself in his coffin. I tried to cheer him up, but nothing I said made a difference. Mother sometimes got depressed too, just trying to help him."

I listened as Alan continued to talk, and I knew God was bringing resolution to these shadows of the past. And somehow I knew part of the healing lay in the renovation itself — just as we were renewing the physical environment, so God was restoring the inner life. How good it would be to hand the salon back to Alan's father all clean and newly painted, as if giving it a fresh start. Even the outside environment was becoming beautiful in His timing!

Over the next weeks, Alan would don an old coat and paint when business was slow, and I, nearing the end of my pregnancy, worked mostly on my hands and knees, varnishing skirting boards and doors. Gradually, the dismal colors disappeared and the place began to sparkle. As a whole new atmosphere settled over the place, Alan's depression simultaneously began to lift. God was doing a work!

Soon I was counting the days until our baby's due date, Aug. 18—the same day as Alan's 29th birthday! I was thrilled with the thought of making him a daddy on that special day.

But with just two days to go, on Aug. 16, I awoke with a slight backache and a wonderful feeling of exhilaration. Somehow I knew today was the day! I told Alan, but he looked at me skeptically. Paying no attention, I hastily cleaned up the apartment, and I went down to the corner grocery store with joy.

"My baby's going to be born today, I just know it!" I told the ladies in their white aprons at the counter. They looked at me askance, and one lady shook her finger at me.

"Oo-Aye, you'll be looky if you 'ave that li'ul wun before tamara!" she said thickly.

I knew better. Right after lunch I went into labor and the midwife was quickly summoned to our home. By mid-afternoon it was all over, and tiny Joy Kristine lay nestled in her daddy's arms. As we looked together at her olive skin, dark hair and rosebud lips, our hearts almost exploded with thankfulness to God.

I had never seen Alan so excited about anything. We were so pleased with our tiny daughter that every day when a customer came into the salon, Alan would go through the same spiel about his new daughter that looked so much like him. How much love this little girl was bringing, both to us, her grandparents, and the rest of Alan's family! She filled our apartment with such love and joy that any remaining shadows vanished from our lives.

Another delight for me was the experience of my first white Christmas, but Alan warned that I would soon be crying because the snow wouldn't go away. How right he was. The once-beautiful white snow turned to dirty slush from the soot of hundreds of chimneys, and then iced over, making all travel hazardous. Laundry I hung on the outside lines froze in moments, along with my fingers. It turned into Liverpool's coldest winter in 35 years and every day was a struggle to stay warm.

Over the next year, Alan diligently gave himself to the hairdressing business, and as satisfied customers began passing the word around, the clientele expanded. Alan had so wanted to build up the business to encourage his dad, and I knew he felt happy at a job well done. But in the midst of it all, that old yearning to be involved in evangelism again began to return to both of us.

We were attending a church a few miles away, and began to share the Gospel in street meetings near the church on Sunday afternoons. Even during the snowy or wet weather, Alan and I traipsed around outside, singing, testifying and preaching. Often we saw people listening from their windows, but when we knocked on their doors and invited them to church, few came. Each day Alan grew more and more restless and dissatisfied.

One day, Alan poked his head into the kitchen as I was preparing the noon meal. "I'm fed up with just cutting hair," he announced. "I'm going to see that Huyton is evangelized!"

Within a couple of weeks we selected a date, rented a local hall for an evangelistic meeting, handed out advertising leaflets, and waited for the big night to arrive.

We arrived early at the dingy old hall, ready to welcome a rush of people. We started up with good rousing songs to charge the atmosphere with the Lord's presence, but it soon became obvious that our "crowd" was already present – Mom Williams, one blind lady, and a middle-aged couple.

Not to be deterred, Alan preached vigorously on the need to be born again. To our delight, afterward the middle-aged couple gave their hearts to the Lord. The blind lady, we learned later, was already a Christian, and Mom Williams was only there to hear her son preach, though we had been praying long and hard for her conversion to Christ.

The next weeks, we continued instructing the newly saved couple and helped them settle into a local church. I began visiting the blind lady to read to her, and Joy claimed her as another Grandma. God had turned our apparent "flop" into a small victory.

But even so, Alan was devastated. He searched his heart for days afterward to see if he had sinned in any way, but came up blank.

"I know God has called me to preach – so why isn't He blessing me?" he questioned. "Maybe I just have to wait for a special anointing to come on my life when I turn 30."

"What on earth are you talking about?" I asked with a frown. Alan went into the bedroom and returned with his daily diary. He proceeded to show me a long list of Bible verses about people who had been commissioned by God for special projects at age 30, including Joseph and Jesus himself. He looked at me earnestly.

"I believe God is going to do this for me," he affirmed. My eyes widened. Alan would be 30 in just a few days!

"I'm going to fast and pray for three days, starting two days before my birthday," he said. "My dad's well enough to work at the salon now, so I'll shut myself in the spare bedroom. I won't come out 'til God meets me!"

I flinched at the thought of him missing Joy's first birthday, but held my peace in respect for his diligence. The morning of August 15, Joy and I kissed Alan before he locked himself in the room for an encounter with God. What was going to happen in there? Curiosity was killing me! I'd read books about men of God having experiences like Alan was expecting, and I was half afraid that if it were too powerful, I might lose the Alan I knew and loved.

The three days dragged on, despite my busyness taking care of Joy. Now that her grandad was working in the salon, I watched with tenderness as Joy brought him so much happiness. Though

Dad Williams still battled depression and worried endlessly about his health, I could see he was an affectionate, loving man, and I grew to love him. I enjoyed trying to tease his feeble appetite with tasty meals and New Zealand scones, and now I threw myself into that to keep my mind off Alan.

At last on Alan's birthday, the day when he was to emerge, I busied myself around the upstairs area, waiting for the glorious moment. Would he come out looking like Moses, with his face shining with the glory of the Lord?

As the door slowly opened, so did my mouth. Alan's shoulders were slumped, and his sunken, disconsolate face wore three days of scruffy beard. His dull, hollow eyes now peered at me dejectedly.

"What happened?" I asked as sensitively as I could. "Did you see the Lord?"

In the tense moment of silence that followed, I wanted to shake him alive. A tear ran down his cheek, and a look of pain ran deep in his eyes.

"Nothing..." he said at last. "Absolutely nothing!"

I reached out to hold his limp hand. How could this happen?

At last Alan went to take a shower and shave, while I put Joy down for a nap and prepared a light meal for Alan to break his fast. We ate in silence until Alan haltingly began to tell me what he'd experienced.

"I started by asking God to examine my heart to see if there was any sin in my life. Then I confessed everything I could think of," he explained. "I couldn't feel the Lord's presence at all, so I prayed everything on my heart.

"I read the Bible, but it seemed lifeless. I was also reading an old devotional book, and other times I just fell off to sleep. The whole time the Lord seemed so far away." Alan looked out the window thoughtfully.

"Only this morning, after repeating most of the same prayers, did something happen. I was reading the devotional again and my eyes fell on the words, 'Lord, I lie at your feet, willing to be used or not.' It broke me, Luv...," Alan's voice broke with emotion.

"It was so hard, but I literally lay on the floor and repeated that as a prayer to God. This was the only clear thing I had received the whole time – but it wasn't what I expected."

He stopped again and looked out the window at the street below.

"You know, Luv, sometimes I feel like I'm in a fire, and God is refining me like gold. All I seem to be able to think of is being used, DOING! It seems God is more interested in me BEING. I sometimes feel God has forgotten I'm here. I feel so...unimportant, unless I'm rushing around doing evangelism."

I nodded with understanding – but I didn't know what to say. The next day we talked about it again over breakfast, and I was full of questions.

"What about all those verses on turning 30?" I asked. "Wasn't that God speaking to you?"

"I must have been deceived," he answered. "I guess you can make the Bible say what you want if you're not careful."

Over the next days I pondered his words, and one thought kept coming to my mind. Of course we wanted to serve God in missions and evangelism, but maybe serving Alan's parents here in Liverpool was just as important to God as going out to evangelize. We never had felt England was our mission field, but maybe for a season this was God's highest plan for us. I wasn't sure, but I asked God to show us His path for our lives.

Our time in England had stretched out to almost two years, and Dad Williams was well enough to take over the salon again full time. Alan found a job at another hairdresser's to let his father have all the business, but we began to feel we had done what we came for. We didn't know what we would do back in New Zealand either, but it grew more and more apparent that the time to return had arrived.

I dreaded another bout of constant seasickness, but we booked passage to leave England in March of 1962 aboard the Rangitane. At least I wasn't pregnant this time! Ronald was now back in

Liverpool, so he agreed to drive us all night to the Tilbury dock in London to catch the ship.

Little Joy had become her grandad's delight, and we knew it was particularly hard for him to see her go. The night we were to leave, we went over to see Mom and Dad Williams one last time. Sitting once more in their now-familiar living room, we tried to put off the inevitable parting just a little longer as Dad Williams clutched Joy on his lap in obvious sorrow.

As we got up to say goodbye, Dad Williams grew quiet as Alan and I hugged his mother one last time. Handing Joy over to me, Dad Williams grabbed Alan by the shoulders with tears in his eyes.

"Why did you do it, Son?" he asked in a voice ragged with emotion.

Alan looked puzzled. "Do what, Dad?"

"Why did you put so much work into the shop and building up the business?"

Alan looked him squarely in the eye. "Dad," he began, "when the time comes for you to leave this life, I want to be able to say I did everything I could to be a good son."

Visibly moved, he hugged Alan again tightly. "Thank you," was all he could say, his usually deep voice just above a whisper.

At last Dad broke away to hug me affectionately and then clung again to his darling granddaughter. All our eyes were filled with tears when at last we went out the door and settled into Ronald's car.

Our parting at the London dock was equally painful. Ronald and Alan hugged one another one last time, choked with emotion. How these brothers loved each other! Ronald couldn't bear to see the ship leave, so after a final nod, was gone.

As the Rangitane set out to sea, I looked back on England's shores with a twinge in my heart. How I loved my new Liverpool family! We hadn't had any idea we would be in Liverpool two full years, and we were still anxious to get into ministry – but I realized again how good it was to have served Mom and Dad Williams. God's ways again had proved higher than our ways.

We still had no idea what we would do when we returned to New Zealand, but a mounting sense of expectancy filled me as I wondered where the next field of ministry would lie.

PART II

The tension of waiting for the verdict was driving Alan mad. He turned and fidgeted in the Athens courtroom, and finally leapt to his feet and announced to me that he was going to take a walk. "I can't just sit here." With that he pushed through the crowd to the adjacent hallway.

Alan had been consistently positive through the four-day trial, but the strain had pushed him to the brink of exhaustion. Where were those judges? Could it possibly take so long to figure out that these men were not criminals?

The so-called victim, young Kostas Kotopoulos, was now an adult himself and had spoken eloquently in defense of the Athens Three. Their attorney had also testified powerfully of their integrity. But did those three stoic judges really listen?

At least we had a chance to present our case. So many Christians in oppressive countries had suffered far more than we. Countless thousands had been arrested, tortured and even put to death. Alan had been arrested and harassed many times by the police for his street preaching, but God had always been his shield and defender. Surely He would come through for us now.

Glancing at the clock on the wall, I saw the hands moving with irritating slowness, as if mocking me. Beside my feet was Alan's little suitcase, packed with his Bible, tracts, personal items and some prized tea bags. If Alan really did have to go to prison, we were ready. It would be just another of the many separations we'd endured while serving God together.

Cook Islands. Samuel, three; Alan; Joy, six; Fay; Stephen, nine months.

8

Almost Paradise

The separations began soon after we returned to Auckland from England. Alan took a job on a cargo vessel called the M/V Moana Roa, making regular voyages to Rarotonga, the main island of the Cook Islands in the South Pacific.

This time Alan had been gone three weeks, and Joy and I arrived early to watch his ship pull into Auckland Harbour. Alan warned us not to come early. As chief steward, he had duties after docking. But I could never wait at home all day, knowing he was back. He would be home for just 10 days this time and we wanted to make the most of it.

Joy, now two-and-a-half, stood beside me dressed in her blue winter coat and pants. "Daddy coming on the ship?" she asked with a twinkle in her expressive hazel eyes.

Touched by her obvious excitement, I swung her into my arms and squeezed her.

"Soon," I replied warmly.

How I loved her! Being a seaman's wife could be lonely, but having our little girl with me made the gray, misty days much brighter. I longed to have another child, and soon after returning from England I rejoiced to learn I was pregnant again. But my hopes were dashed when, while Alan was away at sea, I suffered a miscarriage only eight weeks into the pregnancy. This loss sent me running to the Lord once again for comfort, and I prayed earnestly that God would give us a son, just as He had for Hannah, mother of the prophet Samuel.

When the Moana Roa emerged from the mist and pulled up to the wharf, we could hardly contain our excitement. Alan poked his head out the door and waved at us. After another long wait the gangway was set up, and Joy and I bounded on board. Alan swung Joy around in his arms, and kissed me eagerly.

As we rode back home on the bus, Alan seemed quieter than usual as he sat with Joy sleeping on his lap.

"Is there something on your mind?" I said.

"I've got a surprise," he answered. "Are you ready?"

Full of curiosity, I eagerly agreed.

"You know how we've prayed for the Cook Islands since I began going there on this ship?" he began. "Every time I go, the former pastor Papa Raui tells me there's such a dearth of spiritual life there that they badly need someone to come preach the Gospel in real power and authority.

"After praying all this time, I...I feel God is saying to put feet to our prayers. I think the Lord is calling us to go there as missionaries." He looked at me a moment in silence. "Well, what do you think?"

I returned his gaze, not knowing what to say. Of course we had always longed to serve God on the mission field – but I had just committed to being a Sunday School teacher at our local church. I was enjoying my new niche, and I hated starting something I couldn't finish.

"How did He speak to you?" I said after a moment.

Alan explained he had been praying about the Cook Islands before he began reading in I Corinthians. One verse was especially highlighted:

"For a great door, and effectual, is opened unto me, and there are many adversaries." I Corinthians 16:9

"In spite of the problems, I just believe this is a door God is calling us to walk through," he concluded.

"I'll have to pray about it," I said quietly. For us, going out as missionaries meant making a life commitment to a nation. Was the Cook Islands the place God had for us?

Over the next weeks, I toyed with the idea, constantly committing it to God. I had had so many exciting plans for the Sunday School, and felt nothing at all about the Cook Islands – but Alan's leading was so strong. We had always planned to go to the mission field, but was this it?

When Joy and I again kissed Alan goodbye at the dock before his next trip aboard the Moana Roa, Alan searched my face.

"You still haven't heard anything from God yet?"

I shook my head. "Nothing."

He flashed a grin. "Well, my feelings have only grown stronger. God must know what He's doing!"

As I watched Alan's ship disappear on the horizon, I could only wonder. How could I move so far away without knowing for myself that it was God's will?

Over the three weeks that Alan was gone, I continually sought the Lord, but still heard nothing. I began to think that because I was joined to Alan in marriage, God expected me to follow Alan's leading. As I meditated on it further, peace flooded my heart.

"Lord," I breathed, "If Alan comes back still convinced we are to go, I'll take it that you're telling me to go along as his helpmeet."

But besides the peace I now felt in my heart, a new exhilaration also filled me with the good news I had yet to tell Alan – I was pregnant again!

This time while Joy and I waited for Alan to return, I could hardly wait to talk to him. As I suspected, he was more excited than ever when we met him at the dock.

"You'll never guess what happened!" His eyes were ablaze. "God gave me a vision about the Cook Islands!"

All the way home on the bus, I held back my own news and I listened attentively to Alan tell the story. He had been praying with a Christian friend when in his mind's eye he saw a thick, stone wall around the Cook Islands. Amidst the vision, he heard God say, "An impenetrable wall of spiritual darkness is surrounding the islands. The Gospel hasn't been preached there in its fullness for the last 100 years, but as you go there to preach the Word and pray, cracks in the wall will appear until it eventually comes down."

Then it was as if he saw the wall crack and fall down before his eyes. "I can't wait to go back!"

He now looked at me in excitement.

"Well, it looks like we're going!" I cut in, telling him not only what I decided, but also the news of our expanding family. Alan could hardly contain his joy.

So, in May 1965, Joy and I also boarded the Moana Roa with Alan to head to the Cook Islands – only this time we were all passengers. My pregnancy brought on violent seasickness once again, and all I saw of the five-day trip was the ship's cabin walls and bathroom. I knew that God had called us to go, but how I wished we had another way to get there! At least this wasn't as long as our previous voyages.

On our fifth afternoon at sea, I was lying on my bunk when Alan burst into the room. "We're here!" he announced, reaching out his hand to help me up.

I was weak from lack of food, but managed to drag myself up and follow Joy and Alan as he carried some of our luggage upstairs to the deck. Now, as I stepped into the bright sunlight, all discomfort was forgotten as I breathed in the fresh air and remarkable beauty now before me. Brilliant green mountains rose up from a deep aqua sea, and coconut palms, pushing up from the white coral sand, swayed in a gentle breeze. Breathing deeply, my whole being came alive at the breathtaking sight of our new home, the island of Rarotonga. Here is where we planned to spend the rest of our lives.

"It's almost like paradise!" I said to Alan. In response, he smiled wryly.

The Moana Roa couldn't pass through the coral reef, so soon a black longboat came out to take us to shore. As we hoisted our luggage over and hopped on, all I could think of was the verse God had given us: "For a great door and effectual is open to me..."

Alan tugged at my arm. "We're going to take this place for God!" he declared, resolutely pointing his finger toward the island. How he loved the challenge! And no doubt a challenge did await us, considering the last part of the verse: "and there are many adversaries."

At the dock, a small group of both brown-skinned Rarotongans and whites now greeted us, all Christians Alan had met on previous trips. Helping us out of the boat, they gathered up our luggage and a lady quickly swept Joy into her arms.

"Alan Kia Orana — welcome, welcome," said a short, round man, who showed several missing teeth as he smiled broadly at us. Alan introduced him as Papa Raui, and I instantly liked him. Papa Raui was the former pastor who had begged Alan to come preach the Gospel on his island. Now an orange farmer, Papa Raui owned a large plantation, and had invited us to stay with him and his family.

Then in traditional island welcome, lei after lei of tipani flowers (plumeria) were put around our necks. My senses reeled with the perfume and rich colors. We'd never had a welcome like this before!

Once we got to Papa Raui's home, Alan and I were introduced to Mama Raui. She had a large motherly figure and a smile as wide as Papa's. I would have loved to sit down and chat with her, but Mama Raui spoke no English and I spoke no Rarotongan, or Cook Island Maori, as it was officially called. Papa Raui had to translate everything for us. I tried to put Mama Raui at ease, but initially she seemed quite shy of me.

Joy was now almost three years old and her light brown hair and outgoing personality obviously intrigued the islanders. She made friends with everyone quickly, and it didn't take long for her to captivate the heart of Mama Raui. While the socializing and conversations continued, I took a stroll around their simple island-style home.

The center of the home was a large living room that opened off to several bedrooms having only curtains for doors. Only netting covered the windows, and the brown walls were decorated with woven fans and a large collection of family photos draped with shell leis around the frames. Also adjoining the very back of the house was a shower cubicle and a three-walled kitchen that stood open to the orange groves extending from the back yard.

I soaked up the serene beauty of the island, but didn't at all like being soaked with sweat from Rarotonga's fierce humidity. Another unnerving thing, was the thought of living with the small lizards that I saw darting all over the walls. Papa assured us they were harmless and beneficial because they killed mosquitos. I decided I'd have to get used to them, but obviously, it would take a while to become accustomed to this new culture.

That evening, when most of the others had left, Mama led us to a large table and placed before us a big meal of taro root, green taro leaves cooked in coconut sauce, and chicken cooked in the umu (hot stones in the ground). I was hungry after my forced fasting at sea, so I couldn't wait to try this exotic food.

In contrast, Alan sat eyeing everything cautiously. As radical as he was, food was not one of his daring areas. I kicked his foot under the table and leaned toward him. "You'll offend them if you don't eat what's in front of you," I whispered. He kicked me back and made a grimace.

No sooner had I giggled than Mama came back to the table carrying a platter displaying a huge gray pig's head, complete with copious hunks of fat. The very sight of it made our stomachs turn, but not wanting to offend, we each took a few meager bites of the pig's head. After that, we both felt queasy for rest of the night!

Foreigners were required to hold a paying job in the Cook Islands because there was no typical missionary status, so Papa Raui had arranged for Alan to work at the government-run freezer, a place to store frozen foods from New Zealand. Sunday mornings we attended one of the four churches on Rarotonga, and Sunday evenings we began holding evangelistic street meetings, rotating between each of the five major villages on the island.

Papa Raui had a small team of mostly young Rarotongans who had become Christians through his personal evangelism, and they now joined us in singing and testifying before the crowds that gathered. Papa Raui served not only as interpreter for Alan's preaching, but also humbly took his turn holding a kerosene lamp on a pole as the sun went down. I helped lead the songs of worship on my piano accordion. The Sunday evening meetings became the highlight of our week, and a real outlet for Alan.

Living with Papa Raui and his family was special, but soon it was apparent we needed more than our one room. Our second baby was due soon, and I thought how relieved Mama would be not to have to watch us eat the nutritional salads I'd begun to fix for our family. Papa told us with a big grin that one day he had found his wife in tears, for fear we would die in her house from "eating only green leaves!"

At last Papa arranged for his widower friend Papa Jimmy to rent us half of his big house. The place was closer to the central village of Avarua, which made it much easier for us to travel to various villages to preach.

Late one Sunday afternoon in November, after we had been on the island for five months, the evangelism team stopped by our home for the usual prayer time before going out to evangelize. I prayed with them, but soon felt such pain in my lower back, I decided to stay home that night.

Within an hour after Alan and the team left, I was seized with a contraction and quickly called for an ambulance. I got to the hospital just in time. I had hardly settled into my hospital bed before I heard the glorious sound of new life.

"It's a boy!" announced the kind, native midwife, her voice full of joy. I was perspiring profusely, both from the humidity and giving birth, but joy flooded over me as I realized God had answered my prayer for a son – our little prophet.

As the nurse placed him in my arms, I saw that he was blue and speckled from the speedy labor, and I pressed my lips to his cheek.

"You poor little thing," I whispered. When Alan burst through the swinging door a moment later, he was bewildered.

"I can't believe it! I only just left you – how could you have a baby that quick?"

Smiling from ear to ear, he leaned over to kiss me, but his smile turned to surprise as he caught sight of our son.

"That's not our baby, is it?"

I burst out laughing. "Well, he's the only one here with white skin," I joked. "I only just made it, that's why he's a strange color. He reminds me of someone I know well – he came at top speed!"

The next day Alan registered our new son with the name Bryce Alan Williams. The baby and I were doing well, but the day we came home from the hospital, I began to feel uneasy. When Alan returned from work that night, I voiced my feelings.

"I felt exactly the same all day!" he said in amazement. We knew this was a signal to pray. First Alan took out our daily devotional booklet and began to read the portion for today's date:

"Wherefore it came to pass, when the time was come about after Hannah had conceived, that she bore a son, and called his name Samuel, saying, 'Because I have asked him of the Lord.' " (I Samuel 1:20)

We looked at each other dumbfounded. Had we given our new son the wrong name? We had prayed for a son and often referred to the unborn baby as Samuel, but apparently we hadn't taken the scripture literally enough. This was our Samuel!

Humbled, Alan now held little Samuel up to give him back to the Lord, just as we had done with Joy. Remembering the story of Hannah, I prayed in kind: "Lord, for this child I prayed, and I give him to you. His whole life, he shall be given to you."

The next day Alan paid a visit to an irate government registrar, who made it clear no parent had ever before changed a child's name the next day. Bryce Alan became Samuel Alan Williams, and we sent telegrams a second time to our immediate family to tell them of the change.

Within weeks, I joined the evangelism team again, and we went from village to village, preaching Christ in the dusty streets. We found that most Rarotongans were religious about church attendance, but lacked a personal relationship with God. Although an attentive audience of 50 to 70 people always gathered to listen, no one ever came forward to receive Christ. We ached to see a response to our labor.

One warm evening, just as another brilliant South Pacific sunset was fading, we set up for our meeting by a rock wall, lined with leafy trees and vines in a small village not far from our home. As usual, a crowd quickly gathered and relaxed as they listened to our songs and testimonies.

Then, just as Alan was moving into a fiery Gospel message, a huge man staggered out of the shadows. Pushing his way through the crowd, he barged up to Alan and thrust his large clenched fist just two inches from Alan's nose.

"I'm the king of this village!" he roared. "Get out of here, and leave my people alone!"

Our young Rarotongan interpreter for that evening, Teariki, went gray with fear. Many young people in the crowd shrunk back in fear at the sight of this Goliath of a man. By comparison, Alan appeared as a little David.

"Keep interpreting," Alan instructed from the corner of his mouth.

Standing at the edge of the crowd, I frantically began praying, holding baby Samuel closer to my chest and tightly clasping three-year-old Joy's hand. Darting his head around the huge man's fist to see the crowd, Alan continued preaching as he saw people watching and listening intently.

"Stop!" the man roared again.

Alan looked up into his towering face and said strongly and respectfully, "Sir...you may be the king of this village, but I've been sent here from the King of Kings! He told me to preach the Gospel and I cannot stop!"

The earthly king pulled his arm back to take a swing, but all at once two local policemen grabbed him from behind. As they took him away, the crowd in unison seemed to give a large sigh of relief.

"Phew," Alan quipped across the crowd to me, "That was close! Just as well – I've already relinquished my teeth!" Later we learned the man was a king by birth in the old island order, but the government system had taken his authority away. At the time he confronted Alan, he was drunk from "bush beer," a home-made brew made with fermented fruit in kerosene tins. We had heard the drink could turn people crazy, and tonight's incident seemed to verify that.

To conclude the meeting, Alan delivered impassioned pleas for those in the crowd to come forward to accept Jesus as savior. Again we searched the crowd for some sign of movement, but those in the crowd stood still as statues.

We went home that night thankful for God's protection, but more disappointed than ever that we still saw no fruit. Were we doing something wrong? The Rarotongans in the team assured us we weren't, yet everything we did seemed to no avail. Would we ever see the crack in the wall?

We didn't know the worst was yet to come.

Alan and some of the team that came from New Zealand to Cook Islands.

9

Putting In The Sickle

Sitting in our primitive island kitchen, I sighed deeply as Samuel again refused to eat the meal I offered him. Almost two years old now, our snowy-headed son was horribly thin after suffering for three months with diarrhea. The local doctor couldn't cure him, and my constant efforts to tempt his appetite met with no response. Little Samuel's troubles seemed to plunge my already-sagging spirits even further.

Since coming to this "paradise" two years ago, we had moved seven times. Now we were renting a small, prefabricated house in Rarotonga's Avarua Valley. Still we had seen no one come to the Lord in a personal way, and to make matters worse, some people were now opposing our work.

One of the few bright spots in the past year was the birth of our second son, Stephen, who now was sound asleep in his homemade crib. I thanked God for this happy, placid baby, who seemed to smile no matter what our circumstances.

All of us had been plagued with viruses and parasites since coming to the Cook Islands. It seemed to be the hardest for Samuel. He had severe colic all through his first year and was extra sensitive to the tropical humidity. As a result, I felt like I never got a good night's sleep, and was constantly tired and cranky.

I sank to a new low when baby Stephen was hit by a bout of chicken pox. He developed such severe complications, at one point we even feared for his life.

At least, I told myself, five-year-old Joy was doing well in her first year at school. But even the thought of having her bright mind challenged failed to lift my spirit.

When Alan came home on his lunch break, one look at his brooding face told me his mood matched mine. He refused my offer of lunch and stared at me with obvious displeasure.

"You know, I'm depressed enough myself – but when I look at you, it makes me worse."

His words hit like a smack in the face. As Alan sulked off into the next room, I didn't have the energy to respond. Looking at the flies buzzing over our sweaty bodies and the plate of food Samuel still hadn't touched, I sighed again. I hated it – the heat, the constant broken nights, the sickness. I had to admit, what Alan said had a ring of truth – I wasn't very exciting to come home to. But wasn't there something in the Bible about helping one another up if you're down? What happened if you were both down? Whatever had happened to this "paradise" I once loved?

Later that evening, when the children were in bed, a welcome breeze wafted through the louvered windows into our small living room. We sat there in silence for a while until Alan turned to me.

"Sorry for the way I spoke to you today, Luv."

"You're forgiven," I said, patting his arm.

"It's just that...if only I could see some fruit. I preach my heart out and people smile and call me a good olometua (preacher), but there are no visible signs of people coming to Christ. I'm just fed up! Sometimes I...I...just want to leave this place!"

"That makes two of us," I replied. "But you and I both know

we can't do that." Alan jumped up and started to pace back and forth.

"We both know it was God's will to come here," I implored. "Remember, God said the wall would seem impenetrable – but that if we prayed and preached His word faithfully, eventually cracks would appear and the walls would fall down."

"Well, we've done that, haven't we?" Alan tossed back, still frustrated. "Look at all the time I've spent fasting and praying at the pastors' college. Two years of it, twice a week at lunch times, and what do we see? Nothing!"

He slumped into a chair, shaking his head and throwing his hands in the air. "You know, I feel like a failure. I didn't get the chance to tell you what the doctor said about my stomach pains. I'm getting a nice little ulcer...me, the Christian missionary! What a great testimony!

"He told me either I learn to relax, or I'll end up with several ulcers. That's great, isn't it?" he said sarcastically.

As I watched my husband continue to wag his head in despair, my own problems seemed small. Somehow being a sounding board helped me forget my own depression.

"Do you want to pray?" I said at last. In answer, he threw himself face down on the linoleum. Soon his chest began to heave with sobs of deep pain.

"God!" he cried. "I just can't cope! I'm a failure. I'm sick, the children are sick, and I want to leave! You'd better get someone else to do the job. It's...hopeless!"

On and on he sobbed until at last he lay silent for what seemed a long time.

Feeling helpless, all I could do was pray under my breath. My heart went out to him, but I knew only God could give him the comfort he needed. Of course it had been rough for me too with the children so sick, but at least I had the daily fulfillment of mothering.

Suddenly Alan's broken voice pierced the silence, quietly at first. "Lord...I'm not sure what you're doing with me, but – if You see I can't be trusted to reap, if You know there's something proud in me, then keep me sowing. Please Lord, You know my heart better than I do."

I was relieved as I sensed Alan's old fight coming back again. Rising to his knees, his eyes were still red and wet as he began to speak out to God all the promises He had given us.

"All we see are the adversaries, Lord, but You said it would be an effective work!" He was almost panting now. "We stand against the adversaries – the forces of evil!"

Alan's voice grew louder and louder as he prayed on, but I had long since stopped worrying about the neighbors when Alan prayed. Jumping up, he began to pace back and forth again as he spoke angrily at the adversaries that blocked the spread of God's Word and ways on the island.

"We resist you, Satan," he challenged, stamping his foot. "God said, an EFFECTIVE WORK! EFFECTIVE, do you hear, Satan? You won't win! You won't!" He was shouting so loud now I thought the neighbors might call the police, but it didn't matter. All at once it seemed something broke in the atmosphere, and our voices blended in praise to God. We both shouted words of triumph and lifted our hands in worship to our wonderful God.

"Lord we believe YOU, not the circumstances!" Alan proclaimed joyfully. "No matter what! We will stand fast. We're here for life, if that's what you ask of us!"

Over the next months we continued in prayer and pressing through setbacks, while Alan continued to lead our faithful evangelism team each Sunday night.

One morning just before Alan left for work, he came up to me with a strange look.

"I can't understand it…but as I stepped into the shower this morning, I felt God was saying we are to leave the island in one year," he said. "We really need to pray about this together."

I stared hard at him. "But I thought God called us here for life!"

"Well, I did too. Maybe God wants to steer us in another direction."

The thought had never crossed our minds that God might call us elsewhere. We had so firmly believed our life calling was to the Cook Islands, we had settled in to the point of adopting the culture in every way, attending a year-long course of language school, and even trying to start a Bible School. But when we later discussed the matter at length and prayed together, we both couldn't shake the conviction that God was moving us on.

A few days later, Alan discovered that there was a one-year waiting list for anyone wanting to book sea passage back to New Zealand. Recognizing he truly had heard the voice of the Lord, Alan quickly added our names to the list.

Our next confirmation came when Alan bounded home with a telegram. Usually a telegram meant bad news, but his cheery face told me otherwise. I playfully tried to snatch it from his hand.

"Who is it from?"

"You'll never guess – it's from Neville Winger, of Orama Christian Fellowship!"

Neville's Christian conference center was located on the Great Barrier Island in New Zealand, and now fond memories of he and his wife Dottie flitted through my mind. While in Bible School, we had all been involved in evangelistic meetings together.

Alan began to read: "HAVE A BURDEN TO SEND A TEAM TO DO EVANGELISM stop CAN YOU HOST THEM? stop. NEVILLE WINGER."

Alan's eyes were shining, because to our knowledge, no such team had ever been allowed on the island.

"This could be a part of God's plan," he said. "We've laid a foundation of trust with the people and leaders here. Surely God can use us now to get this team in."

My mind began doing cart-wheels as I anticipated how God might at last be answering our prayers. I also relished the thought of visiting with fellow New Zealanders. I felt so isolated on this tiny island sometimes. Of course I had beautiful island friends, but their needs were often different from mine. Also, I had been deeply affected by the recent loss of my closest Rarotongan friend, who had died from typhoid fever. I so needed to talk it through with someone, and I ached for good conversation with my fellow New Zealanders. Alan, on the other hand, was such a loner, he didn't seem to need people as much.

As I was reflecting on all this, a verse of scripture popped into my mind: "They that sow in tears shall reap in joy." (Psalm 126:5 KJV) Was the Lord saying that the literal tears we'd shed over our sick children and seeming lack of fruit would now reap a harvest of joy? But as I shared it with Alan, he tried to pull me back to reality.

"Hey, wait a minute. We don't even know if they can get on the island yet!"

But already my spirit was leaping in faith that this was God's will — nothing could stop His plans.

Sure enough, our visit to Mr. Albert Henry, the Prime Minister of the Cook Islands, brought further confirmation. Mr. Henry already knew us because he attended the same church, so when we presented the possibility of an outreach team coming, he only asked us a few simple questions before giving his permission. He even agreed to notify the immigration authorities to prevent any delays. The only condition was that we take complete responsibility for their housing and conduct while on the island.

After thanking the prime minister profusely, we restrained our joy just long enough to get out of his office. Once we were safely hidden behind a red hibiscus hedge, we let out a loud whoop and danced around in joy, scattering a few stray hens.

"The wall is coming down at last!" I cried.

Over the next few weeks, we purchased tents for the team of about 15 to stay in, and set them up in a circle around our house. Our curious brown-skinned neighbors watched as Alan carefully erected outdoor showers by nailing wooden apple boxes together and using large perforated tin cans for the shower heads, with garden hoses inside. Rarotongan friends set to work weaving coconut fronds to make the roof and walls of an outside dining and meeting room area in our yard.

The morning the team was scheduled to arrive, I hurriedly fed and dressed the children, and then strapped chubby-cheeked Stephen into his stroller. Samuel stood on the back of the stroller, while Joy and I steered it over the bumpy road, carefully holding freshly made Tipani leis in our spare hands for our guests. We met Alan outside the government freezer where he was excused from work for the rest of the day, and in great anticipation, we all made our way to the pier. Now it was our turn to welcome people to "paradise," and we hoped our prayer and preparation would make it so for them.

Almost any solid ground would have been paradise for the team after several days aboard an old red tub called the Maga Dan. They eagerly scrambled ashore from the longboat, and it was thrilling to see a few familiar faces, including two older women who immediately began to grandmother our children. I was beside myself to have these friends from home to welcome, serve and work alongside.

I came up to Alan as he was shaking hands with Jeff, the even-tempered team leader, and was introduced to him and his wife Gail. In humility, Jeff offered full leadership over to Alan, and I knew God was honoring Alan's own humility – although he loved preaching and leadership, he had taken the time off work in expectation of simply serving the team in any way possible and using his influence to set up meetings. As I listened to the two of them talk together, I knew God was forming an anointed partnership.

The first morning of the outreach, the entire group met together for prayer, including a few of the Rarotongans. Alan received an unexpected impression from the Lord that we were to start our outreach toward the east and not the west, as we previously planned.

As the team followed that nudge, the Lord began to work powerfully, and we all experienced a strong awareness of God's presence. Whereas in the past the people listened but made no response, now large numbers responded to the word of God and came forward to receive Christ publicly.

Our two leaders moved as one and all of us benefitted from the unity that flowed down from them. Now doors previously closed to us swung wide open. The head of all the schools on the island allowed us to have meetings, and the island leaders in every village now allowed us to show films as well as preach.

One evening at dusk, the entire village stood in response to the message of salvation. Amazed, Alan instructed them to sit again as he explained once more that he was asking for people to repent of sin and give their lives to Jesus. To his amazement they all stood again. After repeating the process a third time, sure enough everyone stood again. It was truly a move of God's spirit.

A faithful young Rarotongan Christian who was a member of our team, had often shared how her heart ached for her backslidden husband to return to the Lord. During one of our meetings, he came rushing in, weeping in repentance before God down the aisle of the local movie theater we had hired. The night before he had two very frightening dreams that his wife was taken to be with God first through a fire and then a tidal wave, but he was unable to follow her. God's Spirit was moving in a powerful way.

On the way home after one such meeting, several weeks after the outreach began, I was overcome with emotion as I looked into Alan's contented face.

"I can't help thinking back to those dark moments we've had here," I reminded him. "We could have missed all this if we'd deserted our post."

All too soon, the month-long outreach came to an end. As we said goodbye to our new friends, we were glad we would be following them back to New Zealand in a couple of weeks. Eager as I was to return to my homeland, I knew it meant a sad parting with our dear Rarotongan friends.

We now fretted over who would care for the new young Christians? We took comfort in the fact that they already attended church and knew the Bible from childhood. Hopefully with their new understanding of a personal relationship with God, they would grow quickly. Besides, we were so sure it was right to leave, we had to trust God to send others. We had been the pioneers, laying a foundation in prayer and spiritual warfare, and now others would take up the leadership.

Sure enough, as the remaining weeks stretched on, we saw that we could safely leave the work in the hands of a young Christian school teacher who was gifted at nurturing Christian growth. Also, a young Canadian named Herb Risto, who had been on the New Zealand team, was interested in coming back to serve in the Cook Islands.

When our departure day arrived, we paused over a cup of tea before boarding the Moana Roa. It didn't seem possible that three years had gone by – but the children were now six, two-and-a half and one-year-old – living proof of the passage of time. Apart from a few parasitic passengers in our bodies, we were not too much worse for wear – a testimony of God's faithfulness!

When the phone interrupted us, I assumed it was someone wanting to say goodbye, but Alan reacted with surprise as he answered it.

"You won't believe this," he said, shaking his head in amazement. "There's a seat on the Hercules airplane which leaves for New Zealand in one hour. You and Stephen can go by air."

"It's a miracle!" I gasped. Getting a seat on the old military plane was usually impossible, and even more so now, with a long waiting list of New Zealand government officials waiting to get home.

"But…how did anyone know we wanted a seat if we didn't even try?"

"Don't just stand there trying to work it out, go for it," Alan laughed. "It sure beats five days at sea, with your sailing history."

I hesitated. "What about you and the children?"

Alan laughed harder. "You wouldn't be much use to us lying horizontal, now would you?"

So an hour later, I was boarding the bulky gray plane with Stephen in my arms, and waving a tearful goodbye to our beloved island friends. I would miss them so much, but I had an overwhelming sense that we had done all God had asked us to do.

"See you in New Zealand," I called to Alan from the top of the boarding stairs. He waved back, but was distracted about getting all our belongings on to the ship for the afternoon sail. Soon we were soaring over the island and I was in awe once again of Rarotonga's stunning beauty. Like an exquisite, green emerald in the azure sea, it grew smaller and smaller in the distance. I gazed back nostalgically. It really was a "paradise" ...well, almost paradise!

Children from the evangelical ministry at our home in Mangere, New Zealand.

<h1 style="text-align:center">10</h1>

Roots Downward, Fruit Upward

Setting down the tray of steaming tea, I sat quietly across from my husband in our comfortable living room. His eyes were staring into space and I could sense his frustration. Lately both of us felt like we were languishing, and we had been crying out to God for direction.

It had been five long years since we returned to Auckland, and the victory we experienced in the Cook Islands seemed a fading memory. Alan now worked at Air New Zealand as a cabin services employee, and we owned our own small house. But even in our comfortable life, the question lay always before us: When would we be back in missions?

Besides taking care of our three growing children, now ages 12, 9, and 7, I had found fulfillment with a flourishing children's ministry we had begun in our home. Of course, Alan still occasionally preached and taught in our church, but it wasn't the same as serving the Lord full time in missions. To cope, Alan buried himself in his job and withdrew into himself more and more. Now in one of his depressed moods, he wouldn't meet my gaze as I poured the tea.

"What is it, honey?" I said gently as I handed him the cup. "Do you want to talk?"

He shook his head. "I just feel God has put me on the shelf." It was a feeling he had expressed before, and I knew it was far from the truth.

When we first returned to New Zealand, we thought we'd be going right back to the mission field. Instead, we were surprised when the Lord clearly directed us to Isaiah 37:31: "And the remnant that is escaped of the house of Judah shall again take root downward, and bear fruit upward." Our first step in putting down roots was to find a house. We looked first at a modest, government-owned house in Mangere.

We felt right at home in a neighborhood filled with South Pacific Islanders. But, not wanting to be presumptuous, the five of us knelt down in the bare kitchen and asked God if this was our new home.

As we waited before the Lord, a scripture came to my mind: "A city set on a hill cannot be hid." (Matthew 5:14.) As I shared it with the rest of the family, Alan pointed out that this gleaming white house was situated in plain view on a corner opposite an elementary school.

"I think the Lord is saying we'll be witnesses for Him in the area," Alan suggested. We agreed, and soon moved in.

We had lived there about nine months when we began child evangelism meetings each week in our living room. The numbers grew so fast we erected a garage in the back yard to fit the 50 to 80 children who came each week. Many of these children, who ranged in age from five to 11, learned of Jesus' love for them for the first time. Joy, Samuel, and Stephen, who had already given their lives to Jesus, joined right in with us, enjoying the fun with their friends and helping wherever they could. God was indeed blessing with upward fruit.

One special day, I felt God gave me a glimpse into our future. While I led the children in a song, I was looking at the sea of faces before me when for a moment, time seemed to stand still. All at once, the picture before me seemed to change. It was as if I were looking at a multitude of children from many different nations, and I knew one day I would be ministering to them.

Now, as we sat here in our living room so far from the missionary life, such a vision seemed impossible. Still, I kept it tucked away deep in my heart, trusting the Lord to bring it to pass.

There were other blessings as well. Alan, who had been plagued with intestinal parasites after returning from the Cook Islands, was completely delivered from the symptoms at a healing service. Then after Alan's parents immigrated to New Zealand from Liverpool, he was thrilled to see the answer to 15 years of prayer: Both of them left the Jehovah's Witnesses and gave their lives to Christ.

Meanwhile, Alan's higher salary enabled us to begin buying our home. But as the roots went deeper, Alan only struggled more. Why wasn't God sending us back out among the nations?

Now, as I looked at the depression in Alan's face, I tried my best to encourage him.

"How can you say you're on the shelf?" I said. "Every time you speak, people say how much it helped them, and it's obvious God speaks through you."

"Well, I know God is with me, but I can't feel it," he protested. "I just don't understand why He hasn't sent us back onto the mission field."

"Well, that doesn't mean God has rejected you. God has His own timing." In answer, Alan just sat there silently, fighting his own inner battle. I felt so helpless, I wanted to shake him. "I don't understand it either, but all we can do is pray and trust God."

With a shrug, Alan retreated to the small office he'd converted in the tool shed, his favorite place for prayer and Bible study. I closed my eyes and lifted him in prayer. I'd said everything I could say. God was the only one who could give him the answers he so desperately needed.

Over the next few days, I went on about my motherly duties while continuing to pray for him. When my friend Marge Tee invited me to a widely publicized missionary rally in Auckland, I knew Alan would be working late, so I elected to go with her myself. I felt confident leaving 12-year-old Joy in charge of the household until Alan got home.

My heart was filled with anticipation as we drove downtown to the meeting. Brother Andrew, a Dutch evangelist well known for his mission work behind the Iron Curtain, was the guest speaker. Missions! How I loved hearing what God was doing overseas.

A large crowd jammed the auditorium, so we had to sit near the back. Soon Brother Andrew was introduced, but when he walked up to the podium he gave only a few welcoming remarks.

"Before I speak, I'd like to introduce Loren Cunningham, the founder of an interdenominational missionary organization called Youth With A Mission," Brother Andrew said.

I had heard of Loren Cunningham before through our mutual friends, the Dawsons, and was familiar with the mission group called YWAM (pronounced why-wam). As the large-framed American walked to the podium and flashed his winning smile, I sat in rapt attention.

"One day as I was looking at a globe of the Earth, it was as if I had a dream in my mind's eye," Loren explained passionately. "As the waves of water began lapping over the shore, they became waves of young people. In obedience to Jesus' Great Commission to take the Gospel to all creation, the waves of young people went out again and again, until the entire globe was covered."

Loren paused, his face glowing. "Since 1960, YWAMers have been going out in both short and long term missions in fulfillment of this vision. Now works are started on every continent."

As Loren began telling stories of what God was doing through

YWAM, my heart began to race. Could we do something like that?

"We now have a new vision to purchase a ship to serve the nations with evangelism and mercy ministries," Loren was saying fervently. "While carrying food, supplies and medical personnel aboard the ship to bring relief in crisis areas, we will also train young people on board."

"Marge," I said nudging my friend's arm, "that's exactly up Alan's alley!" She agreed with a nod. I listened eagerly as Loren explained the vision for this new ship to serve the nations.

As Loren concluded and Brother Andrew went to the podium, all I could think about was the ship. Even through Brother Andrew's dynamic message, I couldn't wait to go home and tell Alan! What a perfect way for him to combine his desire to preach with his experience and love of life at sea.

When I returned home, I ran inside hoping Alan was still awake, and found him reading in bed.

"You'll never guess what I heard tonight! There's going to be a ship to take the Gospel to the nations!"

"Is that right?" he said with obvious interest. "Tell me about it."

Soon I was spilling over with the news, and we determined to find out more about the new ministry. When we went to bed that night, Alan lay awake mulling over all I'd said, and it was exciting to see a spark of hope in his eyes.

We were even more excited when a few weeks later Alan received a letter from our dear friend, Reona Peterson. A fellow New Zealander, Reona now served in YWAM as Loren Cunningham's personal secretary in Lausanne, Switzerland. Reona said that while praying with others about the ship ministry, they had felt impressed by God to ask Alan to pray about joining the crew.

Holding Reona's letter tightly, Alan waved it at me.

"Do you think this is really for us?" he asked. "I'd probably be away for long periods, and now that we have three children, it would be hard to have me away at sea."

I looked at him soberly. "Yes, it would be hard. But I've known this was for you from the night I heard Loren's message. It's almost as if God designed it with you in mind."

Alan's lips broke into a grin and he nodded in agreement. "It's true," he agreed. "When I became a Christian, I only knew of one other Christian seaman on the coastal ships. It's marvelous to imagine a whole ship with Christians plying the seas with goods for the poor and doing evangelism in ports."

Over the next few weeks, we kept praying about it as a family. Samuel and Joy responded with their usual enthusiasm about Alan going to the ship, and although Stephen was quieter in his response, he also agreed.

One evening I came in and heard Alan talking excitedly on the phone, obviously to someone from YWAM. When he hung up, his face was glowing.

"That was an American named Wally Wenge," he began. "He said he's negotiating the purchase of a New Zealand inter-island ferry called the Maori – and he wants me to join the crew as chief steward."

Alan said the ship was located in Wellington, only 400 miles south of us.

"This has to be the Lord!" I answered, and Alan agreed. So, the decision was made!

A few days later, Alan gave notice to his superiors at Air New Zealand and began preparing to go. The ship's new crew was now renovating and preparing it for sea, so our whole family could have gone – but it was decided the children and I would stay back five more months until the warm New Zealand December, when their school year ended and my children's ministry was in recess.

Alan packed up our small Volkswagen beetle and we all kissed him goodbye. As he waved farewell and headed down the road, I knew it was the beginning of a new phase in our lives.

Alan's phone calls over the next weeks radiated with enthusiasm. The crew was busy cleaning the ship's cabins and praying over every aspect of the ministry. He said he couldn't wait for me to meet the ship's captain and his wife, Ben and Helen Applegate, who had had a vision for a ship like this for over 20 years.

"Oh, by the way, the ship will carry whole families, serving the Lord together," he added.

"Oh, no!" I threw a look heavenward and groaned. Me? Actually living on a ship? I began to laugh incredulously. "If that's what God wants, He'll have to heal me of seasickness or I'll never survive!"

Alan tried to assure me that he would make the first trip alone to get a cabin ready for us all, but my heart was still beating fast. How could I live on a ship permanently?

Joy, Samuel and Stephen were excited at the thought of living on the ship, and our prayers each evening grew more intense. They could hardly wait for school to end so we could join the rest of the crew. I was praying for God to make me willing to go to sea again, and the grace to be able to live there.

Alan had been working on the ship just a few months when his father suffered a fatal stroke. Alan made arrangements to come home quickly for the funeral, and we were so thankful his dad had walked with the Lord for two full years, a time described by Alan's mother as a "honeymoon."

Of course it was natural for Alan to be grieving, but somehow I sensed something else bothered him too. A few days before Alan was to return to the ship, we were having our afternoon "cuppa," when Alan confided that fund-raising for the ship wasn't going well. A Christian man in England had already paid the deposit of NZ $48,000, and about NZ $26,000 in donations had also been received; but the rest of the money, about NZ $480,000, wasn't coming in as hoped.

"We don't have long until the new deadline," Alan said. "The Union Steamship Company has already changed it several times, and unless we pay it by then, they told us the crew will have to vacate the ship."

I looked at him blankly. "But how could we go so far, only to lose the ship?"

Alan shrugged, and I could see the deep concern in his eyes.

"Surely God wouldn't let that happen."

"I certainly hope not, Luv," he said.

After he headed back to the ship, the question weighed heavily on my mind. What was really happening? Of course we couldn't actually lose the ship – not after putting down such a large down payment. But I couldn't get that frightful possibility out of my mind. I found myself praying about it constantly.

A few days later, I answered the telephone to hear Alan's voice more serious than ever.

"We've all been told to vacate the ship, Luv. At least they gave us an extension for the final payment – I guess God is going to do the last minute deliverance again." He was trying to sound light, but a sense of foreboding filled me.

A couple of weeks later, the long December school vacation at last arrived, and Alan came up to Auckland to take us back to meet the crew over the Christmas holiday. He told us the money still was not coming in, but the team was in good spirits, trusting God for a miracle. As we loaded up the car, I was filled with both joy and misgivings. Would I be accepted by all these people who had worked so hard to prepare the ship? It was that old, annoying fear of man again. To combat it, I turned each anxiety into prayer as we drove the 400 miles to Wellington.

The team was staying in dormitory rooms at a local university that was in recess for the summer. We settled into our two rooms and Alan took us over to meet Captain Ben and Helen Applegate. We were pleased to find their two daughters, Gaye and Jan, were close in age to our boys.

"It's so good to meet you at last," Helen said with genuine warmth. "Excuse me a minute while I make a nice hot cup of tea." One brief meeting showed me Helen was a gracious and motherly person.

Ben was every bit the Englishman, slim and dignified, with slightly graying wavy hair. I knew he and Alan got on well together because they both had that dry English humor. I could see right away I needn't have worried about being accepted by these loving people.

For the next hour, we sipped tea and nibbled Helen's freshly baked scones, while Ben caught me up on the ship news. The payment deadline was already past, and Union Steamship Company said it was too late. Still the team was hanging on for a miracle. In the meantime, Alan and other Bible teachers helped to keep up morale among the crew with daily Bible teaching and prayer. I could tell Ben and Helen were committed prayer warriors, and their love for God permeated the conversation. I was going to love working with these two!

The next morning, Alan took me to a meeting hall where we were to have the daily prayer time with the rest of the crew of about 50. He introduced me to the crowd, and though I still felt a bit on edge, I relaxed as we divided into groups and began praying fervently for the finances still needed to purchase the ship.

In our prayer group, we began speaking out prayers of faith. Then the atmosphere grew very still, and for long moments we waited before God with our eyes tightly shut.

A middle-aged woman next to me broke the silence. "I saw a vision of a white gleaming ship sailing the ocean. It was beautiful, with white paint gleaming in the sun."

Alan looked around the group. "I believe this means God's ship will stand for the purity and holiness of the crew and the ministry," he said seriously. "I perceive God will require a high standard of us."

I had only seen the Maori in a photograph, but I knew it was olive green. A sinking feeling gripped me. Could there be another ship God had in mind? "This must mean the Maori is to be painted white in the future," I suggested.

Our group went back to prayer as I continued to ponder what the vision might mean. I wondered what living up to that high standard would mean for us all.

The next four weeks slid by quickly. Although the deadline was clearly past, still our prayers grew stronger. We had often seen God come through at the last minute. Why should now be any different?

One day as the crew assembled for our daily meeting, I took a seat near the back, enabling me to keep tabs on the boys as they played outside with the other children. Alan had been meeting with Captain Ben and Wally, and I looked around to see the three of them heading down the aisle to seats in the front row. I caught Alan's eye as he passed, and the look on his face filled me with dread. It couldn't be! After all the labor, prayer and faith, God couldn't let us down!

The meeting room grew quiet as Wally stood up to face us. His usually smiling face was grave.

"You all know how gracious the Union Steam Ship Company has been to us through this whole situation," he said with solemnity. "They extended the payment deadline for the Maori several times, until finally they could extend it no longer. I know we've all kept believing God for a miracle, but I'm afraid I have some bad news."

I listened unbelieving, wanting to deny what I knew would come next. "No God! Please don't let it be!" I whispered under my breath.

"I'm sorry," Wally said tensely, "but the Maori has just been sold to someone else for scrap. There's no hope of getting back our deposit."

The words fell on us like a collapsing building. We were stunned. A loud buzz of distraught conversation burst across the room. Some of the families had sold homes, and men had given up excellent jobs, giving their all for the ship ministry. Some couples now stared at each other in utter disbelief. What ever had gone wrong? In an effort to quell the fears, Alan sprang to his feet.

"Look, let's stay steady here, and not lose faith in our mighty God," he said loudly, bringing everyone to attention. "We've lost this ship, but that doesn't mean we've lost the vision of the whole ministry, does it? Do we believe God spoke that vision to us or not? If we do, we need to be strong and hold on, no matter what we face."

I looked at his brave face as he strove to lead us all in the crisis, continuing to speak words of hope and strength to the crew. He was putting their needs before his own, and my heart went out to him. But how would he react once the dust settled and the full impact of the news finally sank in? We had waited so long to get into ministry again. Now what were we going to do?

"Oh, Alan…Alan," I whispered to myself. "I hope you can take your own advice in the days that lie ahead!"

11
Embracing The Cross

It was a Sunday morning two weeks later, just six weeks since the children and I joined the crew, that our family again began loading our belongings into the car to go back to Auckland. We and the rest of the crew were all still in a daze as we sorted through the questions flooding our minds.

Losing the ship was a huge blow to the leaders of Youth With A Mission, and my heart especially went out to Wally Wenge, who had led the fundraising efforts with such integrity. For Alan and I and the other YWAM leaders, our last two weeks had been filled with counseling and praying with the bewildered and even angry crew members, helping them sort it all out.

Some of the crew decided to remain in Wellington, living for a time in a campground under the direction of the Applegates. Ben and Helen gathered them like a hen with chicks.

Dear Ben and Helen – how my heart ached for them! Their

faith for a ship ministry had already been tested through two decades, and now what a disappointment. Yet it was so like them to put aside their own grief and minister to others. They had been reaching out to Alan and me too, and were trying to help us gain some understanding of what had happened.

Ben told us part of the answer had come to YWAM's founder Loren Cunningham, whom I had heard speak alongside Brother Andrew that first night. Loren had also been working hard to back Wally up in fundraising, and while at a staff conference in Seoul, Korea, he'd had an encounter with the Lord while praying alone in his room.

In his mind's eye, Loren had seen a vision of himself exuberantly announcing the purchase of the ship to a crowd of applauding YWAM leaders. It was a joyful moment, until Loren's attention was drawn to the side. To his horror, Jesus was standing forgotten in the shadows, obviously grieved. Immediately Loren knew that instead of giving God the glory, we as a mission had been focusing on the ship.

Deeply convicted, Loren wept for an hour afterward, telling the Lord to take the ship rather than let us take God's glory. I watching Ben's solemn face as he paused in the story.

"It seems God is challenging us to get our eyes back onto Him," Ben concluded. Alan and I exchanged glances. Was that what God was doing? Taking Loren at His word? It certainly gave me something to think about over the last week.

Now, with the car all loaded, I rounded up our children who were saying their own sad goodbyes to newfound friends, and we started northward. Joy, Samuel and Stephen were also disappointed with the turn of events, but were apparently taking it in stride. Soon they fell asleep.

Alan was very quiet, and I guessed he was experiencing the same as I – loads of questions that buzzed in my head like annoying flies that wouldn't brush away. Even with Loren's story, there seemed to be no concrete answers, and it was bewildering. We had just begun to have our lives entwined with the rest of the crew, and now we were ripped apart! What was it all for? And would we ever see the Applegates or the rest of our friends again?

I worried about Alan. What would he do now? I knew he wouldn't be happy at a secular job again, but what else was there? On and on the questions tumbled in my mind, and my anxiety continued to mount.

But even in my fretting, I remembered something I told the crew during a time of prayer. As I had observed the children, I saw how even in this crisis they continued to play happily, trusting in the security and love of their parents. It never even entered their minds to worry about where their next meal would come from, or where they would sleep each night; they knew their parents would look after them.

"We need to be like them," I had told the crew. "God is our father, and He loves us no matter what! We need to leave ourselves in His arms, trusting Him to look after us."

As I thought again about the truth of those words, I relaxed in the car seat next to Alan, picturing myself in God's arms. Father would take care of us! I hated what was happening, but I was thankful for leaders who wanted to give God the glory above all else.

I glanced over at Alan. His eyes were transfixed on the road, and I knew he was deep in thought. He seemed to be taking it all so well – almost too well.

We had been home just two days when I awoke with a sense of foreboding. Alan always rose earlier than me, but when I made my way to the small study, I found him sitting in his chair staring into space. His face was drawn and a melancholy gloom had settled over him.

"Alan, what is it?" He didn't stir.

"Just leave me alone," he said after a long silence.

"But, Alan!"

"You heard me. I don't want to talk about it."

Feeling helpless and frightened, I turned and left. For the next three days Alan rarely came out of the study. I was growing desperate to find a way to snap him out of his depression.

On Saturday I decided to try a different tack. The children were away for the morning with friends, and I seized the opportunity to barge into Alan's study.

"I'm not putting up with this!" I said sharply, flinging my hands in the air. "I can't stand you not talking and withdrawing like this!"

Alan sat still as a sphinx.

"Alan, I can't take it any more!"

Finally he stirred in his chair and sighed. "Well, we'd better pack it in then," he said sullenly.

"Pack what in?"

"Everything...our marriage."

A rush of nausea overwhelmed me and I bolted out the door. Running back to the kitchen, I couldn't keep the tears from spilling out of my eyes. I had never seen Alan so low! Why, oh, why, didn't I just pray, and keep my big mouth shut? We'd ironed out problems before, but divorce was never an option. We hadn't even spoken of it before!

I literally ran the three blocks to the small prayer meeting that was going on at our local church. The intimate group listened supportively as, through tears, I openly shared what had happened.

"I'm so afraid!" I confessed. "I think Alan may be suicidal, and right now I need you to stand with us. We even feel embarrassed to be back here after everything we said about the ship ministry before we left."

Several of them put their arms around me with great compassion, and, as they all gathered around, earnest prayers were offered on our behalf. As they prayed, an amazing thing happened. I was filled with a supernatural peace, as if nothing were ever wrong. An hour later when I returned to the house, I ran in to find Alan making tea in the kitchen. His whole countenance was changed and I ran into his arms.

"I'm so sorry for what I said, Luv," he confessed. "I must have been out of my mind."

"Me, too." We clung tightly to each other. "I just wanted to shake you out of the depression. I'm sorry I went about it the wrong way."

"It's just that...I felt so disappointed." Alan held me away and looked into my eyes. "After waiting all this time for ministry...now there's nothing again. It's all over. I feel like God is a million miles away." I hugged him again, as if to share the pain.

"It's just like when I was a lad," he continued. "My dad would promise to take our family on an outing, and then he wouldn't feel like it and change his mind. We'd all be standing there dressed in our best clothes...and I was so terribly disappointed!"

Resting in each other's arms for long moments, we then turned to the only One who could help us.

"Lord, I know you are greater than any earthly father," Alan prayed. "I don't understand why all this happened, and I feel bewildered and disappointed. Please help me to trust You." I pulled away from Alan's arms. "You know what comes to mind, Darl? It's the verse someone read out in the meeting, when we lost the ship." I quoted it from memory: "'For the vision is yet for an appointed time, but at the end it shall speak, and not lie; though it tarry, wait for it, because it will surely come, it will not tarry." (Habakkuk 2:3)

I stopped and met his eyes. "Do you think this means we will get the Maori back some day?"

"I don't think so," Alan answered thoughtfully. "I know all things are possible, but it's already sailed away for Hong Kong where it will be used for scrap. But according to what Loren said, God will resurrect the vision some time in the future."

"Hmm...I wonder if that vision about a white ship means another one after all?"

We continued to talk it over, and although we still didn't have all the answers, we had put it in God's hands, and we could trust Him to work it all out.

The next Sunday at church, I knelt at the communion rail as my pastor served me the emblems. Staring into the crimson grape

juice in the tiny communion glass, I shuddered inside as I meditated on Jesus' shed blood. Death was such an ugly thing! Jesus'
own death, and now the death of this ministry. All at once I heard
that still small voice speaking into my mind, a voice I had come to
recognize as God's:

"Embrace the cross, Fay," the voice seemed to be saying. "Don't
run from it. There will always be resurrection after death."

"Yes, Lord," I whispered. It wasn't easy, but in the midst of so
much heartache, we were learning that resurrection can only follow a complete death. Like Jesus, we had no choice but to accept
the death God had in mind for us, but I knew I could hang on to
the promise of resurrection in the months ahead.

Alan soon got a new job at the airport, and we thanked God for
providing once again. Several weeks had gone by when a family
from the Maori crew came to stay with us for a week before returning to their home in the United States. Bill Mansfield, an American
seaman, and his Canadian wife, Beth, had become precious
friends. They and their 13-year-old son John and three-year-old
daughter, Heather, had become like family to us.

Bill and Beth had not been Christians long, and one night at
dinner we were fascinated as they told us how they were traveling
throughout Europe when they gave their lives to Christ. They had
almost immediately felt God calling them to serve Him on the
ship, and we were impressed with their speedy obedience.

As we began airing feelings of disappointment about the Maori,
Bill pulled out some photographs of small boats, telling in his
deep voice of his vision for a small boat ministry. "We could put
small boats on the larger ship," he explained in excitement. "Then
when we got to a group of islands, we could send the small ones
where the large ship couldn't go."

"This is great," Alan agreed, with new enthusiasm in his voice.
"I've had exactly the same thought. Every time I pray for the thousands of Indonesian islands, for instance, I realize how great small
boats would be."

Bill and Alan continued to discuss the plan with great animation, and I couldn't help thinking how good it was to see their eyes shining once again. Was God giving us a new direction?

We had been back home for about six months, when Bill and Beth paid Alan's airfare to a week-long staff conference of Youth With A Mission in Desert Hot Springs, California. No sooner had he gotten home and given each of us a big hug when he nearly burst with the news.

"Loren Cunningham invited us to go to Hawaii to begin our small boat ministry!" he said excitedly.

"Hawaii?" I said. "Tell us!"

Alan said that when he and Bill explained their vision to Loren, he invited both of our families to move to Kailua-Kona, Hawaii, where a new YWAM center was being established. It could be an ideal place to begin a small boat ministry as part of Youth With A Mission.

Joy and Samuel, always adventurous, bubbled over with enthusiam, and even the phlegmatic Stephen seemed excited. Sitting down in the living room, we bowed our heads and prayed.

"Lord, we commit this new plan to you, and we give you all the glory," Alan declared.

"Yes, Lord," I agreed. "Show us if this is the next step!"

Knowing it was in God's hands, we began waiting in anticipation. Was God really sending us to Hawaii? I loved the idea of being in ministry again, but now a new concern nagged at my heart. What about the children's education? I began to fret about how they would do in American schools.

Alan also continued to pursue the Lord for confirmation. One evening he came home from work and immediately sat me down in the living room. He then went on to describe a vision the Lord had given him during a slack period at work.

"I was crouched alone in a small service truck, waiting for the next plane, when I sensed the Lord talking to me," he recounted. "It seemed He was putting before me a choice of two roads. The higher road was hard and less secure, but full of challenge and rewards. The lower one was more secure, and He would still bless me on that road."

He stopped and looked at me as I caught my breath. Which way had he chosen?

"Luv, I was actually torn," he went on. "It's tempting to stay here, especially for the kid's sake, now that we have a house and I've got a well-paying job...

"But I made a choice for the higher road. I believe the Lord wants us to go to Hawaii!"

I let out a sigh of relief. "Oh, good!" I said. "I know that's what we're supposed to do."

I hesitated for a moment, and explained that I'd been going through a test too. "I've been worried about the children's education, but the Lord just gave me the answer. He said, 'Fay, I love your children more than you do. If you take this leap of faith, I'll be there to catch you.' "

Alan put his arm around me and smiled. "If He's going to send us to Hawaii, He must have plans in mind for the children too," he said.

We saw the importance of following God together as a family and not just dragging our children along, so the next step was to gather them to discuss and pray together about this new direction. Joy was now an enthusiastic, energetic teenager of 13. Samuel at 10 was as intense as ever, and at eight, our quieter, more contemplative Stephen helped calm down the atmosphere of our rather noisy and boisterous family. We spent a half day discussing the pros and cons, sharing our thoughts and praying, and the children confirmed what Alan and I had already been feeling.

That evening we all got together to watch television for a family treat. To our amazement, onto the screen came a brand new program, "Hawaii Five-O." We all burst out laughing. Alan sprang off the sofa like a clown and began quoting from one of his Bible messages about guidance in an exaggerated tone:

"God guides us in circumstances, through confirmation of others, from the word of God, and through Channel Two!"

Hawaii, here we come!

Our family in Kailua-Kona, Hawaii.

12

The World In Our Hearts

On November 12, 1975, the five of us found ourselves buckling our seat belts and sitting back to enjoy an inter-island flight, the last leg of our eight-hour journey from Auckland to Kailua-Kona on the Big Island of Hawaii. We had always thought Hawaii meant Honolulu, so this inter-island flight was a surprise. I had a feeling being in Youth With A Mission was going to greatly enhance our knowledge of geography.

The last four months in New Zealand had flown by. Our church had agreed to help sponsor us financially and rent out our house, and some trusted friends took over the neighborhood children's ministry. We were exhausted from packing and many emotional goodbyes, but it felt so good to be going into full- time missionary work again.

I thought often of the verse the Lord had highlighted from the early days of my relationship with Alan, Ecclesiastes 3:11: "He hath made everything beautiful in its time; also he hath set the world in their heart, so that no man can find out the work that God maketh from the beginning to the end." During all the ups and downs of the difficult early years of our marriage, I could see now that God's ways and timing were always best. It was such a comfort to know that God was making everything beautiful in its time.

"Multiplied nations...The world in their heart." I had never thought much about that part of the verse, but now I saw God's purposes were much greater than my limited vision. The Lord truly HAD put the world in our hearts, and now, through joining YWAM, He was calling us to look on the fields that were ripe unto harvest. I was also reminded of the vision God had given me about ministering to a multi-racial sea of children. Was this the place I would see that fulfilled?

As eager as Alan was to be in full-time ministry again, he still wondered how Hawaii fit into his desire to be a pioneer missionary. But the Lord had repeatedly assured him that he could make a far greater impact by multiplying his life through teaching others. Young people from around the world came to Hawaii for training, and as they absorbed the lessons of Alan's life, widespread multiplication would occur as they then took the Gospel worldwide.

Our plane began to descend toward Hawaii's Kona coast, and I remembered vividly my first breathtaking glimpse of Rarotonga 10 years before. I couldn't wait to see the beauty of a tropical island again.

But as the flight captain announced our landing, I was horrified when I looked out the window.

"Alan, we're about to land on the moon!" I said aghast. Instead of the lush, green vegetation I expected, acres of barren, grayish-brown lava rock stretched below us. This was certainly no paradise!

But before long, my disappointment turned to joy when our friends, the Mansfields, greeted us at the airport. As they drove us into the tiny town of Kailua-Kona, I let out a sigh of relief at the sight of coconut trees, brilliantly colored bougainvillaea and hibiscus, and the same pungent tipani flowers I had loved in Rarotonga, known in Hawaii as plumeria. I thanked God He hadn't taken us to the moon after all!

On the way, Bill treated us to our first American culinary experience, a meal at McDonald's. In New Zealand, we didn't have "fast food" places like this and eating out was very expensive. At first, I worried how Bill could pay for us all, but when I saw the modest prices, I relaxed. I was going to like America!

The Mansfields told us the YWAM facilities included a farm situated a few miles up the hill and a preschool on the south end of the island. Bill explained that the YWAMers all shared meals together at the farm, where 70 students from all over the world were currently being trained in the School of Evangelism (SOE). The only other YWAM facilities were rented housing, and we would be moving into one of the Kona Kai apartments where most of the staff lived.

Our ears perked up when Bill told us Loren had a much bigger vision for YWAM Kona. Although we were making do with the current properties, Loren believed God wanted it to become a large training center where students could receive godly principles in a variety of disciplines and then be sent out as missionaries all over the world.

"We are already looking at a possible site. There's an old unused hotel called the Pacific Empress would just be perfect!"

"I suppose it's quite expensive?" Alan ventured.

"They're asking way beyond what we could afford, but as Loren says, if God's in it, He'll show us what to do," Bill replied.

Alan and I exchanged glances. We all seemed to be remembering the hard lessons we learned when we lost the Maori. This time we would have the chance to walk through the challenge God's way!

The next day we settled into our apartment and that night, we met the rest of the 100 or so YWAMers during their usual cafeteria-style community supper. As we got in line and took our plates, Alan and I looked at each other in surprise at what looked like a piece of cake sitting on the meat dish.

"Oh, that's not cake, it's corn bread," a pretty young American girl assured us. Alan made a face and Stephen decided he wasn't hungry.

"Mum, look!" Joy whispered in a horrified tone. "They're putting green jelly (Jello) on the meat!"

"Come on, let's just be thankful for what's put in front of us," I said. We tried to make the best of it, but it was a wonder any of our family ate that evening. Stephen did go without, but for the rest of us hunger won out as we tried to eat around the melting green juice the Jello had become. After all our unusual meals in Rarotonga, I was sure we could survive these new American meals.

We ate at long communal tables, and I was immediately impressed by the sense of community and common purpose that was expressed by our new acquaintances. Like a piece of blotting paper, I soaked in the warmth and friendliness surrounding me, and the children also quickly began making new friends. Of course for Alan, a loner by nature, the idea of community living was less appealing – he was more interested in when his ministry could get started!

After supper, Alan introduced me to Loren Cunningham and his vivacious, blonde wife Darlene. It was an honor to meet them face to face. Then, as groups of us stood talking in clusters, a pleasant-looking man appeared through the crowd and stuck out his hand to me in greeting.

"I'm Len Griswold," he said as we shook hands warmly. "I wanted to let you know we're beginning the first enrollment of the International Christian School, or ICS – a new YWAM school for our staff children."

My mouth fell open.

"I can't believe it!" I said, now smiling broadly. "That's wonderful news. I was so worried about the children's education before we came, but the Lord said He'd catch me if I took a leap of faith. I never expected Him to catch me like this!"

Len went on to explain that the Hawaii state education department had just approved the new program, and that the school would be held right in our Kona Kai Apartments. I thanked God over and over for His obvious provision.

When I shared my good news with Alan and the children, Samuel objected it was still their holiday time. I tried to explain that while it was now the summer vacation time for New Zealand schools, the American school year had just begun. Poor Samuel! Public school had never been easy for this intense 11-year-old, but I had a feeling the more loving atmosphere in ICS would be good for him. At the same time, Stephen and Joy didn't seem to mind cutting short their vacation.

The next day they had their first day of school, while Alan and I boarded the bus with the others and headed up the hill to the farm. There in the School of Evangelism, students learned about God's character and ways and how to make Him known to a needy world.

At first, I thought it seemed strange to hold a school on a farm, envisioning green fertile hills, sheep, and cows, but as we drove into the property, we were greeted by the same inhospitable lava rock, covered here and there with scrubby weeds.

The lectures were being held in what had once been a greenhouse made of plastic stretched over metal frames, and the plastic now sagged and parts of it flapped loose in the hot sun. As Alan and I sat in on the lectures that morning, it was evident that this humble setting was being daily transformed into a sanctuary through the teaching of God's word and intercession for the nations. That alone made the farm special. Another special thing for me was meeting so many people from different parts of the world.

That afternoon we were told that besides sitting in on the daily lectures, Alan would be in charge of food purchasing because of his ship steward experience, and I would help in the kitchen. Of course Alan was anxious to get started in the small boat ministry, but it seemed apparent that we needed to take one step at a time, laying a foundation in prayer and trusting God to bring it about.

We loved our new community and threw ourselves into our

work, but it was not without its trials. We had been in Kona only a few weeks when the YWAM community planned to celebrate the American Thanksgiving Day feast, a first for our family. Invitations went out to various friends in the Kona community, and soon I and the rest of the kitchen crew began preparing the various dishes. It was obvious from the excitement in the YWAM community that this was a very special event.

The night before the feast, I returned to our apartment to find Alan racing about, anxiously making phone calls.

"What's up with you?" I asked.

"Not enough turkey, that's what's up!"

I looked at him in surprise. "What happened?"

"The guest list swelled far beyond what I understood when I ordered the meat yesterday," he explained. "We're in a right mess now because it's too late to order more."

Alan hated bad organization with a passion. As we discussed possible solutions, the only answer was to have the staff and students eat after the guests. We hated the thought that quite a few would have to go without, but there was nothing else we could do.

The next day, the small farm kitchen was buzzing with activity under the direction of John Fabergenic, a Yugoslavian student who was a former army cook. I and the rest of the crew were chopping vegetables for the dressing when Alan shot into the kitchen.

"I'm sorry, John, I've tried everywhere, but I can't find any more turkey! Everything is closed."

To my surprise, John didn't seem at all perturbed, but shrugged his shoulders.

"Oh, no problem," he said nonchalantly. After Alan left the kitchen, John began giving instructions as if nothing were wrong.

"We'll just have to pray for God to multiply the turkey!" he concluded. I raised my eyebrows to my co-worker. Was he serious? The thought had never crossed my mind!

Soon I was busy helping John lay the slices of turkey roll in the large trays, pouring thin brown gravy over each. The deep trays were only half filled, and I felt bad for Alan – even though it wasn't his fault, he was still the one responsible for not ordering enough food.

"Okay, let's pray!" John said, calling us together around the trays. I stared at him as I reluctantly came near, and I felt phony as I bowed my head. He really was serious!

"Lord, you see that we don't have enough turkey," John began matter-of-factly in his slight accent. "We know you don't want anyone to go without turkey any more than we do. I'd like to ask you to multiply it so there will be enough. Thank you Lord!"

I quickly opened my eyes to see if John were joking, but as he raised his head and opened his eyes, I could see he'd prayed in all earnestness. Could something like that really happen? It was definitely new to me!

But an hour later as the turkey trays were removed from the oven, my mouth fell open and my eyes blinked hard. The trays had gone in half-full, but were now up to the rim! I was shocked and humbled at the same time. After we enjoyed the scrumptious feast, we saw that we even had enough left over for the next day! I was ashamed of my unbelief for what could only be called a miracle.

As the weeks began to pass, the children quickly adapted in the ICS, and Alan and I thrived on being in ministry again. Besides food purchasing, Alan was now serving on the leadership team, and he was more fulfilled than ever.

Christmas came and it was now time for the SOE students to go on a two-month evangelism outreach in various parts of the world. Pangs of sadness gripped me as I tried to join in the festivities at the Christmas/farewell party at the farm. At the end of the evening, it was so hard to say goodbye to these beautiful young people I had come to love. Tears began to flow as I hugged each one. These individual representatives of the world were now definitely in my heart!

Darlene Cunningham was standing nearby, and I was surprised to see that her eyes were dry and she was as bubbly as ever.

"How do you stand this every school?" I asked her, drying my eyes.

"Oh, I'll see them all again," she said with her vibrant smile. "You never say goodbye to YWAMers! You meet them all over the world!"

I thought to myself, I'd have to remember that or I'd never survive the emotion of saying goodbye to so many in YWAM! I took comfort in knowing that in just a few days a new group of students would arrive for a new school, and Alan would help lead the next SOE in March. God was putting new challenges before us! That night as we went to bed, I thanked God again, not only for bringing us here but for His marvelous preparation time. He had led our family in such similar principles and calling that being in YWAM was like slipping on a perfectly tailored glove. It now seemed the ministry we had waited for over the years was encompassed within the YWAM slogan: "To Know God And Make Him Known." Within that saying, the whole world was the limit.

Moving in to the Pacific Empress Hotel on Hawaii's Big Island.

13
Testings

After the New Year, the next major challenge God put before us was to begin praying and planning for the release of the new property, the 45-acre Pacific Empress Hotel overlooking the town of Kailua. Housing was already scarce, and Loren and the other leaders called staff and students to begin praying regularly for God's direction.

One evening when I joined Alan at the dinner table, he seemed particularly excited.

"I've just been praying with the leadership team about the property, and we believe God gave us an amount to offer!" he told me.

Alan explained that as the four-member leadership team waited before God, each one separately believed God was leading us to offer only $1.8 million for the Pacific Empress, an amount far below what they were asking.

"Even that will be a stretch of faith," I responded, knowing full well that we had no money or collateral for such a large offer.

Soon after Loren submitted our bid, our staff and students began holding regular times of prayer for the release of the property. As one of the leaders, Alan had the challenge on his mind continually. He began taking extra time for prayer, often with fasting as well. He was already so thin, sometimes I worried about him; but he knew God was calling him to it, so I left it alone. Many times he stayed out on our apartment lanai well into the night, pacing and praying fervently.

About that time, as the YWAMers were corporately praying for acceptance of our bid and the needed finances, our family faced a parallel battle on the home front.

As YWAM missionaries, none of us received salaries, not even Loren and Darlene. We believed we were called to live by faith, individually and corporately. Yet we were still responsible to pay for housing, food, the children's school fees, and other expenses. Although our family received a small sum from our local church in New Zealand, we depended largely on our quickly dwindling savings. Alan especially felt the pressure of providing for his family, and living costs in Hawaii were particularly high.

One night as Alan and I shared our frustrations in making ends meet, a thought suddenly struck him.

"You know, Luv, I've got an idea," he began. "Why don't we try living in tents up at the farm? It wouldn't be so bad, and think of all we could save without having to pay rent!"

"That's a great idea," I agreed. A few others had stayed in tents while in Kona, and I enjoyed camping. I knew between the both of us we could make it comfortable.

Alan looked relieved, so the next day we presented it to the children. Joy was less than enthusiastic about being away from her best friend, but the boys only thought of how much fun it would be to build forts at the farm.

Later, when I prayed and asked the Lord to direct us, He led me to the Bible story of Isaac and Rebecca. When asked if she would go with this man, Rebecca immediately agreed. Later Isaac "took her into his tent." I chuckled as I remembered the times I told

Alan I would follow him anywhere – even if it meant living in a tent. I knew I needed to follow him now!

So, the next few evenings after our day's work, Alan and I traveled up the hill to the farm to erect a large wooden frame over a wooden platform already on the site. Then we put thick plastic over the frame to make a waterproof covering that extended completely over two tents that sat side by side with a small storage passageway in between. The temperature was cooler at this elevation, and we were sure the azure blue sea and vivid sunsets would make it a great place to live.

There was one problem that we hadn't counted on. Strong winds kept blowing down portions of the already secured plastic. It was annoying to have to keep fixing it, but we were undaunted. We secured the tents and the covering as well as we could, and at last were ready to move in.

First we settled the children into their tent, and then began sorting out the other one for Alan and me. We were quite pleased with our efforts. It was so peaceful here at the farm, and I knew Alan enjoyed the cooler weather and being able to just be a family again. Alan and I hugged each other in delight before calling out goodnight to the kids. Soon we drifted off into a blissful sleep.

Early the next morning the cool, invigorating air helped us jump out of bed. Alan went to shower at the farm house, but within moments he stuck his head back in the tent.

"Did you hear any strong winds last night, Luv?"

I shook my head. "No, and the air is still now. What's wrong?"

"Looks like a strong wind broke off some of the plastic again, but I didn't hear anything either," he said. "And there's no time to fix it now. I'll have to do it tonight."

That evening after supper, Alan set about repairing the plastic before we nestled in for another night. Surely this strange weather would soon be over! I rolled over contentedly in the refreshing night air.

About midnight I awoke to the sound of strong winds and torrential rain. Alan was still fast asleep beside me, and to my relief, the plastic seemed to be holding. I drifted off again with the cozy thought that we were all dry and snug.

All at once I was jolted awake at the sound of my daughter's voice. Alan was already sitting up next to me.

"Dad!" Joy yelled again, with fear in her voice. "There's something in the tent! And it's right next to my bed!"

Alan and I bolted to our feet, feeling our way in the blackness. When I located a flashlight, I shined it into the other tent, I saw Alan and three bewildered children standing beside a giant plastic balloon of water hanging from the roof next to Joy's bed. The weight of the water had pushed the plastic roofing right down to the floor.

At Alan's direction, the five of us gathered around and tried to push the trapped water up and out, but the balloon was so heavy, we couldn't budge it. To make matters worse, the wooden frame was creaking, as if the whole roof was about to collapse.

"What can we do, Dad?" Joy asked.

Alan looked at me. "I guess all we can do is poke a hole in the plastic to let the water out. At least we can try to save what's left of the wooden frame and keep a few things drier."

Samuel fumbled for his pocketknife and poked a hole in the plastic. Water gushed out all over our belongings, soaking the children's tent as well as our things in the storage area.

Not knowing what else to do, we all crawled back into our damp beds, but there was no way I could sleep. Saturday morning dawned with a dreary drizzle that further dampened our spirits. Only the boys thought it was fun. I stayed in the tent until mid-morning when the sun began to peek through. We had an important meeting scheduled that evening, and I began to panic at the prospect that all our clothes might still be wet.

As we carried wet loads to another tent, Alan began merrily singing, "Bless the Lord, oh, my soul…" Each time he passed, my mood got darker and darker. My intuition told me there had to be more to this than I had seen, and somehow Alan's "super spiritual" reaction didn't fit. It was as if he were evading something God was trying to do.

Stopping on the wet, ankle-deep grass, I put my hands on my

hips and looked him squarely in the eye.

"You can bless the Lord all you want," I snapped, "but I want to know what is going on here! Something just doesn't add up!"

Surprised, Alan stopped singing, but said nothing as he continued moving our belongings back and forth in silence. What was going on?

All afternoon a misty rain continued to fall, and I found myself growing upset with Alan for getting us into this mess, and I didn't fully understand why. Alan was acting so strangely, as if everything was all right, when it obviously wasn't. Then I was confused because God had definately given confirmation for us to move up here.

I looked over at Alan, and realized my emotions had gotten the best of me.

"Sorry I got angry with you, Darl," I said at last.

Alan looked at me and smiled a bit sheepishly.

"That's all right, Luv, I understand. Look, I'm not sure what's going on here either. I think we'd better spend some time with the Lord, don't you?"

How thankful I was that Alan forgave easily, a quality I loved him for! The children were still in their first tent, so Alan and I huddled together on our damp bed to wait on the Lord. After a moment or two, Alan stopped and began to turn the pages of his Bible.

"I feel we should read Matthew 6:24," he explained. "Why don't you read it out loud?" Finding the place, I noticed even the pages were damp.

"No man can serve two masters," I read aloud. "For either he will hate the one and love the other, or else he will hold to the one, and despise the other. Ye cannot serve God and mammon."

Alan shook his head. "Oh no! I've done it again!" He slapped his knee in frustration.

"Done what?" I asked.

"I've been fretting and stewing about money, instead of God's work," he admitted. "All along, I've had the nagging feeling that I should be living down with everyone else, being available to them, not isolated like this."

Alan bowed his head and began to pour out his soul before the Lord, and I realized again the extent of his struggle with insecurity over finances. Placing my hand gently on his shoulder, I prayed aloud that he would be freed from fear once and for all. I knew fear would always be a stumbling block in our lives if it weren't dealt with now.

"You know, Alan, I think God must have set up this whole situation to teach us a major lesson. It reminds me of the story of Jonah, at least the water part of it!"

He looked at me and we both began to laugh at the absurdity of it all. God had a sense of humor too. But in the midst of it, He was trying to impress us that He would provide if we got on with His work His way.

Later that afternoon we found out our old apartment at the Kona Kai was already rented out. Now only a more expensive furnished apartment was left. But we knew we were to take it, because that was where God's people were living.

An important lesson had been blazed on our hearts. Ever after, we sometimes lived right on the edge of what we needed, but we always tried to do it God's way. And we saw God faithfully provide for our needs.

By April, we temporarily moved into a YWAM house while Alan helped lead the next School of Evangelism and I continued to work in food services. Prayer for the new property grew more fervent than ever, with the SOE students joining in. Often we would all pray into the wee hours of the night, and sometimes the very sins that were clearly seen on the island, such as materialism, greed and apathy, were highlighted in our own hearts by the Holy Spirit. We began to see that for us to make a spiritual impact on the islands, God was requiring us to be a spiritually clean people. We needed to get our lives in order.

A great camaraderie developed during these days, cementing many deep friendships and laying foundational principles into our lives. Strong loyalty, constant generosity, and dedication to intercession for the nations were only a few of those principles we were learning. It was a true time of pioneering in the mission, as we prayed and fought side by side for the land.

One day Loren called us all together for an important announcement. Sitting among the staff and students I had grown to love, I watched their faces as Loren began.

"I'm afraid I have some disappointing news," he said. "Someone else has just bought the property. But remember, this hasn't taken God by surprise. Let's turn to God and ask Him what our next step should be."

I could see shock and disappointment on many faces, but this time it was apparent we were taking the news differently than when we lost the Maori. We had kept yielded hearts all along, and as we now turned to the Lord, we lifted prayers of thanksgiving and worship to an all-knowing God. We somehow knew the property would one day be ours, and we trusted God to do it His way.

Later our disappointment turned to joy – the deal fell through and the property was up for bid again. We rejoiced that even in the midst of what appeared as the loss of the property, God's word had again proven true. We knew we were to continue praying for the property no matter how long it took.

Alan and Bill Mansfield still had the small boat ministry on their hearts, and every Sunday night they held a small prayer meeting to lay a foundation. Bill had purchased a 27-ft sloop named the First Timothy, and planned to lease it to YWAM for the purpose of training students in sailing and navigation. Plans were also made to eventually begin a six-week Small Boat School to train a crew for the ministry.

By the summer, the SOE students and many staff left on an evangelism outreach to the Montreal Olympics while Alan and I stayed behind to lead the people still in Kona. We were a bit disappointed not to be going ourselves, but I soon saw God fulfill a promise he had made to me back in New Zealand.

A young man named Dale Kauffman, a student in the SOE, believed God was calling him to involve children in evangelism through song and choreographed drama presentations. He and his wife Carol invited me to work alongside them in preparing for the first King's Kids outreach during Kona's 1976 Bicentennial celebration July 4th.

Several other staff and some 15 YWAM staff children from different nationalities joined the team to put on a children's musical about self-worth called, "You're Something Special." Staff member Olive Alexander wrote a drama to accompany it. I was chosen to play the mother and was thrilled to have a dramatic outlet. I loved working with Dale and his family, and so did Joy, Samuel and Stephen.

I watched happily as Dale drew out Joy's untapped musical talent, and she was chosen to sing a solo in the musical. When the big day arrived for the first performance, we all gathered at the Old Airport Beach where Bicentennial festivities included a carnival of rides, games and many booths. YWAM had a booth selling Samoan treats, and Alan and other staff were on hand to watch our performance.

When the drama began and we burst into song, a large crowd quickly gathered, many of them children. Samuel's blond hair, bleached even whiter by the Hawaiian sun, bobbed up and down as he moved with the music. Stephen, a handsome eight-year-old with an acute sense of timing, carried out his dance steps with natural expertise.

Joy looked stunning. Her olive skin and light brown hair stood out beautifully with her royal blue island costume. It gave me such joy to see my radiant 14-year-old daughter and the others lifting their arms and voices to God. I found myself spontaneously thanking and praising Him too. What plans He must have for these children!

Then, as I looked at the sea of children's faces before me, both in the performance and watching from the crowd, it suddenly hit me. God was fulfilling the vision He had given me back at the children's ministry in New Zealand! Back then I couldn't imagine how God would bring together an interracial group of children, but now it was my daily reality. I could only worship Him more as I saw His faithfulness. God had planned it all along.

That was the start of a regular King's Kids ministry each summer that began to flourish with Dale as the leader. We had several other short outreaches that year, and later began preparing for a larger outreach the next summer.

Alan's ministry was also moving along. That fall, he and Bill Mansfield began the first Small Boat School, followed with a two-week evangelistic outreach in Maui. Alan taught on godly character as it related to ministering on a small boat, and Bill, a trained bosun, covered the practical aspects of boating.

Beth Mansfield and I were both very supportive of the ministry, but it really was Alan's and Bill's vision. My history of seasickness made me less than excited about getting on a boat. I now began to believe God had used the vision of the small boat ministry just to draw us to Kona, and that was later confirmed as Alan's ministry expanded to other areas.

His gift as a teacher was now becoming recognized, and after the New Year, he took an eight-week speaking tour overseas at Loren's recommendation. Visiting other YWAM schools in Europe, Cyprus, and the mainland U.S., Alan began teaching not only on evangelism but on character training and the faithfulness of God.

To his delight, Alan found that as he shared about our hurtful childhood backgrounds and experiences of healing, God used him to help set others free. Soon Alan was deluged with invitations to speak at YWAM schools around the world. God was multiplying his life, just as He had promised, and the small boat vision was left for others to fulfill.

Of course, I was thrilled for Alan, but it troubled me at times to feel so isolated from him. I enjoyed cooking, and serving in King's Kids made me feel like a released jack-in-the-box – but I missed working side by side with Alan as we had during our earlier years in evangelism.

I remembered how before our marriage, God had impressed me that we would serve Him with "one heart and one way" (Jeremiah 32:39), yet all too often our paths were separate. Balancing family time could be difficult, and often while the children and I were so involved with King's Kids, Alan would come home from a trip right when we were putting on a performance. I felt torn between the ministry and being there for Alan. I began to pray more earnestly about it.

One Sunday, I walked out to a quiet place under a tree, and turned my heart earnestly to the Lord.

"Father, you said we would serve you with one heart, and we have that, but what about one way? Please show us what you meant and bring it about."

As I continued praying, gradually a new peace came upon me. Even though I didn't understand it, I somehow knew our times of working apart were for a reason. I didn't know how long it would take, but I trusted the Lord to bring our paths of ministry together again.

Meanwhile, corporate prayer for the property continued. The property was bought a second time, and though we were initially disappointed, it only intensified our prayers. When that deal fell through we rejoiced again.

One hot, humid day in July, 1977, Alan came bursting into the kitchen where I was helping prepare the noon meal.

"We got it! We got it!" he shouted. "The property's ours!"

Stunned, I looked at him wide-eyed as he rushed up and gave me a hug. Everyone in the kitchen rejoiced as Alan explained that the property was sold to us for our original bid, $1.8 million! Over the next days, everyone was ecstatic as plans to move in were underway. Over and over in my mind went Psalm 126:1, "We were like them that dream", echoing the cry of the captives of Zion when they were released. It truly was a dream come true, and we thanked God for His faithfulness.

But we found the battle for this "promised land" wasn't yet

over. The present-day "giants in the land" were illegally-housed squatters who had taken over an area in the old hotel. Alan and a rugged, prophet-like man named Rod Wilson were chosen to be our Joshua and Caleb, being the first to stay on the land and confront the squatters.

When informed that they would have one week to move off the property, one of the squatters threatened to barricade himself in with a gun.

On the eve of the seventh day, Alan and Rod began to move in and spent the first night on the property. That night they stayed up until the wee hours praying for the last squatters to leave peacefully. To our delight, they all moved out the next day without a squabble, clearing the way for the rest of us to move in.

When we and other families drove onto the property with the first load of our belongings, I happily took note that four buildings, 99 rooms, and a total of 45 acres now belonged to Youth With A Mission of Kona. Tropical grasses had overgrown the property, railings hung from sides of buildings badly needing repair, and old bottles, tins cans and wads of paper littered the grounds – but to pioneers like us, it was a sight to behold. The children took off exploring, and I noticed Darlene Cunningham clasp her hands with delight as she anticipated life without housing problems.

As Alan and I began carrying our belongings into an efficiency apartment in Building Three, Alan let out a frustrated roar toward the unoccupied field next door. We had been in Kona less than two years, and were moving for the sixth time.

"This is my last move before heaven!" Alan groaned.

"Don't even say such a thing!" I warned. Sure enough, the very next day Alan ate his words and we were moving again. Loren asked that we move to the building nearest to the entrance of the property so Alan could keep an eye on security.

There was so much work to do on the property that even with schools and ministry in full swing, we began working on Saturdays too, challenging the years of tropical growth that covered the property. Rats, lizards, centipedes, scorpions and cockroaches scurried before our troops as we marched in with machetes, rakes, shovels, brooms and spray. Brilliantly colored bougainvillaea shrubs were so overgrown we had to wind chains around their thorny branches and stumps just to lift them.

But the biggest surprise came when we removed one patch of massive overgrown bougainvillaeas in an outdoor pavilion area. Completely hidden underneath the brush were sets of outdoor tables and chairs, as if arranged for the next meal on the day the Pacific Empress had closed! It spoke of a bygone era.

A new school began on the property that fall, and some of the new students who began helping may have wondered why we were so happy. Alan pointed out that work is worship too, and with that in mind, we gladly worked in our spare time. It was a privilege to suffer the blisters and insect bites in the hot Kona sun to help build a new sanctuary where students from around the world could worship God, learn of His character and ways, and be equipped to take the Gospel to the nations.

Our family's third Thanksgiving in Hawaii saw the beginning of what became a yearly tradition for YWAM Kona. Loren announced that he believed God wanted us all to make banners and celebrate with a Thanksgiving March around the property and whole neighborhood, singing, playing instruments, and thanking God for His provision.

When the big day came, outsiders may have thought our little band was crazy as we marched out the gate and down the road singing as we went. Even as we came back onto the land and stumbled over rough terrain, we praised God and claimed through our songs that one day there would be more buildings where huge boulders now stood.

I eventually left my job in the kitchen so I could use my gardening talents to beautify the property. I joined landscaper Fritz Klein in cleaning up the old neglected gardens, rebuilding broken garden walls, planting banks with ground cover and pruning the old gnarled shrubs.

Gradually, the old hotel was beginning to look and feel like home. There was so much to do, but I loved my new job so much I hardly wanted to finish each day.

It was during these clean-up days the Lord showed me a story from Joshua 4. After Joshua led the people of Israel safely through the Jordan, God told him to set up 12 stones as a reminder in the future. Verse 21 said, "When your children ask their fathers in a time to come saying, 'What mean these stones,' then you shall let your children know…" (King James).

I shared this with the leaders and they believed it was right because another staff person had received the same words. So some young men placed the 12 heavy stones in the garden, in front of Building One. We hoped all our future staff and students' children would ask, "What mean these stones?" We could then tell them what great things God had done in bringing us into this land.

Often we gathered together as a staff up in an old building on the back of the property, and Loren would begin describing what he saw up ahead. One night, as Loren described buildings, new schools, and hundreds of students, I sat next to Alan transfixed on the edge of my seat, my creative juices now flowing. I just wanted to be involved in all of it!

Alan cautioned me that all these goals were still at least 10 years down the road, but I just smiled at him and shook my head. For me, it was already real. I could feel it and see it. I wanted to stay here forever and help bring the vision to pass.

14

A Time To Die

I was carrying a pile of dishes to the cupboard when Alan burst through the door of our apartment on the new property. It was all I could do to hang onto the dishes.

"Whoa! What's your hurry?" I protested as he charged into our living room.

"I want to go to Argentina so badly." He began pacing in circles, his hands jammed deep into his jean pockets.

"After leading the prayer meeting for this outreach for over nine months, I just have to put feet to my prayers."

I smiled lovingly at this husband of mine. Right now he reminded me of a race horse straining to be released at the starting gate.

It was February, 1978, and the "Mundial" or World Cup Soccer Finals were to be held this summer in Argentina. YWAM volunteers from around the world planned to converge on the South American nation with one purpose: to spread the Good News of

Jesus Christ. The international games would be held in five major cities, with thousands attending from around the world, so it would be a strategic time to reach a large cross section of people.

YWAM regularly participated in evangelism at sporting events like this and the Olympic Games, and Loren Cunningham had asked Alan to lead the Kona prayer meetings to lay a strong prayer foundation for the outreach. With only four months to go, Alan had a bad case of itchy feet.

I followed Alan out to our lanai, where he stood staring out over the vivid blue sea. I put my arms around his wiry frame from behind and hugged him tenderly. As usual, his shirt was damp with perspiration, and I breathed in the pleasant aroma of his after-shave. He lovingly covered my hands with his.

"Luv, I want to preach the Gospel in Argentina so bad it's...it's like a fire in my bones!"

"I know," I said gently. "I want to go too, but you know as well as I do, we filed for our permanent resident visas and aren't allowed to leave the country."

The last time Alan left the country, he didn't know trips abroad were forbidden to anyone applying for a resident visa. After being held up several hours in Honolulu and receiving many warnings and an order to go to court, Alan was finally let back in.

"We can't risk ruining our chances and be forced to leave." I desperately wanted to stay in Hawaii and be part of all God was doing, and I knew Alan did too.

But two afternoons later Alan came home with news I didn't want to hear.

"Today, Loren asked me to pray about leading a team to Argentina!" His eyes were full of excitement.

"But..."

"I know...the visas. Look, Loren knows about all that too, but when he was praying he strongly felt that I should lead one of the teams. Of course, he left it up to us to pray about it."

"We'd better be really sure," I said, "or you could end up in immigration court again. Last time you left in ignorance, but not this time. It could be a black mark for us and possibly the whole of YWAM."

I knew I was beginning to sound preachy and Alan's face confirmed he was tuning me out.

As I continued to pray over the next days, a constant nagging invaded my thoughts. What if God were asking our family to leave Hawaii? One night after a staff meeting, I was so anxious I went to Darlene Cunningham. Explaining the situation, I asked her to pray for me.

"I'm afraid we might have to leave Kona," I concluded, tears springing to my eyes. Darlene put her arm on my shoulder and began to pray quietly. Then, after a moment, she looked into my eyes.

"Fay, I believe God's got everything under control, and even if you do go away, I believe you'll return here some day. This scripture came to mind for you."

She looked up Hosea 14:7 and we read it together: "They that dwell under his shadow shall return; they shall revive like the corn, and grow like the vine; the scent of it shall be like the wine of Lebanon."

I didn't know exactly what it meant, but it was comforting to know God had a plan. I went home that night encouraged and with new hope in my heart.

Eventually I felt settled that even if Alan went on the outreach, the Lord was leading the children and myself to stay in Kona for the summer, serving our YWAM family. With so many other workers going out, we were needed to fill in the empty spaces.

A week later, after the children had left for school, I was about to go to my landscaping job when Alan beckoned me to sit down with him on the sofa. He had our big Thompson Chain Reference Bible in his hand.

"Luv, I need to share something with you," he said solemnly. One look at his steely blue eyes told me this was serious, and a knot formed in my stomach.

"I believe the Lord is showing me some very heavy things about going to Argentina," he began.

Bracing myself, I moved to the edge of the sofa.

"I do believe I'm to go on the outreach to Argentina," Alan said slowly, "but look at these verses the Lord led me to this morning."

I leaned forward to look over his shoulder, and Alan's deep voice was husky as he began to read Jeremiah 22:10,12: "Weep not for the dead, neither bemoan him, but weep sore for him that goeth away; for he shall return no more, nor see his native country...But he shall die in the place where they have led him captive, and shall see this land no more."

Out of the corner of my eye, I saw Alan stop and look for my response, but I could only stare numbly at the page. He continued reading verses 26 and 27: "And I will cast thee out, and thy mother who bore thee, into another country where you were not born; and there shall ye die. But to the land to which they desire to return, there shall they not return."

"Lord!" I murmured inwardly as I sat re-reading the words. My head began to swim as my eyes stayed transfixed to the page. "God, are you actually saying Alan is going to die in Argentina?"

After a long silence, Alan at last searched my eyes. "Well?"

I took a big breath. "I...I came here hoping God wasn't going to tell us to move...but this!" My voice was shaking with emotion. "It's the strangest thing, but I almost feel as if God is standing right here beside us like a polite gentleman, asking for our permission, waiting for our response."

I instinctively placed my hands over Alan's and fingered his gold wedding ring. "Remember all the times we've told people to hold relationships with an open hand? Now it's time for us to really do it!"

My eyes grew moist as I studied Alan's face. He sat solemnly quiet. How did he feel? After all, it was he who had to face the thought of actually dying! I couldn't tell, and I knew he probably found it hard to voice his own deep emotions.

Before Alan and I were married, I had instinctively known such a radical and fearless preacher could some day be a target for martyrdom. Over the years I accepted that he might some day die for the Gospel, but it had always been tucked away in a file marked "future." Now it was here, hitting me in the face.

Nagging questions based in fearful insecurities now bombarded me. How would I survive without Alan? How would I bring up the children alone? I knew deep in my heart God would take care of us, but I could only imagine how excruciating it would be.

"What else can we say, but yes?" I said at last. The fronds on the large coconut tree outside our lanai clapped in the breeze, the only sound breaking the stillness. Then Alan slipped to his knees, and I quickly joined him.

"Lord, we hold nothing back from you," Alan began. "How can we hold anything back from you? You're our Lord, our Master, and if my death will bring You more glory, we say yes to you, God, we say yes!"

"Yes, Lord," I whispered. "We give you everything."

Then we lifted up our faces and worshipped the God we loved so much that we would give our lives for Him. Suddenly, an unexplainable peace came into my heart, and I opened my eyes to see Alan. His facial muscles were now relaxed, and I knew he felt it too. God had heard and registered our response.

Usually we shared everything with the children, but this time Alan and I both strongly felt we were not to mention it to them. As the summer quickly approached, we sensed that the grace of God was giving us supernatural strength to walk ahead in obedience.

One Sunday in late March, while Alan was away teaching on the U.S. mainland, the children and I decided to drive to the beach for a picnic after church. We enjoyed a nice lunch, and as the afternoon began to while away, I lay on a mat in the sun while Joy, now 15 and an avid bookworm, sat beside me reading her latest thick volume. Ten-year-old Stephen was down by the water's edge, as usual collecting shells and stones. At 12, Samuel had never outgrown his love of climbing trees and was scrambling up the nearest palm tree.

Watching them, my heart was filled with love and gratitude to

God for giving us these happy, healthy children. With not much understanding of how to bring up a godly family, and lots of mistakes, we had relied greatly on the Lord to help us, especially in learning how to say we were sorry. I was grateful as well to have the support of our close-knit community of like-minded Christian families.

Our busy schedules always pulled at us, but Alan and I constantly worked at spending time with our children. As I gazed on them with pride, once again I wondered what would become of us with Alan gone.

From their early childhood, Alan and I had instilled in them the necessity of being willing to die for our faith. Stories of Bible heroes like Joseph, Daniel and David, to name a few, had been a natural backdrop to instill concepts of loyalty, bravery and total commitment. We had always applied the Bible personally in our family times, and all the children had received Christ as their Lord and Savior at early ages. But now, like Alan and me, they would have to make their own decision to let their dad go.

Suddenly a loud cawing sound broke into my thoughts, and I looked up to see a white-faced Samuel making a hasty retreat down the trunk of the palm. A big black myna bird was in vicious pursuit, obviously resenting Samuel's intrusion into his tree! After Samuel escaped and the color returned to his cheeks, we all laughed heartily.

"Why don't we stay here for our family time?" I suggested. The beach area was now almost deserted as the cool late afternoon breeze wafted over us. It was most welcome after the heat and humidity of the day.

Gathering around a rough wooden picnic table, we read the Bible together, followed by some discussion. Just as we were about to bow our heads and pray, Samuel looked up at me, his blue eyes locking intensely on mine.

"Dad's going to die in Argentina, isn't he?" he blurted.

As I stared at him, my mind raced over the reading and discussion we had just completed. Had something triggered that question? But there was nothing.

Samuel's white-blonde cowlick flickered in the breeze. How could he know? We had been so careful not to say anything about it! Samuel the prophet, I mused. It was not the first time he had come out with unusual ideas, but seeing the Lord had cautioned us not to share, I took careful thought how to answer.

"Well, son," I began at last, "What if that is true? Are you willing to give Dad to God freely, for the Gospel's sake? Does God really come first for all of us?"

I looked tenderly at each one. Joy, my duty-conscious first born, nodded her affirmation thoughtfully, but I knew she wasn't experiencing the same reality of it as Samuel.

"Yes," Samuel agreed with a resolute nod.

Stephen sat with his shoulders hunched a little, clasping his hands on his lap. As usual, he was thinking deeply. At last, a little hesitantly, he too said yes.

Flooding into my mind came a memory of a similar time two years earlier when Alan had asked the children how they would respond if God asked him to die for his faith. The response had been the same, although at that time it was a general question with no specifics involved. Today it seemed that the Holy Spirit, through Samuel, was sowing His own seeds of preparation within them.

My own heart preparation deepened on Easter, 1978, as I took part in a musical were were preparing for the local community. Suddenly, I realized anew how Jesus made a calculated choice to go to the cross. "Setting his face as a flint," the Bible called it. During practices, I fought to control the tears each time I saw Jesus choosing to accept the crown of thorns and the cross on His back, going to Calvary for the whole world and for me. Now I really understood. Jesus could have escaped the cross if He wanted, but He chose to obey the Father. That picture of His sacrifice dispelled any temptation I might have had to escape the cross in my life. Alan and I would embrace it, just as Jesus had.

The weeks sped by, and soon Alan was preparing for his departure. One key step for him was updating his will. Back in the late '60s, when we had purchased our house, we had both made legal wills. My meticulous husband had written out a special document on ten steps to take should either of us die.

Now Alan insisted that I familiarize myself with those steps. I hated business matters and was terrified to think of managing things when Alan was no longer here. Finally Alan bullied me into going through the details with him.

We told few others about what we believed the Lord had shown us, but we trusted our secret with our close friends Dr. Bruce Thompson and his wife, Barbara, who had come to Hawaii almost the same time as we had. Bruce and Alan had often counseled people together. Though a trained medical doctor, Bruce was now ministering to the whole person and had recently set up a counseling clinic. Alan now asked Bruce to watch out for us in the event of his death, and he agreed.

We knew we also needed to make an appointment with a very busy Loren Cunningham. His ministry was expanding to the point that he needed to travel constantly to YWAM bases around the world, as well as to other ministries which heard of his reputation as a peacemaker and missionary statesman. But in spite of his busy schedule, we knew that as YWAM's founder and director, he must know what we believed the Lord was saying.

On the morning of our appointment, Loren welcomed Alan and me into his office on the top floor of Building Three. Smiling warmly, he motioned for us to sit and made us feel completely at ease. Alan immediately pulled out his Bible.

"Loren," he began, "we believe the Lord gave us some startling news. We believe the Lord is saying I will die in Argentina."

Loren's brow creased into a deep furrow of concern as Alan began to share the whole story and read the accompanying scriptures. Then, after a few moments of silence, Loren looked from Alan to me and back again.

"Did you hear that a terrorist organization has threatened to send a large group to Argentina to cause havoc during the Mundial?" he said.

The words were hardly off his lips when he fell on his knees and put his face down on the carpet.

"Oh God," he cried out loudly, "I pray for these men to be restrained. Think of the guilt they would incur by killing a man of God, a prophet like Alan Williams!"

Alan and I looked at each other with our mouths hanging open in astonishment. With the millions of thoughts we'd entertained about this issue, we had never given a thought to who would be responsible for Alan's death — let alone prayed for them. How this man knew God's ways!

"Oh, Lord," Loren continued, "I ask you to please spare Alan's life. We need him. Like King Hezekiah in the Bible, please grant him an extension of life." My heart leapt and I moved forward on my chair. Oh, if it could only be so! But I let out a sigh when I realized even Loren's earnestness couldn't convince me differently.

Alan's departure day in June dawned as bright and clear as any Hawaiian day I could remember. The children were eating breakfast in varying stages as they got ready for school. Alan drank his morning tea on the lanai as I kept busy packing lunches. Then Alan went into the children's room, ready to give them their usual morning hug before they were off to school.

As I followed him to their door, my heart was aching. It was too real! Alan Williams was saying goodbye to his three children, not knowing if he would ever see them again. He put up a wonderful act of normalcy, but one look at his eyes told me he was battling to repress the anguish in his heart.

None of the children had mentioned the incident at our picnic three months earlier, and they now seemed unaware of the day's significance. To them, Dad was just off on another trip, a way of life for our family. Being secure in his love, the children never seemed to suffer for it. As I watched him hug each one, my heart was in agony. How could he bear it? "I love you," he said extra tenderly to each one in turn.

Soon we carried Alan's luggage to the car out back of our building. Other YWAM workers were piling their belongings into larger vans for the trip to the airport. Bruce and Barbara Thompson, knowing the pain we were suffering that morning, appeared on the path by our car. It was so like them to be there for us.

As we stood under the shade of the plumeria trees, Bruce grabbed Alan's shoulders, and looked at him with great emotion.

"Brother, I believe I'll see your face again," he said with a slight smile. His sincere blue eyes shone as he looked into Alan's. Maybe it was all just a test! I tried once again to grab a flicker of hope that Alan would return, but again there was nothing to pin my hopes on. It was as if I had an inner knowing that it wasn't so.

Alan and I tried to make light conversation on the 20-minute trip to the airport. Finally, I asked, "What did you think about Bruce's comment?"

"Oh, you know Bruce – Mr. Mercy." A faint smile appeared on his lips. "He can't bear to think I would die, and you and the children be left alone. I really have no conviction it was from God."

We drove the rest of the way in relative silence. I had gone over and over this scene in my mind, wondering what it would be like, and what we would talk about. There should have been so much to say. But nothing was as I imagined it.

At last Alan broke the silence.

"Don't forget the ten steps to follow when you get the news," he repeated again.

"Yes, yes, I know," I said, almost annoyed. How could he talk about that now?

After Alan checked in his suitcase at the airport counter, we mingled with the other YWAMers until at last the flight was called. Then Alan pulled me over to a private place.

"Well, I guess this is it," he said awkwardly. We hugged each other tightly, both shaking as we tried to control the tears.

"I love you," he said, still holding me tightly.

"I love you too," I whispered.

Was this really happening? To the natural mind, it was all crazy, and yet we felt a paradoxical grace to go through it. Finally we let each other go, and his eyes met mine. "I'll see you in heaven!" he quipped, trying to make light of it to hold back the tears.

Then picking up his bag, he walked quickly to the plane and up the gangway. At the top stair, he turned and looked at me once again. In his dear, familiar Liverpool way, he waved with a humorous mock grin — a cover up to make me laugh — before he disappeared from sight.

But I didn't feel like laughing today! As quickly as I could, I ran to the car and began to sob, somehow driving home through the tears. Over and over in my mind echoed the words Alan had often quoted: "If Jesus is not Lord of all, He's not Lord at all!"

Even with all my pain, I was still able to say, "Yes, Lord."

The Williams Family

15

Resurrection

The days passed ever so slowly, and I threw myself into my work and into caring for the children to get my mind off Alan's impending fate. Six weeks after he'd left, I came down with a severe viral flu. I was still bedridden when a friend brought me the first letter from Alan. It had taken 14 days to arrive, and was filled with all kinds of wonderful news about what God was doing in Argentina. Oh, how good it felt just to hold it, finger it, knowing he had touched it too. How many mornings had I awakened filled with dread that it might be the day I heard Alan had been killed.

But now I just reveled in the good report from Argentina — stories of victory, liberty to preach, thousands of tracts being given out, and many coming to the Lord.

And what about Alan himself? I read between the lines of his mild complaints of cold temperatures to discern he was freezing although usually he loved cold weather. Poor Alan had been eating jam made from sweet potatoes, and even horse meat! But his passion to preach the Gospel was obviously winning out above all the trials. How I loved him!

Lying there in bed digesting the news, I held the letter close as a warm glow filled me. All at once a strong impression to read Psalm 91 came upon me. Weakly reaching for my Bible on the bedside table, I propped up my feverish, pounding head and fumbled through the pages to find the comforting psalm. Was that what God wanted to do, comfort me?

I slowly read through the familiar words until my eyes riveted on verses 14 and 15:

"Because he hath set his love upon me, therefore will I deliver him; I will set him on high, because he hath known my name. He shall call upon me, and I will answer him. I will be with him in trouble; I will deliver him, and honor him."

Deliver him? My heart began to beat faster. Was God saying Alan would be delivered after all? Was it all just a strong test, just as God asked Abraham to sacrifice his son Isaac? And what about Loren's prayer to spare Alan's life for a time?

For the first time since Alan read me the scriptures of impending danger, I *knew* deep inside it had all been a test, and whichever scenario was right, we had passed it! Suddenly I was filled with so much joy, I wanted to run and tell someone, but I was sick and alone.

"I worship you, Lord!" I cried, as tears of relief ran down my cheeks. "I praise you for the strength to go through this test!"

After months of giving him up, I knew Alan would be coming home again!

The next morning my fever was down, and though still weak, I decided to get a letter off to Alan. Grabbing my writing pad and pen, I hastily wrote about the scripture I had received, explaining the unusual assurance I had that he was coming back after all. As I dropped the letter in the mail, all I could do was hope it would reach him before he left. Had God shown him the same thing?

Then it hit me! What about Alan's visa? They might not let him back into America! I was apprehensive, but I trusted it to the Lord's hands with newfound courage. After passing this most recent test, the visa problem paled in comparison.

The weeks dragged on, and the only snippet of news I had was a brief postcard from Alan. Besides telling his scheduled arrival time in Kona, Alan asked for prayer about immigration at the border in Miami. I was already praying! Reports had come back that Alan was seriously ill, so I also prayed earnestly about his health.

I longed for any bit of news. So when I picked up the telephone on the day before Alan was due home, and the operator announced a long distance call from Miami, my heart skipped a beat.

"Is that you, Luv?" I heard Alan saying. That familiar Liverpool accent never sounded so good!

"Yes, it's me, Darl!"

"How are you? How are the children?"

"We're fine, and we can't wait to see you," I yelled, as if literally being heard in Miami. "I heard you were sick. Is it true?"

"I'm recovering, but I'm okay. I'll tell you about it when I get back tomorrow. Look, I've just been through the immigration wringer here at the airport. They even had my name in a book here, can you believe that? I'm allowed back into the States, but I have to go back to immigration court in Honolulu later on."

"Oh, no, not again!" I groaned.

We continued to talk for a few moments, but all too soon we had to say goodbye.

After a restless night, I spent the morning making our place spick and span for my fastidious husband. I hadn't been such a fussy housekeeper while Alan was away, so I had a bit to do. But even in my haste, the clock seemed to be going double-slow time. At last, in the early afternoon, I drove YWAM's VW beetle to the airport, pressing the brakes several times to stop myself from speeding. The kids had gone to school so I would meet Alan alone. We had so much to talk about! A time would come to share the whole story with the kids, but right now, I needed Alan to myself.

Parking the car, I raced into the waiting area holding a fragrant, white plumeria lei I had made. As the plane disgorged the usual crowd of tourists and locals, I scanned the passengers until at last I caught sight of Alan's familiar frame emerging from the plane. When he waved my direction and started down the gangway, it was almost like a dream.

As Alan strode through the gate, I could see that his eyes were lined with dark shadows and his olive skin had a yellowish tinge, a tell-tale sign of his recent sickness. But my haggard husband never looked better to me!

Slipping the plumeria lei around his neck, I almost fell into his arms and we embraced tightly for long moments. It was a personal resurrection for the two of us, a happiness we hadn't expected, and one that was sweeter than I could ever have imagined.

"What did you think of the scriptures the Lord showed me?" I asked eagerly.

"What scriptures? I only got a couple of letters..."

"Don't tell me it missed you!"

"I guess so. It was a miracle anything got through to us at all, with the political turmoil in Argentina."

Getting the luggage and loading the car, Alan listened as I excitedly explained what God had shown me.

"You know, Luv," he responded as we began the short drive back, "before the outreach, some other YWAM leaders also believed God challenged them to be willing to die in Argentina. It really seemed that because we were willing to give our lives for the Gospel, we were more radically committed than ever."

"So what's different?" I joked. "You're always like that!"

After a chuckle, Alan explained that they took more risks to be effective for the Gospel, even preaching when the police had advised against it for their own safety.

"I preached every time as if it were my last," he recounted. Alan said the conditions were especially rigorous in Mar del Plata, where it was so cold they met for prayer in sleeping bags. But I saw the glint in Alan's tired eyes as he began to tell of the great harvest of souls and the fervor of the newly saved Argentinians who, after receiving Christ, immediately joined the teams in giving out tracts.

"Darl, it's so good to have you back!" I gushed, leaning over to kiss his cheek. Seeing Alan's zeal, his love for God, and his longing that men may know Him – that was what first attracted me to him. How I would have loved to be with him during it all!

The next few hours, Alan continued to fill me in over his hot "cuppa." He explained that at the end of the outreach, during the reporting time in Buenos Aires, he contracted some kind of flu and collapsed on the floor during a trip to the bathroom.

"They thought I was having a heart attack, but when they put me in an ambulance, it wouldn't start!" he said. "Someone told me later they signaled a bus to give a push, but the bumpers locked. Here I was with intense chest pain, and the ambulance was swaying back and forth to the sound of banging and scraping noises. I said, `Lord, if I'm going to die, don't let me go like this!' After expecting a bullet every day for weeks, I couldn't handle the thought of dying in a smashed ambulance."

Both of us doubled up with laughter, draining all the tension of the last months.

"When at last I got to the hospital, it turned out to be some kind of viral infection in the lining of my lungs," he ended. By then we had laughed so much, our tea had gone cold.

"I wonder if I'm on borrowed time," he said after a moment.

"What do you mean?"

"Those verses about dying in Argentina were so strong. It really seemed to be God," he said thoughtfully. "I still wonder about when Loren prayed for an extension of my life. Was it all a test, or did his intercession save my skin?"

I shook my head. "I'm sure it was all a test, like Abraham with Isaac. The Lord saw our obedience, and now it's over!"

For a few tense moments Alan stood staring into space.

"I don't really know. I'm just wondering, I guess," he mused. "I mean, it really seems as if God answered Loren's prayer. I really expected to die with a bullet or something."

That thought was no comfort to me. I didn't want to walk through the next few years wondering if my husband had merely been granted an extension of life as Loren had prayed.

Later Alan had a happy reunion with the children, and that evening we told them of the test we had been through. Thank God it was all over!

But the trip was not without its consequences. A few weeks later when I met Alan at the plane after his trip to the immigration court in Honolulu, I knew by his face it was bad news.

"So we have to leave?" I asked, wanting to bite my tongue from saying the words.

"I'm afraid so, Luv." He took my arm and we began walking to the car. "I have to leave within a year at my expense, and I can't return for another year. If I don't leave, I'd be deported and possibly never allowed to come back."

Tears came to my eyes as the reality hit me. We really did have to leave my beloved Kona.

"Our lawyer is appealing," Alan added, trying to comfort me. "But that will only give us a bit more time at most." As we started driving back, I turned to Alan.

"Isn't there something we can do? I feel so helpless. It's bad enough to have to leave everything, but I want to know God's sending us out, not immigration!"

"He's got it all under control, Luv. You'll see." But as we rode the rest of the way in silence, I struggled. How could I leave Kona, the work of God here, my friends?

Several weeks later, we were encouraged to hear God was answering our prayers. A vital Christian was put in charge of immigration, a blessing not only to us but to all YWAMers in Kona from other countries. In the meantime, we prayed earnestly as a family that our eventual departure would be at His will, not man's. Sure enough, we began to see the hand of God answering our prayers in a way we couldn't have imagined.

One night at a staff meeting in the Kona pavilion, Loren announced that Don Stephens, the leader for YWAM Europe, was purchasing a ship called the Victoria that was now docked in

Venice, Italy. YWAM's International Council, the top governing body of the mission, now believed the Victoria was to be the resurrection of our vision for the Maori.

Alan and I looked at each other in amazement, and he grabbed my hand. We hadn't expected this at all!

"Looks like this is the answer to our prayers!" he said.

"It would seem so, Darl," I said, shaking my head. With so much happening here in Kona, our vision for a ship had almost been forgotten.

As the meeting closed, Loren stepped off the platform and made a bee-line in our direction.

"Well, you two!" he said with a warm smile. "You need to pray seriously about joining the ship. It certainly seems to be good timing for your situation! Of course, you'd only be on loan from the leadership here."

My spirit leapt, taking comfort in his words as I remembered the scripture Darlene had given me in Hosea 14:7: "They that dwell under his shadow shall return." Did that mean we'd be back some day?

"We hardly even have to pray, Loren," Alan told him. "It's all been a matter of time, that's all." Loren smiled his agreement. God was truly leading us out!

Of course, we did pray about it as a family, but we already knew in our hearts it was right. Now it was just a matter of adjusting to leaving Kona, especially for Joy and myself. Joy didn't want to leave her best friend, and my heart was so attached to seeing YWAM Kona grow and develop, I had trouble letting go. Of course, I was thrilled about the new ship, but God had done so much in our lives here in Kona, leaving it was one of the hardest deeds God had asked me to do.

One morning not long after, I drove down to a local recreation area, the Old Airport Beach. After parking the car, I found a lonely place under a tree and threw myself on the sand. Tears poured from my eyes.

"Lord, I feel like you're ripping everything I love away from me," I cried. "All my close friends and what about King's Kids? Lord, even if I will return some day, I really don't understand why I have to leave."

On and on I cried, pouring out my heart to the Lord, and somehow I sensed He heard me.

"Lord, I trust you," I said at last. "You know I'll go anywhere You want. I'm even willing to be seasick all the time if You don't see fit to heal me, but You'll have to help me. I can't go from here without Your strength!"

Sitting up, I looked out at the white surf crashing on the lava rocks. Even in the midst of my pain, I thanked God for all He'd done in our family since we'd been here. Could God do as much even in a new location? Then it hit me! Maybe I could even start a King's Kids on board the ship!

"Lord, I can't see the future, but I trust it all to you."

So in late September of 1978, our family was once again packing to leave. Alan would first go to a week-long speaking engagement on the mainland U.S., and then join the kids and myself for a five-month stay in New Zealand. There we planned not only to see our families, but to attend to our belongings and re-rent our home before leaving for Italy. We were all still praying fervently to see the release of the needed finances for the trip to Auckland, not to mention the trip to Italy.

Two weeks before we were to leave, Alan gathered us around the table for our usual family prayer time and made an announcement that would have been too much for either one of us just a few years earlier.

"I've got a surprise," he said with a glint in his eye. "I asked the Lord, as my Heavenly Father, if He would let me as your father take you all to the mainland with me and to provide for us to go to Disneyland. And I believe He said yes!"

Excited yells burst forth across the table.

"What about the money?" I said with amazement. "We've only got about $300, and we don't have even enough for our original plan!"

Alan smiled broadly. "Remember what we have been reading

about seed faith? I believe the Lord is telling us to give it all away, like planting seeds, and that He will then multiply it back to us."

For a moment, I almost couldn't believe this was the same man I'd married. It only showed the new freedom God had worked into Alan's life over finances. As I likewise saw the faith on our children's faces, I squelched my own misgivings and sensed that something was about to happen.

Alan went to our bedroom and returned with the $300 cash. As he divided it between the five of us, I noticed such a light in my children's eyes as they anticipated the joy of giving. Then, we each bowed our heads and silently waited before the Lord, asking Him to bring to our minds the individuals to whom we should give. After a moment, Samuel's head shot up. "I know!" he said, and off he went at full speed out the door to give his portion to someone. We all soon followed.

To my amazement, over the next three weeks we saw almost $4,000 come into our hands from two separate offerings and other gifts. God was saying we were on the right track, and we were really on our way!

When the day came to begin saying our goodbyes, I cried with each parting. But God showed me that these were deep, godly friendships, forged on the anvil of love, and they wouldn't disintegrate just because we moved elsewhere.

These last three years in Kona had been the most satisfying time of my life. Based on God's character, I knew obedience to His call would bring more of the same, but it was hard to think about starting all over.

Even in the excitement of having a ship ministry again, I wondered how long we would stay with it. Would I sink my heart and soul into the ministry, only to be uprooted once again? And, the question I most dreaded, what about my wretched seasickness?

My heart was torn as I followed Alan and the kids aboard the plane, and waved a final goodbye to the good friends seeing us off. Our lives were changing once again, but I had no idea what God had in store for us.

The Anastasis

16

A Ship To Serve The Nations

The rhythmic clicking of the train rocked our family to sleep during the last leg of our trip to Venice. Hard as I tried to sleep myself, I couldn't help thinking about the great Italian city that would soon be our new home. Although I'd never yearned to travel, Venice was one city I had always wanted to visit. I could just picture myself standing in its magnificent cathedrals and seeing the romantic gondolas along the canals.

Our last five months in New Zealand had been jammed with activity. We spent our days visiting friends and relatives, sorting through everything we owned, and making decisions on what to keep, sell, or give away. Now it was March, 1979, and with our house rented again, we were at last free to head for Europe.

Our journey via Asia and Switzerland had been long and

exhausting, and we couldn't wait to get settled onto YWAM's new ship, the Victoria.

Arriving at dusk at the Venice train station, our tired and hungry family unloaded our mass of luggage while Alan thumbed through his address book for the ship phone number.

Squelching my own irritability, I tried to divert my three grumpy children by trying to guess what each word meant on the colorful Italian billboards. The advertisements of sunny Italy we'd seen at home hadn't prepared us for such cold evening air, and we began pulling on our sweaters as Alan went to a nearby phone.

"Hello," I heard him shout above the station noise. "Is this the Victoria, the YWAM ship? Pardon? I don't understand. Oh no! Is that right? Camping Jolly? Yes, I've got it! Over the canal? Okay."

He hung up abruptly, and I knew by the look on his face that we were in for a change of plans.

"We're not going to the ship," he said curtly. "No one is allowed on board. Something to do with immigration and the lack of qualified seamen's documents among the crew."

The kids groaned.

"When can we have something to eat?" Samuel complained.

"Yeah, I'm starving," Stephen joined in.

Joy had already discovered a pizza place nearby, but she grimaced when I told her we didn't have Italian money yet.

"Let's stop complaining and concentrate on getting our luggage over the canal bridge," Alan directed. "There's a bus waiting for us which will take us to some camp."

"A camp? What kind of camp?"

"I've no idea," Alan snapped, obviously getting impatient. "I just know it's called Camping Jolly."

As we cut through the last alley leading to the parking lot, a young, blond-headed fellow with a winning smile rushed up.

"Hi! I'm Jim Hamlett," he said. "I'm here to take you to the camp." He led us toward the large YWAM bus, where a young Italian man with jet black hair began energetically loading up our bags and boxes.

"This is my friend, Francesco Di Fabbio," Jim said. "He recently became a Christian and is working with us."

"Ciao," he replied, inducing a giggle from the kids. We climbed aboard and set out to Marghera, a suburb of Venice where the campground was located. Exhausted as we were, still we eagerly hung on Jim's every word as he filled us in on the dormant and dysfunctional ship. He explained that since it was purchased last October, about 25 of our young people, including Jim and Francesco, had spent the winter living on board.

"With the generators and engines not working, we used candles for lights, cooked on a gas ring, and sometimes hopped around in sleeping bags to keep warm."

Alan and I exchanged glances. These were pioneers par excellence!

Jim said the team had temporarily moved off the ship and most were now on an evangelistic outreach in Austria while immigration questions were being worked out.

As we rounded a corner, a sign surrounded by lights and green trees came into view: CAMPING JOLLY. Jim swung the bus into the camp, and I caught sight of a familiar face, vivacious Debbie Smith whom we had known in Kona. As soon as we got off the bus, she began hugging us one by one, and then took us to a tent where a light meal was waiting. We hungrily devoured it, and then followed Debbie to a temporary cabin and flopped gratefully into bed.

Alan and I rose early to find our two energetic sons already gone. As we suspected, we found them waiting in line for breakfast at the large food tent. It was a cold misty day, something we would soon grow accustomed to, and as I cast my tired, puffy eyes over the campground, it struck me how instead of normal summer camp wear, everyone wore winter clothes.

YWAM appeared to have taken over the whole place. We learned the campground was now mostly filled with about 300 short-term YWAMers from Discipleship Training Schools in different parts of Europe. We wouldn't meet the rest of our ship crew until they returned in a few weeks from the outreach in Austria.

After breakfast, we moved our belongings to one of the family-sized tents at the back of the property. The campground had large shower facilities, but we soon discovered that it couldn't provide enough water for all 300 of us. The singles were housed in two enormous tents which slept about 40 each; one for guys and one for girls.

Joy, now 16, gratefully accepted the offer to stay in the girls' tent, much preferable to being squashed in with her two brothers. The boys, now 13 and 11, shared the tent with us. In one corner, the boys helped me set up a study area for their schoolwork brought from New Zealand. Once settled, the boys set off to meet other kids their age, while Alan and I went out to keep an appointment with an American named Mark Spengler. In his early 30s, Mark was now the on-site leader of the ship for Don Stephens, who would later join us. Mark explained Don was at the time recruiting crew for the ship while phasing out of his responsibilities as director for YWAM Europe.

The delicious aroma of European coffee wafted through the window as Alan knocked on the door of the Spengler's tiny cabin. As Mark opened the door, I noticed his flaxen-haired wife, Eva, tending to their new four-week-old baby girl Mia. Nathan, their blond two-year-old, was riding his small tricycle by the doorway. I couldn't help thinking what troopers they were, living with small children in such close quarters. Eva calmly put the baby to bed and welcomed us with cookies and coffee from her Swedish homeland.

"You've come at a very strategic time, and we're so glad you made it," Mark said gratefully. "We have a captain coming soon, Alan, and you and he are the only ones who have official seaman's papers."

Mark said Alan's papers should help with the immigration situation, and expressed high hopes of being able to move on board again soon. As he continued filling us in, his gifts in organizing and business matters were obvious, and I could see that his sharp brown eyes never missed a bit.

After getting more acquainted, Mark, Alan, and I set out for the Molo Isonzo Pier, where the Victoria was berthed. Mark parked the car and we all scrambled out, full of anticipation. In moments we rounded the corner and caught sight of the regal lines of the ship's bow stretching toward the sky. We stopped and I caught my breath.

"Oh, Darl, she looks so much bigger than on the video we saw!" I exclaimed. "But, why is she tipped over like that?" Alan burst out laughing at my novice attempt at sea language.

"That's called a list!" he corrected. "Hmm, I'd say it's about five degrees or so. Could be empty cargo holds, too much water in one tank, many things. It can be righted."

"Come on, let's go on board," Mark called as he bounded up the steep gangway. The foyer was lit just enough to see large worn patches in the linoleum, something we hadn't seen in the video. It was obvious the ship badly needed renovation, something we hadn't expected, but even so, the latent beauty in the Italian wood panels was evident.

With Mark and his flashlight leading the way, we began passing through long, dark alley-ways, maneuvering around old boxes and planks of wood threatening to trip us. Coming into the reasonably pleasant lounge and dining room areas, we again saw the same ornate wood paneling now lined with Italian paintings.

Heading down to B Deck, we entered the huge engine room which was as still as death. Mark explained that many repairs were still to be done. It was quite a different scene from the picture postcards we'd seen of the Victoria in her glory. Then, as a popular passenger/cargo ship, she had plied the seas between Genoa, Bombay, Singapore and Australia.

We were already feeling the cold through to our bones, and Alan was unusually quiet. I knew he was fighting the same disappointment I felt. By the time we came back up to the forward deck, the rather misty day seemed brilliant in contrast to the eerie darkness we'd experienced in the depths of the ship.

After Mark left us to attend to some business, Alan looked at me with set jaw and clenched lips.

"It will take at least a million dollars and six months before we'll ever get out of here," he said somberly. "Look at the rust!" He paused to point out the numerous brown areas before continuing.

"The ship had been up for sale since 1977, and just sitting in the water with little upkeep. No wonder it looks like this," he said softly, lost in thought. "It will take thousands of man hours."

Although Alan was a trained seaman and knew all too well what was involved, my creative juices were beginning to flow.

"But, Darl, can't you just see it newly painted, with the cabins all decorated?" I put hand on his my arm. "Even if it does take six months, just think – we'll soon be sailing around the world doing evangelism again!"

Alan began pacing the deck, obviously assessing the spiritual war we would have to face to tackle such an immense task. I knew my husband so well, I could almost see the prophetic wheels whirring within his mind as he counted the cost and sized up the obstacles to overcome before this ship would be ready to go out to serve the nations.

I walked over and leaned my elbows on the rail, looking out at the shipyard beyond. Memories came filtering back of our pioneering days in Rarotonga as well as the once weed-filled property in Kona that was now transformed. There were many obstacles in our way back then too, and in God's time and way, with His power, we had overcome all of them!

Full of new resolve, I strode back to Alan.

"Darl, remember all we went through back in Rarotonga?" I began. "And look at how hard it was at first in Kona, yet by the time we left it was so hard to leave! Surely God can get us through again!"

Alan stopped and looked at me with a frown.

"Luv, if you think those battles were tough, they were just preparation! Believe me, this will be the granddaddy of them all!"

It was only a few days later that Captain Hal Burton arrived, complete with his thick seafarer's beard. We were all thrilled to have such an experienced and professional sea captain. Life at Camping Jolly fell into a routine over the next days, as we battled the cold, damp weather to go about our daily lives. All the laundry had to be washed by hand in cold water, and I gladly escaped the frequent rain to supervise the boys' schoolwork each morning in our tent. Meanwhile, Alan was asked to teach on evangelism to the other YWAMers in a large cathedral nearby as they prepared for an upcoming outreach.

One rainy morning, Alan came looking for me in the tent as I helped the boys with their schoolwork.

"Mark just got permission from immigration and the harbor master for Captain Hal and I to move on board with a team. We need to get the ship ready for dry docking so it can be scraped and painted."

"Does that mean without us?"

"Listen, it's far too dangerous to have families on board in dry dock," he asserted. "The ship has to be sailed out of the water onto a cradle of wood blocks, and they've been known to tip over at times. Besides, we'll have to go off the ship for absolutely everything: showers, toilets, food. It would be even harder for you all to live there."

I accepted it, but that didn't mean I had to like it. Alan left after two days and I found myself battling depression. I kept busy helping the boys with their lessons. I even volunteered to work in the kitchen tent, but was let down when they didn't need me. I missed Alan terribly, and though people were friendly, I longed for the warm weather and my friends back in Kona. Somehow this all seemed so foreign to me.

Just a few days after Alan left for the ship, the leaders of the camp announced a real schoolteacher would now run a program for all the children together. Although I was glad for them, I now had nothing to do with the kids gone all day. My depression only deepened.

To get away from the dreary campground, I set off for the

nearby village one morning to look at the stores. Passing by some teenagers, I heard them snickering as they motioned in my direction. What were they laughing at? Was it my shoes, the way I walked? Everything seemed normal to me.

Deeply embarrassed, I ducked into a supermarket and chose a few snacks for the kids. I picked up a jar of honey, but before I could put it in my basket, it fell from my grasp and smashed on the floor. Before I knew it, an irate assistant rushed up and shouted at me in Italian, waving his arms wildly. I apologized profusely and offered to clean it up, but he shouted all the louder.

I felt my face flush hot as customers stared at me, and after more attempts to explain, my mouth gagged in frustration. No one spoke English, and it was hopeless. I hurried to the check-out and then ran all the way back to the camp.

I had to call Alan! I just couldn't cope. Why couldn't I be with him? Reaching the camp driveway, I rushed into the nearby phone booth and dialed the Victoria's number. But when a male Italian voice gabbled something to me I didn't understand, I slammed the phone down. Running to my bed in the tent, I buried my head in a pillow and started to cry. I felt ridiculous, but I couldn't stop. I tried to pray, but I couldn't sense God's presence at all.

At last I quieted down, and heard the sounds of another dreary downpour outside. Shivering, for the first time I realized I'd never been in a country before where they didn't speak English. Was this culture shock? Of course I'd heard the term, but I always thought it was just an expression. Now grappling with a whole new environment and way of life, I knew what it meant only too well. How I longed to be on the ship, with all of us together, or back in Kona where we all knew and loved each other!

A few days later the YWAM outreach began, and I jumped at the chance to participate. In the meantime, I memorized the extension number for Alan in Italian and called him at last. He said the ship was going into dry dock in just a week, and I was encouraged at the progress.

For the outreach, I was assigned to a team led by a lovely young

African couple, Oliver and Margaret Nyumbu from Zimbabwe, who asked me to give them input on street evangelism from my past experience. As they drew me in, I felt needed and began to feel better about my circumstances.

Not long after joining the team, I was reading my Bible alone in the tent when I felt God put His finger on the root of my trials: idolatry! Although I had obeyed God in leaving Kona to join the ship, I had never truly given it up in my heart. It was natural to miss close friends and a fulfilling ministry, but I found myself clutching for it like an idol. Now seeing it for the first time, I wept before the Lord.

"Lord, I repent of putting Kona before You and Your will," I cried. "You are Lord of my life, and I don't ever want to do that again."

Soon my whole outlook began to change. Our first day out ministering as a team changed Venice from a seemingly forbidding, foreign city to our own territory claimed for God's purposes. Through interpreters, we testified and preached to hundreds of people who, although they attended church all their lives, didn't know God in an intimate way. As we spent time praying over areas, singing worship and Gospel songs, it began to belong to us spiritually, and all I had gone through didn't seem to matter any more.

Tourists and Venetians alike saw the message before their eyes as our roving drama team performed an hour-long dramatic dance and mime presentation called "Toymaker and Son." The atmosphere was electric as the allegorical drama depicted man's fall in the garden of Eden and Christ's subsequent death and resurrection. After the performances, many came forward to receive Christ as their Savior, and tears filled my eyes as I grasped for the first time how effective the tool of drama could be. I was hooked, and began gathering ideas for shorter dramas we could use in the future.

For our family, Venice's well known Piazza San Marco, or St. Mark's Square, became our weekend meeting place. While Alan came from the ship, the children and I would take a bus and boat to meet him in the square. There we would spend time catching up before visiting the sights of Venice – the golden St. Mark's Basilica, with its ancient mosaics and paintings, or the picturesque Doges Palace, with its gothic arches.

One weekend, Alan delighted us with a surprise visit back at camp. We had supper together, and when the kids disappeared with their friends, he and I spent time catching up on his work aboard the Victoria.

"It's been interesting to say the least," he told me. "Captain Hal is a professional through and through, and is used to a normal shipping company. Captains usually just ask for what they need, and the company gets it. He's not used to YWAM, where we have to pray for everything and wait until God sends it!"

He grinned widely. "On the other hand, Mark is a seasoned YWAMer. He understands the prayer dimension, and thinks of the ship like a YWAM base. But a ship can't run that way either. Since I'm both a seaman and a YWAMer, God must have put me in between to help them understand each other."

We laughed together. "It's like you're a piece of felt in between two parts of machinery," I said. "Like cushioning to prevent friction."

Alan's surprise visit ended all too quickly, and I continued praying for our family to be reunited soon. In early May, the dry dock work was completed, and we rejoiced when the immigration authorities said we could all move on board. No more Camping Jolly! We had been there just 10 weeks, but it seemed much longer.

Many of the 300 YWAMers at Camping Jolly divided up into outreach teams at that point. Some left for Yugoslavia and Africa while others stayed to minister in Italy. When the ship's original crew arrived back from Austria, we all moved aboard the Victoria.

The monstrous vessel was still sitting out of the water on wooden blocks when we arrived. For the next few days, some of us painted the bottom of the hull, while I cleaned and organized our belongings in a cabin on Promenade deck. The boys settled into a cabin next door, while 17-year-old Joy shared a cabin on the deck just below us.

The old passengers' writing room now became a schoolroom for our children and those of one other family. The ship's large laundry facility was inoperable, so I continued washing laundry by hand in cold water, hanging it over the long lines that Alan stretched along the deck heads outside.

On May 10, we all watched with great curiosity as water was poured into the dock below us. Once again the ship was afloat! Next we were towed about a mile through a canal to the Arsenal, an old Navy dock, where shipyard workers would do further work on the Victoria above the water line.

Alan immediately formed a ship evangelism team, and began doing street evangelism in the city on Sunday afternoons. But we hadn't been in the new shipyard long before it became evident that strikes and political unrest in Italy were affecting the work. With each new day, the atmosphere of the shipyard grew more tense, until finally the shipyard workers went on strike after only a half an hour on the job. With the major work now at a standstill, we could only wait while our own volunteers did smaller jobs on board.

By the end of May, Mark Spengler was visiting Don Stephens in Switzerland when Alan called me and Eva Spengler into the tiny single cabin he had renovated into an office. Taking a seat with them, I saw Alan's expression was serious.

"I've just had a call from Don and Mark in Switzerland," he began. "We have to pray about leaving here, because of the constant shipyard strikes." He let out a big sigh. "We'll never get going if we stay here."

Eva and I looked at each other curiously.

"Where else can we go?" I asked.

"Well, there are two alternative shipyards to choose from," he said. "One in Yugoslavia, one in Greece."

I gulped. "Yugoslavia – that's a Communist country! How

could a Christian missionary ship make it there?" Alan and Eva nodded agreement.

Even though it made the most sense to us to go to Greece, we knew better than to trust our own wisdom. Bowing our heads to ask God for His guidance, we sensed clearly that we were to go to Greece. Later, Don called from Switzerland to say his prayer group felt the same way. Greece it would be!

So, June 30, 1978, Alan and a crew of 12 waved to the rest of us on the dock as an ocean-going tugboat towed the Victoria out to sea. The rest of us would pack into the YWAM bus, spending two days and nights driving down through Yugoslavia to meet them at the Eleusis shipyard in Athens. Alan was to be a pastoral support for those aboard the ship, and I knew he would get little rest. He would be up at night praying over every detail. How often I had heard him, in that Liverpool brogue, quote a favorite paraphrase of Philippians 4:13: "If you pray about everything, you can be anxious for nothing."

Cheers went up from the sides of the Grande Canal as the rest of the crew and the remaining YWAMers from Camping Jolly watched the ship sail past toward the Adriatic sea. Somehow the Victoria looked beautiful to us, even with her five degree list. I couldn't help wondering what the many tourists thought as they watched our enthusiasm over what must have seemed a rusty passenger liner that couldn't even go by her own engines.

But they didn't know what we did. This was God's ship. One day it would sail upright, filled not only with food, clothing and medical supplies for the poor and needy, but people bearing an important message for the nations of the world. But we couldn't have known then just how long we would have to wait before that would come about.

PART III

More than 40 Greek evangelical pastors and missionaries had managed to crowd their way into the Athens courtroom. For me, one of the only good things about having to return to Greece for the trial was the joy of seeing so many of these dear friends. They all had a stake in the verdict, and it gave Alan and me such strength to feel their support and prayers.

I was particularly moved to see young Kostas again just before he was interviewed by our YWAM video news team. No longer a depressed teenager, Kostas had grown into a vibrant Christian of 21. I was glad to see him handling the situation so well.

Despite the years of repression against evangelical Christianity in Greece, people like Kostas were living proof of its growth in this ancient land. Much of that growth had come in just the last five years, and it gave Alan and me great joy to know we had a small part in spreading the Gospel there.

As the minutes ticked by, with still no sign of the judges' return, I thought once again of the day we arrived at the Athens shipyards back in June of 1979. We were all so eager to see the Victoria repaired and set sail to serve the nations. We never imagined that we would be in Greece for three years or that our small crew would have such an impact on this country.

The Fish Miracle in Greece.

17

Greece

My first impression of Athens was the wild traffic as our van weaved through the crowded streets. Drivers honked their horns constantly and tried to hog the road.

"Don't worry about the traffic," said driver Russ Martin, a veteran of many YWAM outreaches in Greece. "There's a saying here that all the bad drivers are long gone!"

And if I thought the Italian language was unusual, the Greek billboards we passed had a completely foreign alphabet, reminiscent of ancient hieroglyphics. Russ began pointing out landmarks in the city, including the Acropolis and Mars Hill, where the Apostle Paul had once delivered his famous message on the Unknown God. I could hardly believe we were actually here.

Stephen sat next to me, quietly looking out the bus window, while the more gregarious Joy and Samuel sat near the front, pumping Russ with questions. Those two were so like Alan, I mused, not a shy bone in their bodies.

All three of the kids had become true pioneers. They had put up with tight financial times, fewer material possessions, and difficult living conditions, but right now I could see only the privileges. Besides having days like today, when they were on the edge of a new adventure, they had often seen the joy of God's last minute provision. They had such close relationships with teens of like mind and goals, and I knew the cross-cultural lifestyle they had experienced would make them valuable instruments for God in the future. We all had been far from short-changed.

As we approached the Eleusis Shipyard, signs of Greece's shipping industry recession dominated the skyline. Huge oil tankers and cruise ships sat empty and rusting in the bay.

Like every shipyard, it had cranes, large metal containers, and all manner of materials piled about everywhere. It wasn't a pleasant place to live, but as we drove in and caught sight of our real "home," the Victoria, it was easy to forget our strange back yard.

With luggage in hand, we boarded the launch for the 15-minute ride out to the Victoria. Then, climbing to the top of the ship's gangway, we could see the reception area on board was congested and buzzing with Greek officials.

"There's Dad," Samuel shouted. Alan, Captain Hal and Mark were obviously doing their best to explain who we were, through interpreters, but it was apparent these Greek Orthodox men had little understanding of other denominations. At least the shipyard owners would be glad for the profit they could make on our repairs.

We were anchored out in the bay between the village of Elefsis and the small inner-harbor island of Salamis. The island's craggy cliffs rose straight out of the sea. I thrilled to see such ruggedness, but also was saddened by the sight of the oil-covered industrial waste which turned the water a murky gray.

As several of us stood there talking, looking over the sea toward Athens, we were struck afresh with God's heart to reach the Greeks for God. We knew we were here for more than just ship repairs.

"Russ Martin said past efforts to evangelize have met with real opposition," I said to Alan. "Greeks won't even receive tracts, and some YWAMers have been spat upon. Apparently the police don't like crowds either because of violent Communist activities, so we may not be able to hold street meetings."

"It's a shame the very birth place of democracy has come to this, but it sounds like an exciting challenge," he replied.

Alan described how that morning he was especially impressed while reading Joshua 8. In verse 18, the Lord told Joshua that if he stretched out his javelin toward the city of Ai, God would give the city into their hands. As soon as Joshua obeyed, the army broke through.

"I just read that chapter this morning!" Mark interrupted, his face alive with surprise.

We were all smiling wide now. It was evident God was speaking.

Pulling out his Bible, Mark began reading the chapter aloud.

"I believe God wants us to do the same thing in prayer," Alan said. The three of us moved toward the rail and stretched out our hands toward the land, as if each holding a javelin.

"Lord," Alan prayed, "You told us in Psalm 2 to ask for the nations as our inheritance! Right now, we ask you for Greece!"

"Yes, Lord," Mark agreed. "Reveal your purposes, and give us your wisdom in how to evangelize this place."

Almost immediately, Alan began preparing to take evangelism teams into the city. Our children were now off school for summer vacation, and with the good weather and abundant tourist crowds, now was the perfect time to move ahead. To manage the huge workload on board, it was decided that our family and nine others would go out in evangelism for just two weeks, and then we would have a new team from the ship join us for the next two weeks.

Through a past YWAM contact given us, Alan and I made a visit to Pireaus to meet a fervent pastor and his wife. They agreed to work with us on the outreach, arranging speaking engagements and even inviting us to stay at their church. God was opening the doors!

In early August, our first evangelism team headed out to Pireaus and we quickly settled into our makeshift home on the floors of the church Sunday School. Alan and I started scouting the nearby waterfront area for suitable meeting sites.

Since Pireaus was the main port for cruises to the beautiful Greek islands, it was a gathering spot for thousands of tourists from all over Europe. They lay around all over the city parks waiting for boats, some even spending the nights, and sexual promiscuity was rife.

"Jesus always went where the people were, and so will we!" Alan declared. Rushing back and eating a quick meal, we gathered up our instruments and portable sound system and began setting up in a park. I was a little apprehensive about the police not wanting crowds to gather, but that didn't deter Alan. After first walking and praying two-by-two over the area, we reassembled and began to worship God in song.

People began crowding around us. And after a few more songs, the crowd was mesmerized as our team began a Greek pantomime of the prodigal son I had written. The spectators laughed, clapped, and even yelled, "Bravo!" in appropriate parts, and Alan winked his approval to me across the crowd. At the end, Alan moved like lightning before the crowd and began preaching about the Bible story of the rich young ruler.

"This young man let money and possessions come between him and God," Alan proclaimed. "Jesus asked him to give it away to the poor and come, follow Him, but he was too entrapped by materialism."

Alan challenged the crowd that no material possession can be compared to the value of knowing God personally. After inviting them to come forward and ask Jesus to be their personal savior, he suddenly dropped to his knees.

"If you want to receive Christ, I invite you to kneel here on the grass with me. Humble yourself before God!"

Whatever was he doing? I was embarrassed, but to my amazement, a tall, dignified Greek man in an expensive gray suit came forward and knelt with Alan on the dusty ground. Moments later, a middle-aged lady in a short fur coat did the same. We didn't know it then, but kneeling and many other rituals were a cultural tradition in the Greek Orthodox Church. God was leading Alan!

A number of young people came forward too, some shaking with the conviction of sin over their lives. As the rest of us prayed for Alan and the interpreter, they led the people in a prayer, confessing their sins and asking forgiveness. As soon as the meeting was over, we gave out tracts to those who came forward and others standing around. Now as some came close to meeting their maker in a personal way, the interpreter said they asked why no one had told them this before.

When at last we made our way back to the church, we were full of unspeakable joy. What a night! Instead of being hard, we found the Greeks eager to respond and hungry for God. Obviously years of prayer by those past teams had broken up the fallow ground until it was very fertile indeed.

That night as we lay on our thin mattress on the floor, I thanked God for allowing Alan and me to serve Him side by side again in evangelism. All at once, I remembered the promise God had given me when we were newly married in Jeremiah 32:39, that we would serve Him with one heart and one way. In Kona, our ministries were so separate that I had prayed in frustration, but now God had truly united us again to serve Him with one heart and one way!

The next two weeks were filled with nightly street meetings, with people always responding. Unlike my culture shock in Italy, this time I thrilled to discover the intricacies of Greek culture. The more Greeks I met, the more my fascination grew. I found them to be a warm, gregarious people who could spark up an argument one minute and laugh over it the next.

After two weeks, we went back to the ship to get more supplies and new team members, and as the pattern continued, sometimes we joined forces with other YWAM evangelism teams there for the summer. The Greek pastor also invited us to minister at a summer youth camp where several came to the Lord, and Alan spoke in their church Sunday mornings.

Alan and I were elated. We wanted to go on forever, evangelizing and training others to do the same. The Lord had put the world in our hearts, and we knew this was only the beginning. We were filled with delight at just the thought of the ship finally being repaired and ministering from nation to nation.

But one morning, after almost a month of outreach, Alan was called to the phone in the pastor's study at the church where we were staying. I was making our bed on the floor when he returned and stood still in the doorway. I looked up to see his face dark and tense.

"What is it?"

"It's Mark Spengler. His son Nathan is seriously ill. We all need to go back to the ship."

Nathan, now two-and-a-half, lay drooped sadly in Eva's arms as we gathered in Alan's office to pray for him. His stomach was seriously distended, and his usually creamy skin was yellow. As Alan implored the Lord for Nathan's healing, my heart went out to Mark and Eva. We had been through so much together, seeking God in detail over many issues to do with the ministry. Now we wanted to stand with them for their little boy.

Nathan's doctor ashore had already diagnosed him to have Hepatitis A virus, and had cautioned the Spenglers to monitor any changes in his skin color. They had no idea Nathan would worsen to this alarming state. It made no difference to us whether God healed Nathan supernaturally or through the physician, but we brought him to the Lord.

We'd no sooner finished praying when Alan's deep, yet tender voice broke the silence. "Tomorrow if Nathan is not greatly improved, I believe you should take him straight to hospital, but the choice is yours."

Mark and Eva agreed. The crew prayed for Nathan all that late afternoon and night, but by the next morning his condition had only worsened. At last, Mark and Eva took him to the hospital, where doctors now diagnosed his illness as Serum Hepatitis B, a much worse form of Hepatitis and listed him in critical condition.

All afternoon, I couldn't find Alan, until at nine that evening he came soberly into the cabin.

"Where have you been? I've been looking everywhere for you!" I said. "With Mark gone, so many people have been asking for you."

He brushed aside my agitation. "I have a secret place to pray down in the hold where no one can find me, not even you," he explained. "Listen, I really believe the Lord wants us all to seek Him together, so I'm going to call the whole crew to a time of prayer and fasting. As I waited on the Lord, He impressed on me that He would use this innocent little boy's crisis to show us some things."

For the first time I felt some relief at the situation, and slept easier that night. What was God going to show us?

The next morning we all gathered in the ship's forward lounge to pray. The first hour began with many prayers for Nathan's healing, and soon we were not just sitting on chairs but kneeling before God. Then Alan stood to his feet and faced the assembly.

"I believe God is saying we have things wrong among us," he began solemnly. "I believe Nathan's sickness is a sign that we are spiritually sick." Alan sat down and the atmosphere grew quiet for some minutes. Then a few people read scriptures about our need for purity.

My heart began to beat faster as I felt the Holy Spirit remind me of something. I nudged Alan beside me.

"I feel the Lord just reminded me about the vision of the white ship He gave us when we lost the Maori," I whispered. "White stands for purity!"

"The Lord just brought that back to me too," he said nodding. "That's confirmation."

Alan stood to his feet again. "I believe the Lord is reminding us that He wants a pure crew to run this ship. We need to be people who live holy lives by the power of the Spirit. In the days to come, this ministry will have a high profile before the public, and we must have high standards. We think we are just re-fitting a ship, but God wants to do the same thing to us!"

As we all began waiting before the Lord, one by one people began to get up and confess areas of personal disobedience. Often because of our diverse nationalities, small and large irritations had been building up, and now people began going to one another to make amends. As individuals spoke out sins or faults, it was encouraging to see people reach out in response with a hug or smile.

As we gathered in the lounge for the second morning, Mark came in with grim news that Nathan's life still hung in the balance.

"His little arms were strapped down to insert the IV needles, and at one point complications arose when his veins collapsed," Mark said. "The needles had to be inserted into his head and then his feet, and it really seemed as if our son was on a cross!"

His words led us to seek God with new fervor as Mark returned to the hospital. That day and the next, the Holy Spirit continued working among us as more sins were confessed and our hearts were further purified. After three days, our prayer time officially came to an end, but we all kept praying for Nathan as we continued the daily business of cleaning and renovating a ship. After two weeks, Nathan's condition was still critical and Mark and Eva decided to take Nathan to Switzerland where more advanced medical treatment was available.

It was hard to see them go, but we knew it was best for Nathan. Alan was left in charge with Mark gone, and we began what seemed an unbearably long wait for news of his condition. Days dragged into weeks, and Nathan's illness continued. Our work on the ship was progressing, but everyone felt heavy-hearted.

One Friday, Alan found me as I was on my way to scrub the back stairs and motioned me into his office. I put down the bucket and mop and felt an uneasy tension as Alan closed the door and turned to me with a serious look.

"You know the ship ministry isn't doing well financially," he began. "We're also low on food and water, and now the launch service to shore will be cut off Monday if we don't pay our bill."

I looked at him in shock and disbelief. "But how can we stay on board if the launch service is cut off?"

"Well, that's it, we can't. Captain Hal can't take the risk of being stranded on the ship if someone gets sick or a fire breaks out."

Everything in me rebelled at his words. It was the Maori all over again! "Alan, I can't believe this. First Nathan, and now this? Everything is going wrong!"

"I'm sorry, Luv, but it's true. It's still a secret, but it looks like we'll have to evacuate the ship by Monday."

Alan explained we needed to keep it confidential until plans were finalized with Don and Mark in Switzerland.

I stared at Alan in disbelief. Not knowing what else to say, I turned and walked out.

I ran straight to our cabin and dropped onto the edge of our bed, my heart and mind swirling with turmoil. Yes, it was the Maori all over again, only now we were in Greece. Where would we all go? Families had sold their homes and given up all to join the ministry, and none of us had money for airfares. How could God allow this?

A short time later, Alan came into the cabin, apparently having sensed my strong reaction. He looked at me in silence, and then walked over and stared out the porthole.

"We couldn't lose another ship, could we?" I said somberly. "I really don't know, Luv," he answered gently. "I really don't know!"

After a moment, I let out a big sigh. I couldn't bear just sitting there moping, so I got up and headed back by Alan's office to retrieve my bucket and mop. Carrying them down the lengthy passageway to the back stairwell of the ship, I filled the bucket with water and detergent at a nearby faucet as my mind wrestled with it all. How would the crew take this? We had invested thousands of man hours in hard labor on this vessel, the kind of dirty work some would do only for God. Was all that going to waste?

Setting down the bucket on the top stair, I began to scrub it with vigor.

"Lord, isn't this the ship vision we waited for?" I said aloud. "What about all these precious people? How could You allow us to come this far and then have to give it all up?"

A strong determination began to rise up within me as I thought about God's character. How could such a trustworthy God possibly let us down?

"Lord, I'm going to clean these stairs better than I've ever cleaned them before, because by faith, I know they will be walked on by this crew and many others in the future. We're not going to lose this ship!"

By now I was speaking full volume, perhaps to convince myself, but as the words left my mouth, pure faith began to fill my heart. God was going to come through, and I knew it. I grabbed the mop and began mopping up the soapy lather, and the next thing I knew I was singing at the top of my voice. It was going to be all right!

The next morning there was no change, but Alan again sat me down in his office. His jaw was set and I saw a look of determination in his eye that seemed to say, "Look out, obstacles!" I could see the Lord had encouraged him too.

"Let's have a celebration meal with the food we have left," he said firmly.

"Oh, Darl, a Love Feast – that's a wonderful idea! Just what we need. After all the fasting and prayer and concern over Nathan, it will do everyone good."

That afternoon, a team of us decorated the dining room tables and helped plan the evening worship service. But even with the joy of preparation, an atmosphere of seriousness clouded our hearts. The evacuation plan was still a secret, but everyone knew our supplies and money were running out. The crew also was still deeply concerned about Nathan, whose life still hung in the balance.

Once the tables were set with crisp white tablecloths and napkins, colorful candles and silk flower centerpieces, Alan came in to see how things were going.

"This reminds me of the widow who fed Elijah with a barrel of meal that never ran out," I said. (I Kings 17:9-16). "As we give our all to God, worshipping Him in spite of the circumstances, I believe He will replenish whatever we need."

Alan agreed, but added his concern that we keep our focus purely on God. "A few minutes ago when I was praying," he said, "I told God we would love HIM, the God of the ship, not the ship of God! It's merely a tool, a huge hunk of metal sitting in the water."

I nodded. "Yes, that's to be our attitude, Darl, but I just know we're not going to lose it this time."

"We'll see," he replied as he went off to get dressed for the meal.

The whole crew gathered for the feast with a cheery attitude of expectancy. All the tables were elegantly set and everyone sensed that this would be a memorable evening. Sitting opposite me at the table, Alan was quiet but strangely buoyant. The worship was about to begin when someone handed him a piece of paper that looked like a telegram.

"Oh, please, Lord, don't let it be that Nathan has died," I prayed, bracing myself. I saw Alan's eyes widen and he whispered something to Captain Hal. I desperately wanted to ask what was going on, but before I could, Alan stood to his feet.

"Let's have a time of worship before the meal is served," he said, and we all stood up as the song leader began the familiar strains of "We Exalt Thee..." As our voices swelled in harmony, Alan leaned across the table toward me.

"Guess what, Luv?" he whispered with a glint in his eye. "A large check is coming from Switzerland, and...Nathan's turned the corner. He's going to be okay!"

As I looked at him in amazement, thankfulness exploded within me and tears of joy welled up. "Oh, Lord, you've done it again," I cried. "Last minute deliverance. What a God!"

I looked from face to face at the dedicated crew members worshipping our wonderful God, many with eyes closed, faces up-turned, and hands raised. As the song rose to great fervor, it was a true sacrifice of praise, direct from their hearts. I felt so honored to work beside these ones who had risked everything, leaving homes and loved ones to follow God's call and live this way, and my heart filled with a new love for them all. I couldn't wait to see their reaction when Alan shared the news.

As the song ended, we took our seats. Alan stood before the group with the look of a father about to surprise his children.

"Before we say grace," he said matter of factly, "I have something I want to share." He lifted up the telegram.

"Money is on its way from Switzerland for oil and our other supplies, and Nathan's on his way to recovery. He's going to make it!"

The room exploded with shouts of joy and praise to God. People began hugging each other and celebrating with wonderful abandon. Alan at last confessed we had plans for evacuation on Monday, and more shouts of praise rang out. We had worked, prayed, mourned, and confessed our sins together, and now we were rejoicing together. We were becoming more of a family than ever.

Several weeks later, the Spengler family returned to us amidst great rejoicing. Nathan was recovering quickly and this was a visible sign of God's faithfulness.

Although Alan and I had always assumed we would return to leading evangelism teams again, by now we found our roles had changed. Even after the Spenglers returned, Alan continued ministering to the crew in the role of chaplain. In addition to my "ship-keeping" duties, I often counseled others at his side.

With mountains of work still to do on the ship and many more thousands of dollars needed to pay for it, we rolled up our sleeves and got to work.

18

Slaying King Og

One day in October, I arrived back at the shipyard after a hectic day of shopping in Athens to find Don Stephen's wife, Deyon, unloading bags from a new camper. Now that Don's responsibilities were completed as director of YWAM Europe, he and Deyon were moving their family aboard the ship.

"Hi, Fay," she called with a friendly voice, her short blonde hair neatly framing her smiling face. I pushed past my old habit of shyness around leaders and smiled back warmly.

"Welcome to the ship, Deyon."

I had only met Deyon briefly at Camping Jolly in Venice, and I was pleased that she remembered my name.

"Don, Heidi and Luke are on board already, and I'm just getting the last bags together."

Turning, Deyon introduced me to their nanny Gigi from Belgium and her 3-year-old son, John Paul. With white blond hair and flawless creamy skin like Deyon's, he was an exceptionally winsome child, but his small blue eyes shifted aimlessly. He had suffered brain damage prior to birth and needed constant care.

I couldn't help but admire the dedication and sacrifice of this missionary family. In spite of the difficulties of rearing their special son, Don and Deyon had gladly given up the security of a home and regular salary to trust God to provide for their daily needs. Now they were sacrificing again to live in the cramped conditions of the ship.

Helping Deyon gather her belongings, I accompanied her to their cabins where Alan was standing in the hall talking with Don. Their two other fair-haired children, nine-year-old Heidi and six-year-old Luke, were excitedly examining their new home.

"So nice to see you again, Fay," said Don, extending his hand in greeting. We shook hands and his caring eyes met mine. Although I realized Don was younger than me, his obvious integrity and authority made him seem more of a father figure. His sensitive leadership began having a positive impact almost from the moment he set foot on the Victoria.

Deyon continued to be warm toward me despite my timidity, and I so appreciated her friendship. Soon after the Stephens' arrival, other key leaders also came to serve our crew of ship missionaries. David and Linda Cowie, a couple we had known in Hawaii, arrived with their small daughter Lisa and joined the ship's leadership team. David, a fellow New Zealander, was a gifted facilitator, so it was natural for him to keep the accounts as the ship's chief steward and purser. Linda, an American born in Colombia to missionary parents, became the principal for the 27 children attending school aboard the ship.

Christian officers were scarce, so we were thrilled to hear Ben Applegate and his family planned to come from New Zealand to join us. His arrival was particularly timely because Captain Hal's time commitment to the ship ministry was coming to an end.

Also joining us were Jack and Myrna Hill and their three children, Canadians whom we'd also met in Kona. Jack's skill as an engineer and his spiritual insight enabled him to take up leadership not only in the engine room but on the ship's leadership council. It was evident God was bringing together a marvelous team.

Each day, those of us on the leadership team grappled with major pioneering decisions, as well as paying bills for the ongoing expenses and repairs. Broken water pipes had to be repaired, and corroded electrical wiring had to be replaced. The ship's hospital underwent major renovations too. Skilled doctors and nurses who joined us now found themselves "operating" with chipping hammers and paintbrushes on the rusted and faded walls of the hospital wards.

In December, 1979, the Victoria went back into dry dock, with the majority of our men staying on board to work. Meanwhile, the women and children moved to a B-class hotel near the Athens coastline called the Pine Hill. The hotel lobby became the children's school and thankfully, the men joined us each weekend.

After we spent our first Christmas in Greece, Ben Applegate arrived with his family, ready to serve alongside Captain Hal. In January, Don initiated the first Ship Discipleship Training School for over 20 students. The daily lectures and prayer sessions were held in the hotel, with Alan and I joining Don, Deyon, and others as staff.

As the ship underwent major renovations, the Lord continued His work on the crew as well. We began to see that the powers of darkness hated this venture with a passion, and were working hard to regain a foothold in our lives.

Even with all the changes God had done in my life over the years, I began to be tripped up again and again in an old battle area I knew only too well. When Alan grew absorbed in his work and appeared to shut me out, those familiar feelings of rejection, either real or imagined, would settle on me like a dark cloud. He explained to me again and again that he couldn't meet all my emotional needs, but no matter what I did, the cycles of discouragement and defeat continued. I knew they were affecting my prayer life, but didn't know what to do.

One warm day in late spring when my bruised emotions were already close to the surface, Alan seemed unusually preoccupied as he went about his daily affairs. I could feel him withdrawing again into his own shell, and although I tried to fight it, I felt so unneeded and alone.

"You're not fit to be a missionary!" the enemy seemed to taunt. "You're so weak, you'll never make it in a big project like the ship."

That was it! I couldn't take these wretched cycles any more. For the first time I saw that instead of trying to change Alan, it was I who needed to change. I had to seek God for an answer.

Alan spent that night on the ship, so the next morning while the children were in school I decided to fast breakfast and lunch. Wandering out to the small Greek hotel garden, I found a quiet spot among the trees where I could read the scriptures and pray.

I closed my eyes. "Lord show me where to read," I prayed. Deuteronomy 3 came to mind.

Quickly turning the pages of my Bible, I found it was a story I had read many times before. But as I read over it again, a forbidding figure I'd hardly noticed before leaped off the pages. The troublesome King Og of Bashan was terrorizing the children of Israel to try to keep them out of the promised land.

Looking at the margin footnotes, I saw his name meant "long necked giant!" My heart was pierced. Was rejection my King Og? It was almost as if I could hear the Lord tease me, "Yes, Fay, rejection is your King Og and he keeps sticking his long, ugly neck into your life!"

As I kept reading, I was comforted to find Israel did conquer this giant, and they even kept his huge bed (equivalent to about 13 feet long) probably to serve as a reminder that even giants can be defeated by God's people.

Fueled with new faith, I saw that although rejection had been a giant in my life, likewise it could be defeated. It was time for me to take on this giant.

Leaving the garden, I remembered a park area on a small hill near the hotel. With new determination, I strode across the narrow road and up the hill, brushing over brightly colored wild flowers along the path. I usually couldn't resist stopping to pick some, but today was different. I had a personal war to fight, a battle more real than one I could see with my physical eyes.

Reaching the top after about 10 minutes, I quickly scouted around to see if I was alone. All I could see was a gray marble monument. Casting my eyes down the path I'd just climbed, I realized that up here, I somehow felt more victorious, as if I'd left all the trials of daily life behind. Planting my feet firmly on the ground, I raised my hands and thanked God for the victory.

"And in the name of Jesus Christ, the Son of God, I address you, spirit of rejection, you long-necked giant! This is your last victory! You will no longer reign over me!"

If anyone were watching, they might have thought I was mad, but I had never been more sane. The more I addressed this personal giant, the stronger I felt. I knew he was real, standing his ground there by me.

"In Jesus name, I slash you with God's word!" I declared loudly. "The Bible says Jesus came to destroy the works of the devil (I John 3:8). Jesus has come, and you must go away. Leave me alone, once and for all!"

By now I was shouting, and I actually swung an invisible sword in my hand. All at once, everything seemed strangely quiet. King Og was dead, and I knew it.

I burst into praise, accompanied with tears of joy. "Oh Lord Jesus, I thank you, I thank you!" I cried. "Only through Your death can I truly know victory."

After singing a song of joy to the Lord, I left the battle scene tripping with a light step all the way down. Now, the colorful wild flowers seemed to be even more brilliant, and I stopped to pick a victory bouquet. I was free!

Over the next weeks and months, that freedom was proven more and more each day. When faced with the same situations, I began to respond in new ways. It was a true resurrection.

Meanwhile, the Lord was using difficult circumstances to bond the crew into a remarkably strong family. The ship got out of dry dock in early June, and we at last were able to rejoin the men. But with no air conditioning, we were unable to sleep in the stifling hot cabins. All of us were assigned areas for sleeping on deck: married couples, single girls and single guys.

When fall came, the cold weather dealt our crew a new misery. Because of the dwindling fuel supply, on weekends we turned on the generators for only an hour each morning. Jokingly calling it "our hour of power," each morning we bundled up against the cold in our warmest clothes and started off with a hot breakfast. Then we filled our vacuum flasks with hot water for coffee and tea for the rest of the day.

This was true pioneering, and in a strange way, we thrived on it. The rough circumstances brought new meaning to the word prayer. Besides laughing and crying together, all we could do was pray! Each of us had to press into God in a new way, and next to worship, humor was our most valuable weapon. Noticing that the ship swung slowly back and forth on its anchor, we dubbed our own private soap opera, "As The Ship Turns."

One major passage for our family was Joy's graduation and subsequent departure for Kona to enter a DTS. It was so hard to see her go for she was not only our first child out of the nest, she was a vital part of our evangelism work and the ship ministry.

The physical ship was coming into order at what seemed a snail's pace, and we sometimes struggled with what to tell those who financially supported our ministry. All we could do was quote the words Nehemiah used when he saw the state of Jerusalem: "And there was much rubbish!"

Numerous areas of rust were now being chipped, treated, and replaced with fresh coats of white paint. Back in Maori days, the Lord had indicated we were to have a white ship standing for purity, and now we had an object lesson growing daily before our eyes. If we didn't deal with our sin, our lives would corrode.

Little by little, we were making progress. Thanks to our plumbers and engineers, the toilet flushing system at last was working.

No more strenuous walks to the deck to hoist buckets of salt water for manual flushing!

Unfortunately, our cabin happened to be at the end of the line when they were cleaning out the sewage pipes. Occasionally, the pressure would build up and cause our toilet to explode like a geyser, leaving a hideous mess on the ceiling.

Others had their rooms flooded as rusty pipes burst throughout the ship, but the plumbers eventually gained the upper hand and gave us a new "luxury," hot water for showers.

The year finished with a particularly encouraging note. On December 16, 1980, our ship was given a new name and new registry. That day we raised the flag of Malta, featuring the Cross of St. John the Evangelist, over the newly christened M/V Anastasis, a Greek word meaning resurrection.

As I watched the deck crew over the next few days begin the joyful task of painting the new name on the side of the ship, I couldn't help thinking how appropriate the name was. Both ship and crew were being recreated with a brand new life. Of course, we would never forget the loss of the Maori, but now this ship was the resurrection! Only the Lord knew how much I personally needed that victory.

That winter, I began to notice Alan withdrawing again, spending more and more time away from people in his study. It had been so long since Alan had had any kind of depression that at first, I discounted it. Then one day I walked into his office to find him staring dejectedly.

"Want to go to lunch?" I asked cheerily. He glanced at me gloomily before casting his eyes to the floor.

"I believe it's time to leave the ship ministry," he said in a monotone.

"Uh-oh," I mumbled under my breath. The ship ministry fit us like a glove. To leave was unthinkable.

"Well, God hasn't told me that," I countered. "You're just down a bit. You don't really mean it." I looked again at his dark, brooding face, and instinctively knew the root of the problem. His lack of involvement in evangelism, coupled with the lull in the ship's visible progress, had left him feeling deeply discontented.

Now looking at him again, I saw he was more depressed than I realized. At least I could look at the situation objectively. Again, I thanked God for the deep work He had done in me.

Alan lifted his head slightly. "I'm not doing what God called me for," he mumbled.

"Darl, not that again," I said, trying to stifle my growing frustration. "We've been 'round this mountain so many times. If you're not doing evangelism, you always seem to be discontent. But you're an absolute pillar in this ministry! Can't you see how much God is using you? Your prophetic input is needed so much right now. You just have to be patient. I know we'll go out doing evangelism again. I just know it."

I had learned long ago that my pep talks didn't cure his depression, and sure enough, Alan lifted his drooped head to give me a desperate and hurt look.

"It would be better if I just went away somewhere when I'm like this," he muttered. He got up to shuffle out of the office, and the look in his eyes was so hopeless, I was filled with panic.

"Look, I'm going out on deck to pray for you," I called after him. "I don't know how to help you, but I know God does."

Once he was out of sight, I tore up another passageway to Don and Deyon's cabin. I was relieved to find them both there and I blurted out what happened.

"Alan is so depressed he wants to leave the ship," I told them. "I know it's not God's will, but I'm scared he'll leave and the children and I will have to follow." Never was I more thankful to God for knitting me together with these trusted friends.

"Fay," Don said in deep earnestness. "I wouldn't want to go on if Alan weren't beside me. He's so vital to this ministry."

"I know that, but you try to convince him," I said as tears streamed down my cheeks. "Somehow he just doesn't think he's valuable unless he's out doing evangelism."

The three of us joined hands and bowed our heads, committing the situation to the Lord. Now more at peace, I thanked them and hurried up to an isolated area of the forward deck. A sense of urgency filled me as I began to pace back and forth, praying all the while. I felt as if I were fighting for Alan's life. Of course, he'd always come out of depressions before. But what if he really left the ship this time?

As I continued praying, I was amazed to see how completely God had set me free from my own rejection. Instead of falling into a tailspin of insecurity at a time like this, now I was able to freely go before the Lord with Alan's great need.

Twice that night, I woke to find Alan gone. Over and over, I kept calling out to the Lord to break through his depression. The next morning, when Alan entered our cabin during the coffee break, his face was somewhat brighter.

"Don just came to see me," he said. "He sees discontent in me too. That's what you said. Is it really that obvious? What's wrong with me?"

But before I had a chance to answer, he went on.

"Don also said he felt you were the one to minister to me, Luv. He said he believed God would give you the key to all this."

Feeling the weight of Don's pronouncement, I grimaced. "I sure don't know the answer right now. But I trust Don's judgment. We need to take time to pray together." I took his hand affectionately, and we agreed to meet later that afternoon in his office.

At the appointed time, we deliberately hung a "Do Not Disturb" sign on the door and knelt beside our old maroon sofa. As we waited in silence before the Lord, only the constant throb of the ship's engines broke the stillness.

After a long 15 minutes, I looked up. "Darl, there's something I need to explain," I said, putting my arm around his shoulder. How I loved and respected this man. My heart ached to see him free.

"You know, I've noticed this discontent through the years, and it's always tied to whether or not you're out doing evangelism," I explained. "It's like a constant cycle. If you're not doing evangelism, it's as if you can't see any other ministry as valid.

"Then when we are involved in direct evangelism, you get so absorbed in it, you hardly notice me, the children, or the rest of the team. You have no time for anyone or anything else but winning souls. It's almost as if you're driven by it."

Alan turned to face me. "I know that's true, but I don't know why."

Again bowing his head, Alan began to pray. "Lord, I don't know why I do this, but I'm sorry for this cycle of discontentment in my life. I repent and renounce it right now in Jesus' name. Please show us the root of the problem and don't let it go on spoiling my relationship with You, my family, and others!"

All at once he broke into sobs. I couldn't keep my own tears back as I watched, but I knew it was a good release after days of such heavy depression. When finally his sobs stopped, we continued again waiting before the Lord in silence.

After a few moments, Alan began flipping through his Bible, apparently looking for a reference that had come to mind. I leaned close to look over his shoulder, and my eyes fell on the chapter heading: "Joshua 12." As I began reading down the chapter, all at once my faith soared. It was another reference to King Og!

"I can hardly believe this!" I said excitedly. "God used the story about King Og to set me free from rejection nearly a year ago!"

Until now, I hadn't wanted to tell Alan the whole story of King Og, until I'd proven I was really free, but now I knew it was time. As I explained how God had led me in prayer to cast the "long-necked giant" down from his throne, a new light began to shine in Alan's eyes.

"So rejection was your giant and discontent is mine," he said thoughtfully. Without another word, he bowed his head before the Lord. I stood to my feet and, in new faith, laid my hands on his shoulders.

"Lord, you are amazing!" I spoke out. "Now please show us where this giant of discontent came from." After a few moments, a picture flashed before my eyes.

"I see you in the early days when I first met you, standing on the Open Air Campaigners platform preaching. What do you think it means?"

Alan bowed in prayer again for a few moments, then jerked his head up with a look of astonishment.

"I see it. I know what it means! Because of my natural preaching gifts and my burden for souls, back then I was receiving praise and affirmation for the first time in my life. It was as if the approval were filling a desperate hole in my heart.

"Soon I began to feel that was the only way I could be approved."

"So, when you're moving in other roles, like counseling or leading crew meetings, you don't feel significant, do you?"

"That's right, I don't," Alan agreed with a look of relief. "I see it all so clearly now."

In joy, we stood to our feet and began to praise God aloud with hands upraised. "Thank you for showing us what we could never see ourselves," I shouted.

Alan raised his voice too. "We thank you, Lord, for the victory! And in the mighty name of Jesus, we take authority over this deception! We resist and cast down the very presence of the giant of discontent, for the Bible says, 'Resist the devil and he will flee'!" (James 4:7)

With the sword of the Spirit, the Word of God, we attacked old King Og. We could almost feel the last vestiges of his oppression being torn down. At last we fell into each other's arms and began to thank the Lord for setting both of us free.

It seemed as if my whole body heaved a huge sigh of relief. The enemy had failed again to thwart God's purposes for our family. And although we were about to face some of the toughest trials yet, we were never again bothered by the terrible King Og.

Joe Portale (L.), earthquake aid in Greece.

19

Earthquake

Across the nation, the domes of Greek Orthodox churches dominated the skyline. These great churches were founded on biblical doctrines, but we discovered that tradition and rituals often superceded spiritual understanding in the lives of many Greeks. Many who attended church regularly had no idea what it meant to have a personal relationship with Jesus Christ. Despite this, our policy was never to undermine the practices of any church or individual, but rather to lift up Christ.

While the ship was docked in the Bay of Elefsis, Alan and I led evangelism teams each Friday night to the villages along the coast. I joined forces with our energetic co-worker Ron Musch to teach street dramas to our teams, and Greek Christians from various churches interpreted our dramas and testimonies. Many villagers responded openly, often kneeling in the streets to receive Christ. And as our interpreters gave the good reports to their own pastors, more churches began catching the vision for evangelism.

We quickly discovered those in the minority evangelical and pentecostal churches felt like social outcasts, and few had dared to openly evangelize for fear of being fined or put in jail. When Alan encouraged the pastors to take their members out in evangelism in spite of the risk, we praised God to see one church in particular take up the challenge. The church members began sharing their faith in the streets and underground railway tunnels, and the harvest was so great that in only a few weeks they had to move to larger facilities. It was a new time for Greece, and we reveled in it.

But authorities in the area had not overlooked our activities. One day the police in Elefsis called the ship and asked David Cowie and Alan to come in for questioning at the local station.

When Alan returned home from the station, I had hot tea ready and was eager to hear what happened.

"They know every village we've evangelized in between Athens and Corinth," he explained, rolling his eyes and head upward in a Greek expression he often copied. "They were very polite, but they wanted to know why we were proselytizing people."

"Come on," I said with some irritation. "No one in YWAM ever forces people to change their religion."

"Yes, but it gave me a great chance to share my testimony. I explained we change people's hearts and not their religion, and they really listened."

Alan slapped his knee with delight. My fiery husband never missed a chance to share Jesus.

Between munches of shortbread and sips of tea, Alan recounted how the men fired question after question at David, wanting to know the purpose of the ship and why we all lived on board with our families.

"No matter how well David explained it, they just couldn't grasp the concept of a ship for Christian work. It's not in their mindset, especially with a volunteer crew."

"So, are the police going to stop our evangelism?"

"Well, I promised I wouldn't change anyone's religion, only hearts, but they're still very suspicious. I know they'll be watching us closer than ever." Alan's chin jutted forward with that familiar look of determination. "But we're not stopping! And, I have a plan!"

"Uh-oh," I squirmed. "What kind of a plan?"

"Instead of going to one village after another in succession, we'll simply surprise them by jumping about haphazardly."

Everyone thought Alan's plan was good, so over the next weeks we cautiously began alternating our pattern. Although we were probably still under the authorities' watchful eye, they didn't make themselves known, and we rejoiced to see more and more people giving their lives to the Lord. A fervent American-born Greek who was a missionary to Greece then continued the discipleship process by enrolling the newly saved in a Greek Bible correspondence course.

On Feb. 24, 1981, I had just drifted off to sleep when I was suddenly awakened with a jolt. The ship began shuddering violently. I thought first it might be the engines starting. I reached out for Alan, then remembered he was staying ashore with some Greek friends. Leaping out of bed, I pulled on my robe and popped my head out the cabin door. Within seconds, Samuel and Stephen in the next cabin also popped their heads out, while other heads appeared out the doors all along the corridor.

"We're going up on deck to see what happened," shouted 15-year-old Samuel, and they shot past me toward the stairway. Moments later an announcement came over the ship's intercom:

"Greece has just experienced an earthquake registering 6.7 on the Richter scale. The epicenter was only a few miles away in Perahora."

We all froze, looking at one another in horror, and then suddenly moved into action. I raced up on deck to find my boys.

"Mum!" Samuel called. "The people on Salamis are screaming and all the lights have gone out!" The small island was a mile and a half from us in the gulf, but I could still hear them screaming.

I began praying immediately, and took comfort in knowing that Alan was quite a distance from the epicenter. With all the electrical problems and chaos, he didn't return for another day and a half, and when he did, he was full of stories of terror and loss. Tall buildings swayed like coconut palms in the wind, and people ran out screaming hysterically. How terrible to face such a catastrophe without God or assurance of life after death!

Although the Anastasis was not yet ready to sail, its very existence was based on bringing relief in such emergencies. It seemed to us there was no better time to start than now. Joe Portale, a man of real mercy, was chosen to lead a team of 12 for our first relief efforts. Gathering up spare blankets and clothes that Greek Christians had given us for future relief efforts, the team filled our old Mercedes van and set out for Perahora. Many of the village's frightened people had lost their homes and were living in tents, so they gratefully received the goods we had to offer. We rejoiced to be there to help in a small way.

A few days later, our crew was shaken up again, only not with an earthquake. I was out on the forward deck during the coffee break when Alan strode up and called me aside.

"Some Greek officials came on board. With so many of us living here without a sewage treatment plant, they believe we're polluting the harbor. All but 15 of us have to vacate the ship."

"Not again!" I groaned. We both knew the sewage treatment plant was badly needed to upgrade our old ship, yet it took second place to the new engine room boiler we were acquiring soon. We had no choice but to move again.

This time we moved to a small resort hotel farther up the coast. Part of our payment was to help clean up the earthquake's rubble and dust, but six weeks later the repairs were done, and we moved again to an even more damaged resort. The kitchen at Kinetta Bungalows was so ruined that our staff had to cook meals under a canopy outside. At least our bungalows were still intact, and the teachers set up school again.

Evangelism outreaches continued and the crew stepped up our intercessory prayer times, but all around, our pace had slowed again. Bills added up quickly for equipment and tools, as well as for the added expense of living ashore. So much more money was needed, but how could we ask for more shipyard help until we paid the bills?

Then we received more disturbing news. So many ships in Greece were being laid up during the oil recession that our space in the shipyard was needed for tankers. To make room, we were told the Anastasis would be taken to the "ship graveyard" in a different part of the bay. There, once-regal passenger ships now sat tied together in forlorn clusters while rust and barnacles slowly devoured them.

I fought back my emotions as the next days passed. How could God's resurrection ship live in a graveyard? Some workers would continue living on the ship as repairs continued, but it looked like the rest of us would be stuck in Kinetta for awhile. Everything within me rebelled at the idea, and for those of us who suffered the loss of the Maori, the old fears of losing the ship began to nag. I could almost feel the enemy's jeers and taunts, and I fought constantly to resist him.

When the Anastasis was finally taken to the graveyard, it nearly broke my heart. All we knew to do was continue in prayer, so over a 40-day period, we began taking turns fasting and praying for the upcoming public ministry that seemed just out of reach. Our five leaders planned to fast a total of eight days each, while the rest of us voluntarily signed up to forego certain meals. It was so encouraging to see our children and teenagers signing up, who also had been praying together regularly during school. They knew we needed a miracle.

One personal answer to prayer came when a professional dancer named Paula Kirby joined the crew. Ever since I'd left Kona, I carried the dream of beginning a King's Kids team on the ship, but I knew I wasn't capable of choreographing the dance presentations myself. Paula eagerly offered to help me.

Since it was already November we decided to invite our staff children to participate in a Christmas musical. We knew Greek law forbade us from evangelism aimed at anyone younger than 17, but this type of program could use children to subtly present the Gospel to the Greek children. The new surge of activity was a small resurrection for me. I was particularly pleased that Stephen, who at 14 was already a skilled gymnast, was also becoming a fine dancer under Paula's tutelage. Samuel had wanted to be in the program too, but found he needed to devote all his time to school-work.

On November 24, I boarded a local bus and met a Greek Christian friend in the center of Elefsis. She took me to reserve the local theater for our musical and we posted flyers in several local schools. When I returned home to Kinetta late that evening, the place was buzzing with excitement.

When I found Alan his face was absolutely beaming.

"An amazing thing happened today," he said excitedly. "After you left for Elefsis, I was in a leader's meeting when Deyon interrupted us with a shout. Myrna had looked out the big window and noticed the whole surface of the water shimmering. Suddenly fish began jumping out of the sea!"

"That's happened before," I interrupted, but Alan stopped me.

"That was always just a few fish found on the shore. We're talking about THOUSANDS!"

I gasped. "Thousands?"

"I could hardly believe my eyes! We all grabbed plastic bags from the kitchen and ran down to collect them. By the time we counted, there were 8,301 fish! It's a good thing our Norwegian cook knows how to preserve fish with rock salt."

Alan laughed as he told me they had bought out every bit of rock salt in all the grocery stores along the coast.

"Some of us thought the fish might have jumped out from being chased by other fish, but when they tried to throw them back, they jumped back out again. Peter, our caretaker, was dumb-founded. He'd never seen anything like it in all his life, and it only happened right in front of our place. Nowhere else!"

I looked at him in amazement. How could all that have happened in the short time I was gone? Alan kept rattling on in his excitement while I began to feel like I'd missed out on everything.

"I couldn't get over the timing," Alan continued. "We're just at the 30-day mark of the 40 days of fasting!"

"What do you think it was all about then?"

Alan said they had all stopped to ask the Lord what He was saying, and that he believed God indicated we were to step up our evangelism. "He's telling us to catch fish!"

"But we're already doing that."

"Yes, but I believe we need to do more. Even though the ship sits in the graveyard, the Lord will come through with the money we need if we're carrying out the Great Commission. I just know it!"

He reminded me of what happened in the Bible when the disciples needed to pay taxes. "Jesus told Peter that the money was in the fish's mouth, and I believe that's what He's saying to us. If we win souls, God will supply!"

I tried to be happy, and yes, it was all very exciting, but all I could feel was disappointment. I had missed a miracle! Here I was, a part of all the hardships, not to mention the prayer and fasting, and now I'd missed the grand finale! I felt cheated and let down.

When Alan left the room, I cleaned up my dishes, berating myself with questions. Had I done something wrong? Had I chosen the wrong day to go to the village? Eventually I went to bed full of discouragement.

The next morning one of the school teachers laughed when I told her of my disappointment.

"You missed all the work of cleaning the fish too," she said cheerfully. "Maybe the Lord wanted to give you a rest! Besides, you were doing something important, Fay."

I smiled weakly in agreement, but as she walked away I still was upset. I decided right then to do what I should have done earlier – take a walk on the beach and talk to the Lord about it.

"Lord," I prayed as my feet trudged through the sand, "I don't understand why I missed this miracle. What did I do wrong?"

Coming to a quiet, lonely spot overlooking the sea, I sat down and waited in silence. After a moment, a picture I had long forgotten flashed before my eyes. Back in New Zealand in the early '70s I had looked out on the sea of children's faces from our evangelism meetings. In the vision I saw those faces change into many nationalities, and God me an assurance that I would one day minister to children from many lands. That vision was now being fulfilled. And it was as if I could hear the Lord whispering again: "Fay, what are a few fish compared to these precious children?"

Deep inside, I knew it was true. I had experienced many miracles in my life already, and what I was doing that day was equally important, preparing to present Jesus to Greek boys and girls. It was part of the special destiny God had given me to fulfill. Now I could almost hear Him chuckling: "You didn't even imagine that faces of Greek children were in that group, did you?"

I was humbled. "Lord, I love you so much! Thank you for putting it into the right perspective!"

As I tripped back along the beach, the sparkling water and blue skies never looked better. I began singing softly to myself one of the songs we were teaching the children: "Joy to me, joy to you, joy is something that we do. Give away pure delight, make someone feel all right. That's what joy really is; let's learn to live! Joy to me, joy to you, and others too…"

It truly was an occasion to rejoice! Not only had the Lord performed a miracle with the fish, now He'd performed a miracle in me.

Sailing day, Greece: (L. to R.) Franciose, Gigi, Fay, Joanne, Alan, George, Bill.

20

Aftershock

Life in the Greek villages was beginning to bustle again as people picked up their lives after the earthquake. The fish episode had given us a faith boost, and since the time of prayer and fasting, major financial donations came in to cover past bills and further repairs. The ship was still tied up in the graveyard, and we were still living in the Kinetta bungalows, but overall, our team was encouraged.

Taking seriously the latest orders to catch fish, Alan stepped up our evangelism activity like a commander of God's army. We began adding more street meetings to our schedule, including a blitz on the nearby village, Theodore. With the cooperation of a kind and elderly Orthodox priest, we began putting a Gospel of John in every home in Theodore as we went door to door. At the end of the week, the priest allowed us to use the best place in the village for a street meeting, the church grounds. The church's head deacon was the first to come forward for a personal relationship with

Christ, and whole families came up to kneel together in repentance.

We knew that this remarkable move of God could not have escaped the attention of the enemy, or the local authorities, but each success only made us more bold to share the Gospel. One hot summer day, the team for the day loaded into our old Mercedes van and set out for the famous New Testament city of Corinth. Sitting beside Alan as he drove the van, I noticed him singing softly to himself.

"You seem extra happy today," I commented.

"I'm just so tickled to be here, where Paul the Apostle preached. As soon as I get to heaven, I want meet him and swap stories."

I chuckled. "I'm sure you'll both have a lot in common."

Setting up our sound equipment by the seafront, we began our singing, dramas and testimonies before the crowd milling about. Alan delivered his usual strong salvation message, and then began "drawing in the net" by inviting people to repent from their sin and receive Christ. I was filled with joy as about 10 people knelt down on the pavement beside Alan. I was so happy, I just wanted to keep doing this forever.

Then all at once I noticed a short, stocky middle-aged man zigzagging through the crowd, gathering literature from our team members. Thinking he was seeking help, I moved toward him until all at once he started shouting at Rita, the interpreter, who was standing next to Alan.

"He's an off-duty policeman, and he's ordering us to go to the police station," Rita explained when I reached them. We tried to explain, but the man insisted. He appeared to have a personal hatred for the Gospel.

Once inside the gloomy station house, the angry policeman stood behind a large darkly stained desk, stretched out his arms and leaned forward.

"Give me your passport!" he commanded Alan, who quickly pulled it from his pocket. With a flick of his wrist, the man rudely banished me to an old wooden bench along the back wall.

Rita stood beside Alan to interpret, but because she kept interrupting to explain to the policeman, he roughly ordered her out of the room. His face was red and sweat ran down over his protruding neck veins.

"You dirty teacher!" he hissed venomously in Alan's face. His rage was so great, for a moment I feared he might have a heart attack. Picking up a pen from the desk, he reached toward Alan's passport.

"I'll cancel your passport. We don't want people like you in Greece!" he hissed.

Alan lurched forward, covering his passport with his hand. "Excuse me," he said firmly, "but I don't believe you have the authority to touch my passport. That's for the immigration department. I want to call my lawyer."

Madder than ever, the policeman recognized his hands were tied, and pulled back from the passport with a spiel of Greek words. The other policemen in the office shifted about nervously, obviously not approving of the senior man's behavior. The man thumped the table and began roaring in broken English.

"Don't...don't you know...I have the power to...put you in prison and take all your clothes off?"

I fought to control a nervous laugh. I guessed he meant something like "strip us of our belongings," but couldn't find the right words. We were in big trouble this time, maybe even going to prison!

"That's all right, as long as you put my wife and me together to keep each other warm!"

Not believing my ears, I screamed inwardly. Alan! How could you? Had his Liverpool humor gone mad?

Suddenly, the policeman started shouting.

"Get out! Get out!" he ordered, herding both of us toward the door. Whether or not he understood Alan's last comment I didn't know, but suddenly he'd run out of steam and authority.

"Don't ever preach here again!" he yelled, shaking his finger at us as he spoke. "And if you want your Bibles back, you'll have to come for them next week. I'm going to warn all the police up and down this coast about you!"

Alan grabbed my hand and whispered in my ear. "Quick, let's get out of here before he changes his mind!"

But before we were out the door, Alan turned back to the policeman. "Excuse me, sir, before I go, could I please see the Chief of Police?"

"What for?" he snapped, but fear passed over his face.

"I want to ask permission to preach in the prison here in Corinth."

"GET OUT!" he screamed, and this time Alan hurriedly obeyed. Once outside, I breathed a big sigh of relief. "That was a close call!" Finding Rita, we filled her in as we almost ran the 200 yards back to the team.

"I'm going back next week to get our Bibles," Alan declared.

"Can't we just forget it?" I protested. "I'm just thankful we weren't put in prison!"

"The enemy won't intimidate me through any man!" he asserted. "And what's more, I'm going back to Corinth to preach when God tells me to!"

I shot a smile at Rita. This was the man I loved! He never lost that fiery passion to preach the Gospel.

The next week, Alan and I did make the trip back to get our Bibles, and after a long procedure, including paying for a signed document from an attorney, we walked out of the police station with our Bibles in hand. I also knew that one day we would be back to preach in Corinth. The enemy had once more lost the battle.

But that wasn't the only run in we had with the police. Not long after, while looking over the map for our next evangelism target, Alan was drawn to a place called Neo Smyrna. He told me it was a suburb of Athens, where the people were generally more affluent and better educated. We later learned that many of the young people there had turned from the Orthodox church and elevated university studies in their minds. These people needed the Gospel, too, and we believed God was directing us to start evangelizing there.

Our first night, we unloaded the old Mercedes near a park in the center of town, and some of the team set up while the rest of us walked the streets in twos and prayed. Once we began our usual songs and testimonies, we were thrilled to see a large crowd gather quickly and start listening intently. Alan then began preaching his heart out, interpreted by a young woman named Hara. But just when Alan raised his arm to invite the crowd to receive Christ, a tall police officer stationed himself immediately in front of him.

"Stop now," he commanded.

"Sir, ple-e-ease let me finish," Alan pleaded. "I'll only be a few minutes longer, I promise. And then I'll stop."

Alan's face, which moments before reflected overflowing compassion for the crowd, now registered obvious frustration. He stood there looking like a skilled fisherman who's full net had been ripped open to let the fish escape.

The policeman shook his head. "Stop now!" Alan looked past the policeman's shoulder at me and mouthed the word Anastasis, our signal to mingle with the crowd and speak to them one on one. Since our time in Corinth, Alan had devised this special pass word in case of any problems.

The team did our best to start speaking to the people and handing out Greek Gospel literature, but as Alan and Hara were escorted down the road to a nearby police station, many of the crowd followed them, making an unplanned procession down the street. I wanted so badly to go with Alan too, but I knew he wanted me to stay with Ron and the rest of the team.

By the time I caught sight of Alan and Hara returning, we were sitting in the parked van waiting to go back to Kinetta. Jumping out, I was surprised to see they were grinning from ear to ear.

"What happened?" I asked as the team gathered around.

"You won't believe it," he said, laughing and slapping his thigh. "The huge crowd that followed us to the station totally took over the chief of police, yelling at him, shouting, and talking all at once." Alan paused as we laughed.

"I didn't know what they were saying, so I just moved aside and sat in a chair, reading my small New Testament," he continued. "Finally, Hara told me the people were demanding they let us go. One man even said, `These people gave us something sweet to eat, making us hungry. What have they done wrong? The drug push-ers come to the park, but you don't arrest them.'

"After the confusion died down, the chief of police came up and said, `GO! GO! GO! The world is for you.'"

We all looked at each other in amazement as Alan laughed loudly. "I love it! It's just like the book of Acts!"

Such incidences only served to bolster our faith, and in the weeks ahead, we continued evangelizing the villages in our haphazard order. One of the villages hardest hit by the earthquake was Megara, a place that had previously been resistant to our evangelism efforts. Now, much of the town had been devastated, and the people were hungry for answers. It was a natural place for us to target.

One night soon after the quake, my eyes scanned the devasta-tion as we drove into the village. Pieces of roofing dangled precari-ously over several buildings, while others looked more like the Leaning Tower of Pisa. As we parked the van and began to set up, I thanked God again for the obvious change in the village's atmo-sphere. Before, the men sat playing cards at the coffee shops and ignored us, but tonight some smiled a greeting. Others looked un-usually thoughtful. I noticed Alan, too, was deep in thought, brooding over his message as we began the meeting. After only two songs, he and the interpreter went to the microphone to ad-dress the crowd.

"Jesus told a story of two men who built different houses, one on rock and one on sand," he said. His eyes swept the gathering crowd. "Unexpected devastation in the form of storms and floods came upon them in the same way the earthquake hit your village. Are you building your house on the rock or sand tonight?"

As Alan skillfully explained the Gospel message and challenged people to take a stand, a hush came upon the whole crowd. After a pause, he stretched his arm out toward them. "You may not have seen the last of the tremors yet," he proclaimed.

Just as he began asking people to receive Christ as their rock and salvation, suddenly a noticeable tremor shook the ground. As everyone looked at each other in amazement, Alan continued calling people to come forward. It was no surprise when an unusually large number did so! Had God given a supernatural sign of His shakings in their lives?

One evening we returned to Megara, and as Alan was preaching I noticed a young man standing in the shadows of a store doorway, listening intently. Probably not more than 16 years old, the young man's downcast yet handsome face told me he was hurting and depressed. I breathed a silent prayer for him, and although he didn't come forward, after the meeting he approached Alan to ask for a free copy of the newly translated Modern Greek New Testament we were distributing. I and others approached as Alan gave it to him with a smile full of compassion.

"What's your name?" Alan asked.

"My name is Kostas Kotopoulos," he answered in careful English, apparently wanting to practice speaking. He explained he lived in Megara with his father and stepmother, and as we continued talking, we learned he was suffering the trauma of a broken home. Although he didn't make a decision for Christ that night, young Kostas seemed drawn to us, and afterward came to each street meeting we had in the village. Soon he made so many friends among the team, he started visiting us regularly in Kinetta. He quickly made good friends among our teenagers as well.

Kostas confided he had been raised in the Orthodox Church and had religious instruction at school, but he was seeking more understanding about this Christ whom we said was a personal friend. Kostas's pleasant-mannered father seemed happy for the new friends his 16-year-old son had found, and he often brought Kostas to visit us at Kinetta. Though Kostas hadn't officially asked Jesus into his heart, his face appeared happier and his eyes were becoming lighter. The young boy became the focus of much prayer among the team as his visits became more frequent.

All seemed to be going well, until one day Kostas mentioned

that his real mother had a different opinion about his visits. She especially didn't like it when she heard the word Christian, and one day even came with Kostas into the small ship office in Elefsis to complain to Don Stephens and Alan about it. But we weren't prepared for the aftershock that was about to hit us.

Without warning, one morning the press swarmed like bees onto the Kinetta property, with Kostas' mother right in the middle of them. Twelve or so reporters from both newspapers and television stations, bearing cameras, microphones, and note pads, began shooting out questions all at once to a group of us who had been enjoying a chat over our morning coffee break.

"Do you believe in sex before marriage?" one reporter asked a Swedish girl roughly.

"Certainly not," she threw back with a flushed face. But already the reporter had swung the camera away. I guessed by this kind of nonsense they were trying to prove we were some kind of cult who were living together immorally. I was relieved when Don and Alan quickly burst through the main door of the nearby building.

"Don't answer any more questions," Don told us discreetly. We were all aware of the way the media could possibly twist our comments to suit their purpose. He then turned to address the intruders in a respectful but firm manner, "If you want to know anything, you can ask us questions, and we'll be happy to show you around our facilities." The reporters willingly followed Don and Alan through the building where our children were having school, and some of us walked behind, praying quietly. The children even sang a Christian song for them, and the whole atmosphere calmed down.

The Greek property owner was indignant about the attack, and knowing our integrity as a group also stood up for us. Over the next few hours, Alan and Don explained to the reporters our purpose for being in Greece, answering the many questions about our outreach activities, and the events surrounding young Kostas Kotopoulos. We hoped for the best, but our worst imagination couldn't have prepared us for what was about to happen.

The next day, 11 Athens area newspapers came out decrying us as a false cult planning to abduct Greek children and spirit them away on the ship. Some of the stories filling the front pages were nothing short of bizarre. The craziest headline was a distorted twist about the fish miracle: "When hungry, they pray, and roast chicken jumps out of the sea." If it weren't so damaging, we could have laughed. We couldn't understand how the legitimate press could write articles fit for seedy scandal tabloids.

The following weekend, a Greek Christian friend told us an hour-long television news program similar to America's 60 Minutes would feature us on prime time. Our friend offered to interpret the show for us, so at the appointed time we all gathered around the television in the Kinetta lobby, prepared to watch our names be smeared in the mud.

"Well, Lord, after all it's your reputation," I breathed, as Don Stephens stood before the crew. He reminded us of the sound advice of General William Booth, founder of the Salvation Army, who said staying in the news, whether good or bad, was good for publicity.

"And remember," Don continued, "if God's enemy Satan is given enough rope, he eventually hangs himself."

We didn't know how prophetic that statement would turn out to be. The room grew quiet as the show began and pictures of the Anastasis loomed before our eyes. Our friend interpreted as familiar shipyard workers recounted our past debts and late payments for services rendered, obviously putting us in a bad light. But the hardest scenes to watch were of young Kostas' mother herself as she dramatically accused us of wanting to kidnap unsuspecting Greek teenagers and take them away on the ship.

All at once we saw a picture of Kostas' mother holding up the New Testament and pointing at Alan.

"You gave this book to my son!" she accused. As the camera zeroed in on the cover, the tension in the room was broken as we all burst out laughing. What better way to let people know about the newly translated modern Greek New Testament than to connect it to a scandal! We didn't know just how much this would prove to be true.

Until recently, the Greek people had great difficulty reading the Bible because it was written only in antiquated classical Greek. Respected Greek evangelist Costas Macris, leader of the interdenominational Hellenic Evangelical Mission in downtown Athens, had made it a personal mission to give his people the scriptures in modern Greek. Costas' father had spent years translating the New Testament, but with little money for advertising the newly printed book, few people knew of its existence.

Costas had tried without success to get it announced on the Orthodox-run state television programs. Now as soon as he saw the cover of the New Testament flashed onto the screen, Costas knew the Greek people's curiosity would be at a high. He dispatched helpers all over Athens to tell bookstore owners it had been highlighted on television. The booksellers now welcomed the New Testament in their stores and in no time, it went into its third printing.

Our ministry was also affected by the scandalous program, but not in the way we feared. The show was so widely watched, when we drove about the area, people would recognize the name "Youth With A Mission" on the side of our van and wave with smiles. One Greek woman telephoned us saying, "I'd be glad if you could help my son." The show had "put us on the map," and we rejoiced that the enemy hadn't stopped God's word from going forth.

But in the midst of our rejoicing, I couldn't overlook that it wasn't just a public battle but a very private one for an anxious mother. I knew from my reading that since World War II, the Greek people had a deep historic scar etched in their memories. At the time, Greek children had been torn from their parents and taken to nearby communist countries. In spite of promises that the children would be cared for, many were mistreated and some never seen again. Kostas's mother did appear to have real fears that we would steal her son away, and although it was hard to understand, I tried to put myself in her place.

Both Alan and Kostas had tried to explain to her several times that the ship didn't accept anyone younger than 18, but the words fell on deaf ears. When Kostas' mother became hospitalized with a severe illness shortly after, we prayed for her often, and even sent flowers, but her difficulty in trusting us was apparent.

Life grew even tougher for young Kostas when we were issued a restraining order forbidding Kostas to visit his friends from the ship. Because Kostas was a minor, we all had no choice but to enforce the law.

One day soon after, I was strolling along praying near the back fence of the Kinetta property when I saw Kostas walking up. My heart sank.

"Kostas, what are you doing here?"

"I took the train because my father wouldn't bring me," he said with a grin. "I miss my friends so badly, I just had to come see them again."

"But you know about the court order," I said gently. "If you get caught, you'll be in trouble and so will we."

I felt like a traitor as I saw his face fall. I tried to explain that we loved him, but that our hands were tied, but he met my gaze with a wounded look. After a moment of silence, I could feel his pain as he turned and slunk off like a hurt puppy with his tail between legs.

Watching him head off down the street, I tried to calm my anger at a system that would let this happen. It was such a big test for someone just starting to trust his life to the Lord.

"Lord," I said softly. "Please don't let this test ruin his new faith in you!"

All I could do was trust him into the hands of a God who didn't let a sparrow fall to the ground without Him knowing it.

21

Like Them That Dream

"**P**repare your baggage for removal!" Alan's voice boomed across the makeshift meeting room at Kinetta where each week we had held our evening staff meetings for the last six months.

As Alan kept reading from Ezekiel 12, I noticed his brow was set in deep concentration. Tonight, he definitely had on what our family called his "prophetic look," eyeing the crowd over top his reading glasses.

Was this scripture in some way signifying an upcoming change? It had been two months since the King's Kids had put on the dramatic Christmas presentation, and with the team now in recess I'd grown restless.

"We need to live with our earthly lives in order, ready and alert," Alan declared, "and not allow ourselves to be too settled.

We need to always be ready for a change."

As Alan continued expounding on the scripture, I thought how appropriate it was for the Williams family. We always seemed to be living on the edge, waiting for the Lord's next command. It was never easy, but we considered it a privilege, and we treasured it.

Later in bed that evening, I snuggled close to Alan in the dark, feeling safe and calm in his arms.

"Do you know something I don't?" I asked. "Your message seemed to have a deeper meaning, especially that verse about preparing your baggage for removal."

"I really don't know," he said at last, a hint of sleepiness in his voice. "I'd never even noticed those verses before this afternoon. But I'm sure God's up to something."

The next morning dawned cold and wet as we started our usual routine. Around nine, Alan walked around the bungalows announcing an emergency meeting in the main hall. We almost never met at that time of day, so something was up.

As we took our seats, Captain Ben Applegate walked to the front of the room and called the meeting to order.

"We've just received an unexpected call from a shipyard on the island of Salamis," he began. "We've reached an agreement with workers there to continue repairs, so we all must move back on board the ship immediately to sail there in a day or two."

As exclamations of both shock and joy filled the room, Alan smiled at me from his place up front. He knew nothing of this yesterday, but God had been telling us to be ready, ready for another resurrection. The Anastasis would finally get out of the graveyard!

Our initial joy turned to panic for many of us we realized how ill-prepared we were for such a hasty move. Captain Ben said buses would arrive in Kinetta in just a few hours to take us to the Anastasis. I wondered how we could possibly pack and get cleaned up so quickly. Captain Ben went on to explain why we had to move so fast.

"There is an immigration law stating that if you come into a country by ship, it can't be moved without all of the crew on board," he continued, pausing to grin widely. "I'm sorry we have so little time, but all we can do is enjoy it, and hope we can stay aboard this time."

As each person flew to their cabin to pack, the Kinetta bungalows looked like a disturbed ants' nest. Then a new announcement came. Everyone was to pack only one small bag for the immediate move, and a cleaning and packing team would come back later to finish. I volunteered for the packing team, and then wondered if I was in my right mind. Did I really want to pack for other people?

But it had to be done, and all of us wanted to be on board when the Anastasis was removed from the graveyard and taken to a regular shipyard. As we loaded our belongings onto the bus, tears of gratitude came to my eyes. God had heard our cries! The ship repairs were nearly complete and that could mean only one thing. We'd soon be on our way!

Two days later, dozens of us, dressed in our warmest winter coats, lined the rails of the Anastasis for the big event. A cold sea breeze whipped our faces as we watched the crew untie the ropes binding us to the other vessels in the bay. I knew Alan was off somewhere praying, and Samuel and Stephen, now 16 and 14, were milling about the crowd in anticipation. How I wished that Joy, now serving God in YWAM Hong Kong, could be here to see this!

As the ship was loosed from the graveyard, I sensed that something was happening in the spiritual realm. The enemy had tried many times to tell us we were too small and the project would never amount to anything, but now he was facing a lost battle. We had gone to death twice for this ministry, but we had never forgotten the God of resurrection. As the ship sailed out of the bay and docked at nearby Chandris Shipyard, it was as if we were being raised to life.

On March 8, 1982, we set out deeper into the harbor for "sea trials," a series of tests and maneuvers to see if our refurbishing was reliable. Our officers and deck men donned their crisp, navy blue uniforms, and the rest of us stood by proudly to watch these skilled crew members going through their paces for surveyors from Lloyds of London.

For me this day was the fulfillment of a dream. In the three years since we'd joined the crew of the Anastasis, I'd often thought of us as God's Navy, and now it was happening.

The surveyors pronounced the ship seaworthy, and even commended the crew's teamwork. We had passed their tests with flying colors!

The Anastasis crew fairly wept for joy at the news that we were free to set sail. With all the main repairs completed and paid for, we now began storing food on board for our voyage to Los Angeles, which would become our home port.

We all hoped to leave immediately, but we still didn't have enough money for the fuel. After slogging away for three long years, we were desperate to get under way. This latest waiting seemed unbearable. All we could do was pray, and we cried out to God again and again.

The days in Salamis now dragged on with torturous slowness. We kept ourselves busy with various small tasks, but our hearts longed for the day we could sail out of Greece. Some four months after the ship was pronounced seaworthy, we were all called to a meeting in the main lounge. Captain Ben stood tall and smart in his navy blue uniform before the full crew of about 350.

"We have just received a check which will cover the cost of the oil we need," he announced. "We'll be sailing in a few days for Los Angeles." All at once, his voice cracked with emotion. Ben, this controlled and dignified English gentleman, was on the verge of tears.

Now tears glistened on the faces of almost everyone as we all clapped, hugged each other and praised our faithful God. He had heard our cries! What a change from the awful announcement Wally Wenge had made nine years earlier when we'd lost the Maori. As I looked from Ben over to his dear wife, Helen, my spirit leapt to realize they were now seeing the fulfillment of all the Lord had put in their hearts so many years before.

Late that afternoon, we all gathered on deck to watch as the fuel barge sailed alongside us and connected the large hoses onto our engine room tanks.

"Those Greek workers must think we're really strange," I remarked to Alan as he came up beside me.

"That's for sure," Alan agreed and he laughed loudly. "In all my years at sea, no one ever watched the oil men."

Over the next 12 hours, the oil kept flowing into our thirsty tanks as singing and hilarious celebration continued all over the decks. How could the barge workers understand the significance of what was happening? How could they have known that for many months our engineers had taken drums to the local gas station and returned with just enough diesel oil to keep us going?

As I watched, a psalm the Lord had given me back in Kona came to mind, and I ran down to my cabin to look it up:

"When the Lord turned again the captivity of Zion, we were like them that dream. Then was our mouth filled with laughter, and our tongue with singing; then said they among the heathen, The Lord hath done great things for them. The Lord hath done great things for us, whereof we are glad. Turn again our captivity, O Lord, like streams in the south. They that sow in tears shall reap in joy. He that goeth forth and weepeth, bearing precious seed, shall doubtless come again with rejoicing, bringing his sheaves with him." (Psalm 126)

July 7, 1982, dawned as a day of destiny for the M/V Anastasis and her crew. Today we would set sail! I opened my eyes and turned in bed to find Alan was already gone. Or had he slept at all? Before most major events, my dedicated husband often spent most of the night in prayer. I lay there smiling as I thought of him most probably walking the decks right now, praying over every detail of our exodus. It was such a familiar sight, some of us joked about how he prayed over every chain in the anchor. Remembering Alan's former depression and desire to leave the ship, my heart was now filled with gratitude that we were still here in God's will, ready to take part in this amazing day.

I leapt out of bed and headed for the shower. While turning on the water for my ship-style two-minute shower, I was astonished to realize Alan hadn't had one day of depression since we had slain that giant of discontent, King Og! Bursting into songs of praise, it didn't even bother me to think I'd soon be downing motion sickness pills my first since joining the M/V Anastasis. When I finished dressing, I found Samuel and Stephen had already left their cabin. Although they did have school today, their teacher no doubt would have her students write up all the highlights of this important day in an essay.

By mid-morning, all was ready. Captain Ben and his officers stood on the bridge, the command center of the ship, while the deck crew stood on the forward deck, waiting the order to pull up the anchor. In the bowels of the ship, the engineers also stood poised for instructions. I marvelled at the quality of men and women God had sent us to work in all areas of the ship, but especially John Brignall, our chief engineer from England. His professional expertise and genius for creating things out of nothing for the engine room, had saved us thousands of dollars since he first came to both work and supervise the refurbishing. I imagined the fulfillment he must be experiencing right now.

Yes! We were ready to go, when the word came that Don Stephens was not back on board yet. He had gone ashore for a final meeting with the port authorities and hadn't returned.

As we stood waiting once again, Deyon Stephens came on deck alongside me with their infant son Charles. I took him from her and cuddled him in my arms, asking if she knew why Don was delayed.

"He just called Ben on the ship radio, and there's been some kind of hold up with the papers," she explained. "Of course, it's a small technicality, but you know what it's like here. It could take a while."

Almost spontaneously, we began to pray and our tension melted as we committed our last problem to the Lord together. Looking up, we both laughed to see Alan leaning on the rail of the deck just above us, obviously praying too as he looked out for the launch that would bring Don back. Ten minutes later we saw it on the horizon and I hurried back to our room.

With Don back on board, I soon heard the engines revving and the loud rumble of the thick anchor chain as it scraped and wound around the anchor winch. We were on our way!

I rushed to the door and nearly collided with Alan as he came in.

"Better start praying again," he said.

"Why, what now?"

"The deckies have just found that a wire rope from the tanker next to us is wrapped around our anchor."

"Oh, this tension is unbearable!" I responded. "It's like the exodus from Egypt. Is Satan having his last fling?"

Alan left, and I began to pace about the cabin, crying out to God and binding the powers of darkness. They weren't going to win!

Walking up on deck, I joined the others hanging over the rail, praying. After what seemed ages, we finally heard the propellers pick up their rotation. The anchor was free! Looking up to the bridge, I saw Alan standing with Captain Ben and the Greek pilot who would guide us out of the harbor. Helen Applegate stood against the rail outside the bridge, and she returned my wave with a look of pure joy.

All at once I felt sad and elated at the same time. We had already hugged our dear Greek friends in an emotional farewell, and as we began to pull out, I saw them standing on shore, waving goodbye.

Just last night our King's Kids team had performed a final musical presentation for Greek officials and friends. Young Kostas had been there to say goodbye, as had our interpreters and others who faithfully joined us in our evangelistic efforts. It was hard to leave them all behind.

Now I waved back to these dear brothers and sisters in Christ, watching teary-eyed as they shrank to small dots on the horizon.

Moments later I heard a familiar whistle, and looked up to see Alan on the bridge. He waved at me to come up, and I quickly ran up the stairs.

"Follow me," he said, grabbing my hand and leading me up to

the monkey island above the bridge.

"No one's allowed up there," I objected, trying to pull back from him. He just shook his head and pulled harder, obviously annoyed with my rigid keeping of rules.

"Today's a special day. We can make an exception."

He smiled broadly until I gave in and began mounting the stairs to the highest vantage point on the whole ship. A warm sea breeze blew through our hair as the ship pushed out of Salamis harbor. We stood arm in arm soaking in the view, and I couldn't help thinking again of Joy in Hong Kong. How I wished she were here with us today! I could see Samuel and Stephen below, standing by the railing with their school buddies. Their excitement was evident by their animated hand gestures.

The brilliantly blue Mediterranean now stretched out before us, and I choked on the lump in my throat. "I'll miss the beauty of Greece..." I said nostalgically. "Of course, I'll miss the people most of all." My voice trailed off as I thought of the hundreds of people who had received Christ during our last three years here.

Tears began to sting my eyes. What a life we had lived! What an awesome privilege to partner with the almighty God! Our future seemed as bright and broad as the sea that now stretched before us.

"Can this really be happening?" I murmured. "With all that's happened, I feel like Pharaoh might try to bring us back." Glancing at Alan, I could see he was still praying as the ship nosed slowly out toward the entrance to the open sea. Next we saw the pilot's launch speeding toward us. After it came alongside and stopped, we watched as the pilot stepped onto it and began heading back. Now we were on our own.

Alan and I looked at each other with too much emotion to speak. Within minutes we were out to sea. It was the close of yet another chapter, but a new one was just beginning. In three weeks we would arrive in San Pedro, California, where new challenges awaited us.

King's Kids.

22

Hearts and Hands To Help

Sitting at the table in our small cabin, I was filled with excitement as I mapped out final preparations for our King's Kids performance in just an hour at the ship's welcoming ceremony in San Pedro, August 5, 1982.

Alan was off somewhere talking to a Los Angeles port official, so I bounded to the upper deck and stood against the rail with the others to watch. I didn't want to miss one minute! My usual seasickness had subsided and since sailing from Greece, Paula and I had taught dances and songs to 15 of our ship's kids for this special public event. My mind was now racing over all the details as we prepared to dock.

Just last night, Don Stephens had called us all together to explain details of the welcoming ceremony and how to meet with the press. Churches up and down the coast had been invited to the ceremony and 3,000 Christians were expected to attend. Looking us all in the eye, Don explained that after three years of relative privacy, we now would need to adapt to a new lifestyle where the ship would become public property and daily tours would be the norm.

"Yes, this is our home, but I want to encourage you, we need to make room in our hearts for people, and even give up our rights to our home," he explained.

We were still trying to take it all in, and didn't understand how public we were about to become but we were soon to find out.

Amid my exhilaration, a new fear hit me. "Lord, what if people worship the ship? Will You have to take it from us again, like the Maori?"

But now as we sailed into full view, I saw thousands of Christians standing on shore, most with eyes closed and hands raised, as their voices blended with the song of worship booming over the loudspeakers. The familiar recording was by Keith Green, who the week before had died in a plane crash:

"Holy, Holy, Holy, Lord God Almighty…"

I praised God as I saw I didn't need to be concerned. Some people were so caught up in the majesty of our great God, they didn't even realize the ship was there.

Leaning hard against the rails, I viewed the decorated platform with an overflowing heart. Seated there was Loren Cunningham, the president and founder of Youth With A Mission, the first one to dream of a missionary ship. With him were Jim and Joy Dawson, two of our treasured mentors from New Zealand days, as well as Keith Green's widow, Melody. What a brave lady! She had obviously taken hold of God's great grace for this moment.

As I opened my mouth to sing along with the next hymn, nothing would come out. Tears of joy and celebration flowed instead. Glancing up at Helen on the deck above me, I caught her eyes. What joy she and Ben must feel today!

As we joined the crowd on shore, I marched down behind the

King's Kids, who were geared up and ready to go. After our two songs and interpretive dances, the crowd responded with more shouts of praise to God. Those on the platform followed with stirring speeches about how God had birthed the ship ministry, and there was no question that He was the focus of the day.

That night, when Alan and I returned to our cabin, we fell into bed happily exhausted.

As Don had forewarned, our lifestyle changed drastically overnight. Tour groups began filling the alleyways of the ship, sometimes to the point that we couldn't get by. That was hard, but as Don had so wisely alerted us, people were our life blood, and we needed them. None of us on the ship received a salary, and thousands of dollars were needed just to keep it afloat. If these people could catch the vision of reaching the world through the ship ministry, perhaps they would help with the ship's financial support base or even join us as crew in the future.

One night, Alan plopped himself down next to me on our small cabin sofa.

"I'm exhausted," he said. "How about a holiday? Once I finish speaking at the staff conference held on board, why don't we plan to get away?"

I looked at my tired husband and laughed. Our family had landed in Los Angeles with six cents to our name, and we hadn't seen any more money come in. No doubt some support money had gotten held up in Greece after our move, but we didn't know when we would see it.

As I looked closer at Alan, I noticed his face was drawn. "Are you feeling all right?"

He looked at me seriously, obviously hesitating.

"Come on, out with it!" I coaxed.

"Recently I've felt some pains in my chest," he admitted. "It's especially when I exercise. Usually it passes in a few minutes, but this morning it was bad. I think I'm just over tired."

"You need to get a check at the ship hospital, Darl." Somehow I couldn't hide the hint of fear in my voice.

"You know I believe we always need to go to God first," he responded. "I'll go to the doctor after I pray about it."

I nodded. "Then let's ask God about this holiday. We can spend some time together while we're away from everything." Reaching out for Alan's limp hand, I closed my eyes.

"Lord, you know we have no money, but we haven't had a holiday since 1980," I began. "We're both tired, and we need some time together and with our boys. We ask you to please provide what we need."

As often as we'd seen God answer prayer, we were still surprised by what happened next. During the YWAM staff conference on board, a woman we'd known from Kona ran up to me. Although we hadn't seen her in four years, she had tears in her eyes as she pressed a check into my hand.

"This is for a holiday," she said. "I've really been burdened for you in prayer, and the Lord told me you needed a vacation."

Deeply moved, I thanked her with a hug and told her about our prayer. As I walked away, I marveled at the Lord's timing. But that wasn't all. The next day we received a message to call another friend. To our surprise, she invited us to stay at her beach house on the coast of California for 10 days.

So as soon as we could, the four of us were on our way. We gladly spent the time taking walks, bowling, roller skating and talking together. All of us spent time in prayer together as well, and we felt a spiritual renewal come upon us. Alan began praising God daily for the healing of his chest pains, and by the end of our time, they had almost disappeared.

Replenished for our next phase of ministry, we rejoined the ship full of faith for our next assignment.

During the next four months of ministry, we rejoiced that the dream of a ship to serve the nations had come to pass. Thousands of visitors took part in the daily tours and activities on board, while the engineer and deck hands continued with the constant upgrading of the ship. Likewise, the dining room staff was busier than ever serving the public.

Alan and I also began taking a team out to speak in local churches about the ship ministry, recruiting both crew and students for the Discipleship Training Schools held on board.

As a YWAM ship, we had long before adopted the mission's mandate, "To Know God And Make Him Known;" but now we also added a motto specific to the Mercy Ship: "Hearts And Hands To Help In The Name Of Jesus."

It seemed every moment of the next year was spent fulfilling those mandates of evangelism and practical service. On January 4, 1983, we set sail to dispense relief goods and spread the Gospel in Guatemala, New Zealand and the islands of the South Pacific.

At the invitation of Guatemala's newly elected President Rios Montt, himself a born-again Christian, we delivered cargo donated by the American public to help the suffering Ixil Indians in that war-torn nation. We were delighted to distribute $1.5 million worth of food, clothing, Spanish Bibles, medical supplies, a mobile dental unit, electric generators, building and farming materials, and even a portable saw mill. Besides unloading the cargo, some of us launched evangelistic meetings on the streets of Guatemala City. Many responded to our invitation to receive Christ and the people mobbed us for tracts.

As we sailed on toward New Zealand, taking seasickness pills was a must for me now, because our work didn't stop once we were afloat. Besides spending time in corporate prayer, we were always polishing our evangelism songs and dramas. Alan had now recruited a committed evangelism team, with Ron Musch helping lead. I juggled my time between teaching dramas to the evangelism team and helping with King's Kids. Of course, some days the ship plunged up and down so much practice was impossible, but we did as much as we could to prepare for upcoming outreaches.

Once the Anastasis reached New Zealand we would team with other Christian groups and churches for an evangelistic blitz called "Operation Resurrection."

The morning of February 5, I literally leapt out of bed, and though still dark, I dressed rapidly and rushed out on the forward deck to watch as New Zealand's verdant green North Island gradually appeared in the early light of dawn. Long stretches of wispy clouds hung like chiffon over the lowlands. No wonder New Zealand's Maori people named it *Atearoa* or *The Land of the Long White Cloud.*

For those of us who suffered the loss of the Maori, returning to New Zealand in YWAM's "resurrection ship" had special meaning. With all its pain and struggle, I was so thankful to have been a part of it all.

The next five months were filled with evangelistic services and presentations held on the ship and anywhere crowds gathered — schools, youth clubs, prisons, streets, malls, and churches. Starting at the North Island, we sailed down the east coast to 15 port cities, reaping a harvest of souls along the way. Each time we set sail, memories of the years of constant work, financial struggles and spiritual warfare began to fade in the joy of accomplishment.

By the end, we had received 95,000 visitors on board, and 100,000 attended land-based outreaches and functions. A conservative estimate showed 5,000 people accepted Christ into their lives. In each place, Christian groups and churches donated goods for us to distribute on our next outreaches in Fiji and Tonga, which had just suffered a devastating hurricane.

A special highlight for us was when we docked at our third port of call, our home city of Auckland. We rejoiced to be able to see our families again, and welcome on board my mother, my older sister, Yvonne, and her husband, Ron, as well as Alan's mother, his brothers, his sister and their families. Seeing them all again after four years brought home the high cost of being called to missionary work. But at last they could visualize what we'd been doing the last four years.

One of the big topics of conversation, of course, was news about our daughter Joy, now 20, who was engaged to a Canadian she'd met in YWAM Hong Kong named Rob Penner. They had officially announced their engagement while visiting us in San Pedro last November, and we were excited about their joint call to continue ministering in Asia. Samuel and Stephen, now 17 and 15, had also taken to Rob well, and we were all excited about the wedding set for May 7 in Hong Kong. Most of the family in New Zealand couldn't travel so far to attend, but at least Alan's brother, Ronald, and his family planned to come.

As the weeks in Auckland flew by, we saw our relatives as much as possible before we were on our way to Wellington, the nation's capital, for more evangelism and presentations. While docked there, Alan and I took a two-week break to fly to Hong Kong for Joy's wedding. That day, as Joy glided radiantly down the aisle on her daddy's arm, I couldn't help thinking how she had always given us joy, living up to her name.

Once back in New Zealand, all of us on the Anastasis began preparing for our next voyage to the Pacific Islands. One morning Don Stephens unexpectedly called the leadership team to his cabin. Once we were seated and sipping Deyon's coffee, Don called us to attention.

"We've been offered the outright gift of another ship called the Petite Forte," he announced to the sound of soft gasps around the room.

"It's a former government ferry from Nova Scotia, Canada, and is now docked in Florida. By tonight, the new owner, a businessman named Keith Larkin, wants to know if we will take it. I believe we all need to pray about it together."

We looked at each other with shock. We had always envisioned having up to 10 Mercy Ships sailing the seas, but right now the ministry of the Anastasis was just gaining momentum. How could we possibly handle another one now? But we had learned long ago that God's ways were higher than ours, and we couldn't follow our own feeble thoughts. We each bowed our heads and asked God what to do, and one by one we agreed God was saying to accept the generous gift.

That night as we were getting ready for bed, Alan said Don had already approached him about being involved in the new ship. "I somehow feel God wants me to have a part in it," he explained. A few weeks later, Don and Alan flew to Jacksonville, Florida, to ex-amine the Petite Forte. At 1,034 tons and 173 feet long, the ship was about a third the size of the Anastasis. Alan and Don were still with the Petite Forte on July 12 when the Anastasis set sail for the South Pacific.

Both Tonga and Fiji had been devastated by a hurricane about eight months before, and we felt a sense of urgency to get our cargo of construction materials and supplies to the devastated ar-eas. These supplies, worth an estimated NZ $600,000, had been donated by Christians, business people and the New Zealand gov-ernment. They included the unusual gift of four fire trucks given by New Zealand's fire department.

I had started taking my seasickness pills before we ever left port, but they proved to be of no benefit when the Anastasis plunged into her first real storm. By nightfall, I was re-living the nightmare of my earlier seasick days. Unable to stay on the bunk for the lurching of the ship, I dragged the mattress on the floor, and after several violent retching sessions, threw myself on it.

The ship settled into a pattern of heaving up and down, up and down, and then spinning until I could hear the foaming waves crash on the forward deck outside my cabin. Each time, the ship creaked and shuddered, and it sounded as if it would tear apart with the strain. With Alan gone, I felt terribly alone.

I also felt bad for the young discipleship students on board, who must be suffering too. And what about the deck and engine room guys? No matter if they were sick, they couldn't leave their posts. I tried to pray for them, but fell into a fitful sleep inter-rupted often by more retching.

Lying there in agony, I remembered the promise I'd made the Lord when He called me to the ship ministry: "I'm willing to be sick all my life if that's what You ask." Now my head was giddy and my stomach ached with nausea, but I knew it was a promise I'd never go back on. Obedience to God was worth any price!

All the next morning, the same pattern continued. Staggering outside to find a deck chair and take in some fresh air, I held the rail to steady myself as I realized the whole top deck looked like a disaster area. Bodies lay everywhere, including those of my two teenage sons! Clutching crackers and bottles of water, people lay sprawled on the decks, on the floor of the large lounge, and in every single deck chair. I wasn't the only one paying the price.

After a couple of days, the storm subsided and we soberly prepared for our arrival in Fiji. Once in port, we off-loaded the supplies and started flooding the nation with the Gospel.

Two weeks later, we set sail for Nuku' Alofa in the Kingdom of Tonga, where Alan at last rejoined us. When he returned, Alan told me the trip only confirmed his belief that we would be involved with the ministry of the Petite Forte. He was also pleased to report that this ship was in much better physical shape than the Anastasis had been when we first acquired it.

After Tonga, we set off to American and Western Samoa, much to Alan's delight. Western Samoa had been a place where he'd spent many days as a drunken brawling seaman, and now to be back preaching the Gospel with a Christian ship was a type of restitution for those ungodly episodes. Many other YWAM teams were in Western Samoa for an outreach during the South Pacific Games, so we preached and worked alongside them. We thrilled to see so many Samoans embrace a new relationship with Christ.

Returning again to New Zealand for a short time, the ship picked up more goods to distribute in Fiji. Our final destination this time was particularly exciting to Alan and me: Hawaii!

The departure of the Anastasis that November day meant more sad goodbyes to family and friends, and to a few crew members whose year commitment to the ship was up. But as we sailed away from New Zealand, we knew ever more certainly that God had sent this ship to the nations, fulfilling not only its destiny but ours.

On December 16, the Anastasis neared the Big Island of Hawaii. Alan and I stood out on the forward deck outside our cabin, drinking in the beauty as we felt the warm tropical air. Returning to our former home in Kona was like a dream come true.

It had been five years since we'd left these islands, and I was filled with nostalgic memories of our pioneering days at the old Pacific Empress Hotel. That facility we so lovingly reclaimed was now the thriving Pacific and Asia Christian University (later to become the University of the Nations). I couldn't wait to see the friends we'd left behind, and I praised God for His faithfulness to us as we'd carried out our separate callings in YWAM. Now we would be laboring again side by side in the Hawaiian Islands.

President Ronald Reagan had instituted 1983 as the "Year of the Bible" in the United States, and Loren Cunningham had invited us to help with evangelism and Bible distribution in Hawaii. Loren had been asked to oversee the campaign in the islands, and it neatly coincided with the 25th anniversary of Hawaii's statehood. Celebrations would abound, and we would enhance those celebrations with evangelistic outreaches on Maui, Hawaii and Oahu. We were riding high.

Now as the majestic slopes of Hualalai mountain appeared in view, I tingled with excitement. I knew that just below that mountain was the small town of Kailua-Kona and our university! Our ship holds carried a gift of New Zealand lumber for new buildings to be erected on the university site.

As we anchored out in Kailua harbor, I was excited to learn a ceremony would be held to welcome us on the beach of the nearby King Kamehameha Hotel. Canoes took us ashore, and Loren and Darlene Cunningham and other friends welcomed us on the beach with open arms. King's Kids of Hawaii, dressed in colorful costumes from different nations, performed a musical dance presentation about God's love for the nations. Loren gave the welcoming address and then introduced us to the Mayor of Hawaii, Herbert Matayoshi. The crowd broke into applause as the mayor presented Don Stephens and Captain Ben Applegate the key to the Hawaiian Islands. We felt thoroughly welcomed!

Our old friends the Mansfields drove us the short distance to the campus, talking non-stop on the way. Everything looked so familiar, yet different too. Then I realized the biggest change was in my own heart. Although I loved Kona and the people here, it was no longer an idol standing between me and God. Now holding my friends with an open hand, I was free to enjoy and love them with all my heart. All at once a banner stretching across the main road caught my eye: "Welcome Anastasis."

"Alan, look!" I said in astonishment.

"I never thought I'd see that here!" Alan responded. "We've come a long way since the old days. Hardly anyone knew we existed back then!"

Walking through the Pacific and Asia University property, we couldn't believe the transformation. Instead of an overgrown hotel being reclaimed by young people with machetes, it was now an actual campus with neatly-dressed students walking to class with books under their arms.

"Darl, look at all the new buildings!" I exclaimed. "Remember the rocks and weeds that used to be piled over there?"

We both laughed, but we were overwhelmed with a feeling of fulfillment. God had used us to help lay the foundations, and others had expertly built upon it. Walking into the familiar pavilion, where we and the Anastasis crew were being welcomed, we exchanged hugs and squeals of delight with many old friends. It was especially good to see Mark and Eva Spengler again, who had served so faithfully on the ship and now were working here. We were amazed to see how their children had grown, especially Nathan who was now healthy and strong after his ordeal in Greece. Of course, some of our old friends were conspicuously absent, having either gone back home to serve in their local churches or out to pioneer Christian works in other nations. Serving in missions meant constant change, and I was finally getting used to letting go.

We too were just passing through Kona, so we tried to make the most of our time there. Our family spent a wonderful Christmas day with the Spenglers, but soon after, the ship sailed to Hilo on the other side of the island. Once there, we held evangelistic services in schools, churches and even on the streets, and joyfully received new believers into the body of Christ.

Our next stop was the island of Maui, where we launched a similar evangelism campaign. We immediately noticed a greater resistance to the Gospel on Maui compared with the other South Pacific islands we'd visited. We thought it might be because of the more materialistic spirit there or the strong presence of the drug culture and Eastern religions.

One morning we were a bit subdued as we carried our puppets and musical instruments back to the motor boat which shuttled us back and forth to the Anastasis. We had just completed a morning of open air meetings under a large Banyan tree in the park near the Maui wharf, but again, our spiritual fishing had brought little.

As we chugged along in the little white motor boat, suddenly I noticed another boat beside us sometimes speeding around us as if checking us out. Looking at Alan, I knew by his face he saw it too.

"That's strange! It looks like a small Coast Guard vessel," he said. "Quick, help me count how many on board. If we're overloaded, we'll be in trouble."

We counted just in case, and were relieved to see we had the right number; but the Coast Guard boat continued to follow us out to the ship.

Before long, two Coast Guard officials came up our gangway and spoke with Don Stephens and Captain Ben. As they took them around the ship, Alan told us it was just a routine inspection, and we all relaxed. The ship had already been inspected for safety by the Coast Guard in California, where we passed with flying colors. Little did we know how radically this short visit was going to change our plans.

A couple of weeks later, in February 1984, Alan joined me at our family table in the ship dining room after a meeting with Don and Captain Ben. He pushed his plate of food aside, and stared at me grimly.

"We've heard from the Coast Guard here in Hawaii, and they say our safety standards are not up to the American Coast Guard laws. Because of families being on board, we have to stop and upgrade the ship's cargo status to passenger status."

I looked at him in shock. "But, we already passed the safety check in California. And didn't Lloyds of London give us a great commendation when we left Greece? And they're very strict with their standards, aren't they?"

"Yes, but now the Hawaii Coast Guard is saying we don't meet the fire safety standards. They say we can't sail in American waters again if we don't get a new sprinkler system for the whole ship."

I let out a groan. "How long will that take?"

"Who knows? We need the money first, plus the manpower to do it! We're talking about an enormous undertaking. Every deck head has to come down so about three miles of pipe can be inserted."

I shook my head. "I can't believe it."

He looked me straight in the eye, and I knew something was coming.

"Well, I've been meaning to tell you, Luv. For some time I've had a strong impression that we personally are in for a change."

My mind raced ahead as I started to guess what kind of change might be ahead for us. Alan still didn't know. Did it have to do with the Petite Forte? But how could we leave the new outreach team who just joined us? How I wished Alan wouldn't pop things on me like this! I knew my security was in God alone, but I sat there for the rest of the meal feeling all wobbly inside.

A few days later, we sailed with heavy hearts to Honolulu where the Anastasis was officially grounded. It was a crushing blow for all of us on board. We had been so elated to get the ship ministry underway, and there were still so many homeless, hungry, and sick people needing our help. The Anastasis had risen from her graveyard only a year and a half ago, and since then God had used us so mightily. Thousands had given their lives to the Lord or were challenged to a greater dedication, and the ship had carried 1,100 metric tons of goods in her holds to date. How hard it was to accept that now, after so much, we were again at a complete standstill!

For me, the only bright spot in this gloomy time was Samuel's high school graduation on the ship. During the ceremony, my heart swelled with gratitude as I watched my snowy-haired son, the valedictorian of his class, giving his commencement speech.

This boy who had struggled so in his early school years had been spurred on to remarkable academic accomplishment through the help of caring teachers in his YWAM schools. I would always be grateful to them. Now Samuel was planning to move to Hong Kong to serve on YWAM staff near Joy and her husband. Thrilled as we were to see him moving out in God's will, it was hard to see our second child fly the nest.

After he left, I began to dwell on the repercussions of the ship grounding. Within the next three weeks, the women and children were moved to a campground on Oahu while the men worked to make the necessary fire safety improvements on board.

With all the changes happening around us, I wasn't surprised when Alan informed me that Don Stephens had now officially asked him to be the director of the little ship still in Florida. Weeks before, this would have seemed impossible. But now we knew it was right to leave the outreach team under the capable leadership of Ron Musch, and accept this new challenge.

Stephen, now a level-headed 17, asked to stay behind so he could graduate with his high school class. Hard as it was for us to leave him behind, we decided it was the right thing to do. He would stay on under the care of Don and Deyon.

Having invested so much love and prayer and sweat in this venture, it was a highly emotional day when we had to say goodbye to Stephen and the rest of our Anastasis "family." I thought I might be used to these partings by now, but I couldn't hold back the tears. At least as part of Mercy Ships, we had the assurance of knowing we'd be in regular contact with our shipmates.

As we boarded the plane for Florida, we looked forward to the challenge ahead of us. But as usual, things wouldn't turn out quite as we expected.

The Good Samaritan. Fay surrounded with Haitian children (Upper R.).
Alan speaks while Fay sketches (Lower R.).

23

The Little Ship

From our first day aboard the Petite Forte, we gave it an affectionate nickname, The Little Ship. The sturdy white vessel with a faded blue stack was anchored in a shipyard near Jacksonville, Florida, where the previous owner had brought it for repairs. Only a third the size of the Anastasis, this former Canadian ferry was in need of refurbishment, but not the total overhaul that her sister Mercy Ship had required.

As we busied ourselves settling in, the task before us was still ominous. We had redecorating to do, money to raise, crew to recruit, goods to procure, and relationships to build with local pastors. We really were starting all over again.

Within the next few months, more crew from the Anastasis came to help us, and we toiled to outfit the Little Ship for its new mission. We had to clean it from stem to stern, make repairs and survey it to make the necessary changes for medical and relief work.

As always, our eyes looked beyond what we were doing and out to the needs of the world: Haiti, the poorest nation in the southern hemisphere, was suffering major political upheaval, and with it being so close, we strongly felt it should be our first outreach target. Alan began meeting with local pastors to inform them of our presence in Jacksonville, and soon we were asked to speak about our ministry at various churches.

With the pioneering of our second ship well underway, a new ministry role fell into my lap. I had always loved writing, and now I began writing news pieces for the regular newsletter sent out by the San Pedro office, the on-shore communication center for Mercy Ships. The more I wrote, the more a new desire welled up inside me to write about all God had done in our lives. I wanted to pass this legacy on to our children and grandchildren. However, with so much to do on the Petite Forte, I put this desire before the Lord, and busied myself with other duties.

We had only been on board a few months when another surprise development hit us. The Canadian government, which had sold the Little Ship to our donor Keith Larkin, was now requesting to charter it back for six months to replace a ferry destroyed in a fire. After praying and discussing it with Don Stephens and the other leaders, we agreed to send it back.

So, we found ourselves on the move again – this time to San Pedro, California, to take temporary leadership of the ship's home office. I was delighted to be settled again, if only for six months. The Mercy Ships offices were in an old red brick hotel that YWAM workers had beautifully renovated. The hotel was in a run-down section of San Pedro, but it was a perfect location for ministering to the derelicts, alcoholics and drug addicts who frequented the area.

As we settled into a new routine, I was amazed to find that after nine years in YWAM, I had no specific job. Renovations were complete and office jobs were covered, and although I helped out with the communal cooking and the weekly evangelistic outreaches, I had extra time on my hands.

One morning while reading the Bible alone in our bedroom, my eyes riveted on Ezekiel 2:10: "And he spread it before me; and it was written within and without: and there was written in it lamentations, and mourning, and woe."

"Lord, what's this have to do with me?" I asked.

Immediately, almost as if He'd spoken audibly, I knew what God was saying: "I want you to write a book. I want you to write down the bad things, the difficult struggles, not just the victories."

When Alan came in, I shared my impressions.

"It's God! I just know it!" he said. "Remember all those missionary stories we read as young Christians? The characters seemed so perfect, we'd feel depressed when we finished. If we tell our story like it is, I believe people will be helped, healed, and thrust into missions."

"But I thought I was just going to write a book for our family. I don't even know how to write a book for publishing!"

Even as I said it, I remembered that my old school teacher said I might write a book one day, and an inner excitement filled me. Surely if God were telling me to do it now, I could!

So, taking advantage of my spare time each day, I sat at the table in our bedroom and began writing the rough draft with a plain yellow pencil and pad of ruled paper. I sometimes found myself weeping as I put the events of our lives on paper, including the lamentations and woes. Words describing God's salvation and deliverance almost tumbled out onto the pages, and God's presence was so real in the room, I began looking forward to these times each day.

That summer, a massive evangelistic blitz was being held in Los Angeles for the 1984 Olympic Games. Alan and I threw our energies into helping train some of the 600 participants who came from various YWAM centers, including numerous King's Kids teams. We were especially excited when Stephen arrived as part of the Pacific and Asia King's Kids team.

YWAM joined forces with numerous other Christian groups to bring a powerful witness for Jesus to Los Angeles residents and the thousands of Olympics visitors. The results were remarkable. Hundreds came to Christ, and our prayers for the crime-ridden city produced immediate fruit. The police reported the city's crime rate dropped dramatically during the Olympics.

We had hardly finished with the outreach activities, when a phone call came that would set in motion events that would change our lives forever.

It was from our dear Greek friend and co-worker, Costas Macris, the leader of the Hellenic Missionary Society in Greece. He reported to Alan that the mother of Kostas Kotopoulos, the 16-year-old to whom Alan had given a Greek New Testament, was now stirring up a legal battle that would soon come to trial. Costas said he, Alan and Don, were being charged with proselytizing a minor and seeking to abduct her son from Greece.

I looked at Alan in bewilderment. "But that's preposterous! The ship left Greece two full years ago, in 1982. We haven't even seen young Kostas since then, and he's never even left Greece. Besides, you were the one who gave Kostas the Bible, not the other two."

Alan raised his eyebrows. "I know, but Don is responsible for bringing the ship to Greece, and Costas Macris runs the youth group that Kostas attended. And it's even more strange that none of us have been officially notified. Even Costas said he only heard about it through unofficial sources."

With so many unanswered questions, we finally assumed it would blow over and dismissed it from our minds. After all, why should someone go to court unless they were summoned?

A few weeks later, I was tidying up our room when I received a phone call from Jeff Fountain, the YWAM leader in Holland. I explained that Alan was away speaking and although Don was in town temporarily, he was out for the day.

"It has to do with the trial in Greece," Jeff said somberly.

"Oh that! We're not taking it too seriously."

"But, Fay, listen," he said with a note of urgency. "We've learned that if Don and Alan don't go back for the trial, it could mean all YWAM workers would be permanently barred from evangelizing in Greece. I think you'd all better pray about it some more."

I assured Jeff I'd have Don call him back and hung up in frustration. How could anyone really take those charges seriously? The whole affair was ridiculous!

But when I explained the situation to Don, he also felt we needed to pray and re-examine the situation together. As soon as Alan returned from his trip, Don stopped by our room to relay the news.

"I haven't got time to go to Greece for something as absurd as this!" Alan responded, waving his arms emphatically. "There's so much to do in the Caribbean."

"I feel the same, Alan," Don countered, "but what about the Greek conditions? If we don't go back, persecution could increase all the more. We have to think about that."

He was quiet for a moment, and then shook his head. "I know you're right. But I still can't believe this. It all happened over two years ago!"

We prayed together about the decision several times over the next few days and Don consulted Deyon by phone. We all agreed the two men had no choice but to go back to Greece. As men of integrity, they needed to take a stand alongside Costas Macris and the persecuted evangelical church in Greece, as well as the European YWAMers who in the future would continue to target Greece as a mission field.

Don arranged for a lawyer, who managed to get the trial date postponed to allow him time to gather facts about the case. The trial was now set for three days before Christmas, Dec. 22, 1984.

In early December, Alan and I took a quick trip to Honolulu to attend Stephen's graduation ceremony on the Anastasis. Our youngest son now planned to join YWAM's video communications team in Switzerland.

The three of us arrived back in San Pedro just a week or so before the trial date and soon, Stephen and I were hugging Alan goodbye at the Port Office doorway.

"Don't worry about me. I'll be back before you know it!" Alan said with his cheeky grin.

I waved and blew him a kiss, but deep down I was terribly apprehensive about Alan's situation. I knew there was no truth to the allegations, but visiting the women's prison in Greece had left me with a dismal picture of the nation's justice system. I had alerted friends on our mailing list to pray for our men, and was hoping the trial would end in time for them to be back for Christmas.

The morning of Dec. 22, I awoke early. By Greek time, the case should have been well over, so I expected a call any moment. Looking out the window, I saw it was a dismal, smoggy day, chilly for this part of the state. Or was it merely the way I felt inside? I hated not being by Alan's side at this time, so the moments began to drag.

By mid-morning, I went to the office to find our friend Marie Tylander from Sweden, one of the few staff who stayed during Christmas.

"I can't stand waiting around, Marie." I wrung my hands. "I can't understand why they haven't called yet. I can't even concentrate on prayer any more. I've already prayed around every angle!"

Marie offered to telephone some Swedish friends who lived in Greece and had planned to attend the trial. Within minutes I listened as she burst into animated Swedish conversation with her friends. Shifting my weight from one foot to the other, I saw Marie's face cloud a little and questions stormed my mind. What if they were found guilty? Then Marie put down the phone.

"My friend said they were at the trial, but had to leave. Apparently it's still going on now, even into the night."

"But what could take so long?" I said with agitation. Marie looked at me and shrugged.

"I can't bear waiting around doing nothing. I'm going for a walk."

I returned a half an hour later to find Mike, our computer man, waiting in the doorway to greet me.

"We've heard from Don," he said with a strange look.

"Well? Tell me what happened!"

"They were given a three-and-a-half-year prison sentence," he said hesitantly.

I gave him a playful punch on the shoulder. "Oh, don't joke now!"

His face was somber. "I'm not."

"Tell me what really happened!"

"Fay, it's true. They received a three-and-a-half-year prison sentence for proselytizing a minor. They're allowed to leave Greece pending an appeal trial, so they'll just make it home for Christmas."

Now my mouth hung open. Three-and-a-half years? I couldn't believe it!

"Marie wanted you to know she already told Stephen the news," Mike continued. "He reacted just like you."

In a daze, I left Mike to call Joy, Rob and Samuel in Hong Kong. Their response aped mine. It was all absurd! We were relieved that at least for now Alan was coming back. I assured them Alan would fill them in on details upon his return.

Alan arrived late Christmas Eve, looking haggard and weary from the long court case and jet lag. On Christmas day, the small group of staff still there for the holidays gathered in our room to hear him recount what happened in Athens. He explained that three judges sat facing them, and there was no jury.

"We had to sit for 12 hours without any real evidence of the charges," he said. "Of course, in Greek law you're considered guilty until proven innocent."

Alan explained that the sentence was based on an old Greek law forbidding proselytizing a minor that was instituted during a dictatorship and never stricken from the books. "The three of us actually received a four-and-a-half-year sentence and it was only reduced at our lawyer's request."

We looked at him in disbelief.

"The lawyer said there has never been a sentence so stiff given for a case like this."

"How is young Kostas taking it all?" I asked.

"It's not easy, but he's doing well, considering. I'm just glad he's still hanging onto his faith in God."

It was a difficult way to celebrate Christmas, but as we later enjoyed a special dinner together, we turned our thoughts back to Jesus' birth. I also thought of Don and Deyon and their family in Honolulu and Costas and Alky Macris in Greece. I imagined their Christmas was much like ours. Now we were all playing the waiting game to see what the future would hold for our men.

But this trial wasn't just about our three loved ones, it was about the persecution of true believers in a democratic nation. Greece, once the very birthplace of democracy, still had no freedom of religion. As we waited for the date to be set for the appeal trial, we began gearing up for a fight in the spiritual realm.

Meanwhile, Don Stephens and the team at the San Pedro office began a campaign to inform the American and international church of the persecution of true believers in Greece and the upcoming appeal trial. They asked for prayer for Don, Costas and Alan, who were now presented as the "Athens Three." A campaign was also launched to send letters and petitions to the Greek government. The response from the public was overwhelming as people around the world started praying for us and the nation of Greece, and letters and petitions started streaming in.

A few weeks after Christmas, the Little Ship was returned to Florida, and Alan and I left to take over its leadership once again. Although the possibility of prison was always at the back of our minds, for now we tried to turn our full attention to preparing the ship for its first outreach to Haiti. More crew from the Anastasis and other YWAM centers came to help, and it was full speed ahead.

Over the next few months we became widely known in Jacksonville because of our appeals on Christian radio, and many local churches rallied to support us. They gathered medical supplies, food and other goods and were a great encouragement. Alan was delighted the ship preparation was going so well, but grew increasingly frustrated that we hadn't heard any more about the trial. One night after a shipboard meeting, I noticed him brooding.

"What is it, Darl?"

He shook his head. "I just don't have time to go to prison, Luv. There's too much to do in the Caribbean! I have such an urgency that we need to work while we can. Who knows when the doors will close in these nations."

He began to pace back and forth in our tiny cabin.

"You know, Luv, most of the time I forget about prison and the trial," he said. "Then when I get all geared up for a trip like this, I wonder if the trial will suddenly come in on us and interfere with what God is doing."

I nodded. "I know. If they could just give us the trial date, we'd all feel more settled."

By November we still had no word, so we sailed down the east coast of Florida on the first leg of the outreach. The Petite Forte now sported a new name on the side of her bow: The Good Samaritan. And she was now living up to that name. Our 25-person crew docked first in Fort Pierce to take on more supplies, and then it was off to Haiti.

Our holds now bulged with cargo including $40,000 worth of medical supplies; 65,000 pounds of dried beef; 64,000 pounds of dried milk; 40,000 pounds of grain; two trailers; three trucks; toothpaste and shampoo products; and 9,000 T-shirts to give away to needy people.

Yet with all we had to share, we immediately found the need in Haiti overwhelming. The poverty there was the worst I'd ever seen. The heat was oppressive, and the spiritual climate was even more so. Curious yet joyless faces stared at us everywhere. It made me realize how small our upcoming crisis was in comparison to the prison of spiritual darkness and poverty these people lived in constantly.

We were happy to be bringing them the word of life. We preached it in parks, schools, and even the forward deck of the ship. For many of these people, it was not a new message. Many missions and churches were already working to spread the Gospel in Haiti. But because the people often mixed Christian practices with spiritism and voodoo, we challenged them to make Jesus the Lord of their lives.

After two intense weeks, we were ready to head back to Florida for more supplies. Our time in Haiti had been fulfilling, but our hearts ached for these people. Their physical needs were so overwhelming that our cargo seemed like a drop in the bucket.

We planned to take a short rest over Christmas in Fort Pierce, and then sail to Honduras in Central America. Once back in Florida, a very special Christmas gift arrived, our son Stephen. He had just finished his year of service in Europe, and now he wanted to spend some time with us. He told us he eventually wanted to return to England to earn money for college, but for now he wanted to serve as a deck hand on our trip to Honduras.

In January, we sailed off to the Caribbean with more food, medicine and other supplies. Our first destination was Porte Cortez, Honduras. After a successful outreach there, we pointed the ship north to Haiti, this time to the capital of Port-au-Prince. Once again we were overwhelmed by the need of this desperately poor nation, and when we returned to Florida, we put out a call for others to help. Like the Anastasis, the Good Samaritan was now becoming known and Florida Christians found our ministry a viable way to participate in missions literally on their doorstep.

Alan and I often discussed how fulfilled we were to be evangelizing and training others again, but the possibility of Alan going to prison always loomed before us. At long last, our uncertainty ended. The trial date was fixed for May 21, 1986, just months away. As the worldwide prayer and petition campaign accelerated to a climax, we also prayed with more urgency for the Lord's perfect will in the matter.

After the acquittal. (L. to R.) YWAM attorney Max Crittenden, Deyon, Heidi, Don & Luke Stephens, Fay, Alan & Joy, Hariklia Gerelymou (translator).

24

The Victory

Sitting nervously beside Alan in the stuffy Athens courtroom, I almost couldn't wait any longer. The judges had been in their chambers for three hours now, discussing the final verdict, and we were waiting on the edge of our seats. Wanting to break the tension, I elbowed Alan with a smile.

"How did we get 'ere?" I joked. It was the old Liverpool family phrase we frequently used in tight spots. As always, Alan responded with a comical shrug.

"Don't ask me!" he said, and we both chuckled. Of course inside we knew it was only God who could have brought us here. We had overcome so many obstacles over the years that this situation wasn't about to shake our confidence in God. We had a rock-solid trust in His faithfulness.

We'd been back in Greece now over a week and had received great encouragement from our Greek Christian friends. It was also good to be back together with Don and Deyon Stephens. They had been such faithful friends through everything.

I could still remember vividly the lunch date I'd had with Deyon just a year ago in Honolulu. After some light conversation, she brushed aside a lock of blonde hair from her forehead, and leaned forward matter of factly.

"What do you plan to do, Fay, if Don and Alan go to prison?"

"It hardly seems possible," I replied, "but I'm open to staying in Greece to be near them."

We went on to discuss seriously the possibility of renting an apartment together so I could help her with the children. Suddenly we noticed two women sitting nearby eyeing us with suspicion, obviously listening to our conversation. They no doubt wondered what kind of criminals we were married to! Deyon and I couldn't contain our laughter.

Even now that scene still brought a smile to my lips, but it was not easy to laugh knowing that prison might soon be a reality for our men. An hour ago, our lawyer told us it was an ominous sign for the judges to take so long. Already the trial was in its fourth day, and proceedings lasted from late afternoon into the night. Oh, how I wished it were over!

Alan's face was rutted with tension lines, a clear sign of exhaustion. During the proceedings, he and the two others had been seated up front in three high-backed wooden chairs to the left of the judges' bench. Not even allowed to cross their legs during the trial, the "Athens Three" had found the chairs a mini- prison of their own.

During the proceedings, the prosecuting attorney had been on his feet speaking rapidly and waving his arms to illustrate his points with typical Greek movements. At first the prosecutor appeared to be vehemently against us, but in the final hours, I wondered if he softened. It was hard to tell because even the Greek gestures for yes and no were opposite ours. I was sitting near my daughter Joy and Deyon, just four rows back from our men, but we had to strain to hear the interpreter's words.

Our most encouraging moment so far came when our lawyer, a

man with a charismatic personality and a flair for dramatic oratory, stood to say his piece.

"Seeing the integrity of these men, I pray that I might some day be like them," he declared. Oh, how I hoped those words carried weight with the judges.

The 40-some Greek evangelical pastors and missionaries who had managed to squeeze into the courtroom to support us were also wonderful affirmation. Don and Deyon, Costas and Alky, and Alan and I felt a constant covering of prayer and support for our families.

I was also comforted by Joy's presence, not to mention the fact that her husband Rob and Samuel were praying for us with the YWAM team in Hong Kong. Until this morning Stephen was with us too, but none of us expected the trial to take so long, and he had to return to his job in England.

My heart ached as I remembered Stephen's goodbye at our hotel. Our usually reserved son fell into Alan's arms sobbing.

"I don't want you to go to prison, Dad," he said through the tears. "But if it's God's will, I accept it."

By then, all three of us were crying, wondering how long it would be before we were together again.

Glancing at the clock on the courtroom wall, I saw the hands had moved with irritating slowness. It was still almost 11 o'clock, hardly a minute since I last looked.

Suddenly, Alan leapt to his feet, and squeezed my hand tightly.

"I need to move about. I can't just sit here," he said with a shrug of his shoulders.

Watching him plunge into the crowd, I tingled at the squeeze of his warm hand. If he went to prison, the lawyer told me I would only be able to see him once a month. And what would I do? I agonized again with the decision I'd have to make very soon if Alan went to prison: Would I stay in Athens with Deyon and her family, perhaps working with the local church? Or should I go back to the Good Samaritan and help the new leader as he requested?

I saw Alan station himself again behind his high-backed chair, but I knew he wouldn't sit in it a minute earlier than necessary.

All at once, the door of the judges' chamber flew open. The atmosphere was electric and the noise of the dingy courtroom stopped abruptly as a steward of the court announced the return of the panel of judges. As they took their seats, we followed suit and I braced myself emotionally.

Glancing to the side, I saw the distraught mother of young Kostas seated to the back and right side of me. Inside I only felt sympathy for this woman and again, I offered up a prayer for her. What would be her reaction to the outcome of this trial? Kostas had testified eloquently on our behalf and now was calmly sitting toward the front with his father.

The chief judge leaned forward on his seat with a stern face. Clearing his throat, he issued a strong warning in Greek. Within moments, the official interpreter repeated the command: "This court will not tolerate any loud noises or disorderly conduct at the announcement of the verdict!"

Straining to hear, I looked at Deyon and Joy again seated nearby, who were also leaning forward in rapt attention. With the flood of prayers and petitions that had been offered up for our men, surely the judges would at least give a lighter sentence this time!

Nervously fidgeting with my wedding ring, I moved to the edge of my chair. It appeared the judge made a final statement, and a ripple went through the crowd. But what was it he said? I strained to make out the interpreter's words, and caught my breath. Did I hear what I thought I heard?

"We find these three men innocent," it sounded like he said. I let out my breath and looked at Joy in shock. Could it be? After all this?

Despite the judges' earlier warning, muffled comments echoed across the courtroom and media cameras began flashing. I longed to run to Alan's side, but I knew I couldn't make it through the crowd.

Instead, I sat stunned, unable to move as my mind reeled with the news. After being given a three-and-a-half-year sentence, could the judges really allow such a complete reversal? It seemed absurd and even embarrassing for the Greek judicial system!

Finally the judges and officials filed out the courtroom and when the dark brown door slammed shut behind them, the room broke into joyful bedlam. Greek Evangelical Christians talked rapidly, flinging their hands in the air, while others embraced with whoops and shouts of joy.

In exhilaration and gratitude, I began hugging Joy, Deyon and Alky Macris. Our three men were surrounded by pastors and well-wishers so I knew it would be some time before I could make it to Alan, but for now I didn't mind. For the last 18 months, I had prepared myself for this moment – for what I thought would be a long separation – and now I would have Alan with me tonight and many nights after this!

Still, I felt strangely numb. I bent down and clutched Alan's bag, and looked up in time to see him shoot a bewildered look at me across the courtroom. His eyes were glazed, and I could tell he was stunned. I had to get to him!

The crowd had thinned out a little, so I began pushing my way through. Reaching Don and Costas first, I hugged them one by one before running into Alan's arms.

"Darl, I can't believe it!" I said excitedly as we stood holding each other. Alan nodded. "Me too." We both knew talk would come later.

Before long, we were jostled out into the foyer for interviews with Greek reporters and a video team from YWAM Europe. I noticed security guards were still milling about as the Athens Three and their families moved toward the interviewing area. Kostas also joined us with a radiant smile. How different he looked! Then we faced the cameras and the interviewer went to each person involved for a statement about the trial.

Our main lawyer was up first. "I'm very pleased with the good decision," he responded with a glow of victory on his face. "It's what I would have expected."

I smiled at Alan. Only two hours ago, this man wore a very different look, one of tense apprehension.

The interviewer next turned to Don Stephens. His face also showed the strain of the last few days, but he broke into a broad smile of relief.

"There's been a lot of excitement, but most important is the victory God has won not just for us, but for Greece and for the Gospel!" he said. "It's brought courage, hope, and faith to us all."

Then the camera swung to Alan as I stood beside him. The reality of the verdict was now starting to sink in, and Alan's tired eyes shone with exhilaration.

"This is a small step for we three men," he said triumphantly, "but a giant step for the church of Jesus Christ here in Greece!"

Next an energetic Costas Macris stood before the cameras, his dark eyes glinting as the interviewer asked about his next step. We knew he and his strong evangelical ministry in downtown Athens would probably feel the effects of the victory most, experiencing a new freedom to share the Gospel in Greece without fear of persecution.

"We need some time to think about our next steps, but certainly the ministry will go on," he said with determination. "We will be planning some evangelistic outreaches for the summer."

Costas Macris was so like Alan. Nothing was going to keep him down. I was sure his ministry would gain momentum rapidly.

Next interviewed was Dr. John Ward Montgomery, an American lawyer who was involved in the case due to his interest in human rights. He said that although the old law had not yet been stricken, he was pleased the judges had properly based the verdict on the facts, especially that the charge of proselytism had been disproved when young Kostas's father admitted to supervising his son's relationship with us.

At last, it was time for Kostas himself to speak. His face was shining with the light of the Lord as he turned to the camera.

"I feel very happy about the result of the trial," he said in his Greek accent. "It's not just because I really love these three men, but because what came out was the truth. I believe I told the truth without trying to protect anyone, and God took control of it."

His face grew solemn as he continued. "What really meant something to me, though, was to see people who would consider it a privilege to go to jail for the name of Jesus," he said. "The final victory is not yet won. Today it was them, tomorrow it could be me. Let's all pray together that the law will be changed so the light of the Gospel could be shined all over Greece."

As he ended with a plea for all to pray for his parents, I couldn't keep back the tears. Looking at Alan, saw his eyes were moist too. It seemed only yesterday we had first met the sad and lonely teenager in the small Greek village, now five full years ago.

"Christ sure makes a difference," I whispered to Alan, wiping my eyes.

Alan nodded. "Someday, that young man will be a real evangelist for Greece, you watch!"

Once the interviews were ended, Alan grabbed my arm and began steering me toward the large wooden doors of the court building.

"Let's get out of here!" he said, beckoning for Joy to join us. If only Stephen and Samuel and Joy's husband Rob could be here now too. We wanted to call them right away with the news.

As we moved out into the main road to hail a taxi, I suddenly felt overwhelmed with tiredness. It was past midnight, and a hot shower and soft bed never sounded so good. Once at the hotel, Alan and I hugged Joy goodnight and closed the door on our adjoining rooms.

As we both finally tumbled into bed, I was surprised to find that after all the tension, sleep would not come quickly. I snuggled into Alan's side.

"Hmmm! This must feel better than a prison cell," I joked. I could feel Alan's rhythmic breathing beside me. "It just shows what can happen when God's people unite around the world in prayer," he said. "I know that's been the key to our freedom. And I know Greece hasn't yet seen the full effect of all this prayer."

Starting to relax a bit, we fell into silence. Alan's breathing grew deeper and he turned on his side.

"We've just been part of a miracle, Luv," he mumbled as he fell asleep.

My arm still draped around Alan, I stared into the darkness, pondering it all. I could only wonder. God had done so much already. What miracles would we see Him do next?

Fay, Alan and Alan's nephew Jared a few weeks before Alan's death.

25

Comfortable Companions

I can hardly believe we actually made it here at the same time," I jabbered, as we found our seats on the plane.

"I told you so," Alan said smugly. "And I even got the seat next to you like I said!"

I punched him playfully. "Oh, I missed you. It's so good to see you again!"

It was now a year since the trial, and Alan and I had been constantly on the go. After seven weeks of ministry in different parts of the world, we had just met again in the airport lobby in Honolulu and boarded a plane for New Zealand.

Now as the plane lifted off the runway, I looked out the window to see Waikiki Beach and the famous Diamond Head growing small behind us. It felt so wonderful to be with Alan again, especially knowing we'd have the next three months together in

New Zealand. We had rejoined the Anastasis crew, but it seemed like we were always being parted.

When we'd said goodbye in early November at the Anastasis dockside in San Diego, Alan was flying off to teach for several weeks at YWAM schools in England. From there he flew to Kona to attend a YWAM strategy conference and to look for possible housing for us. Both of us believed the Lord was leading us back to serve on staff in Kona, a fulfillment of the promise God had given me in 1978 that I would someday return to Kona to live.

While Alan was away, I had sailed with the Anastasis to Lazaro Cardenos, Mexico, co-leading the team of 11 King's Kids for seven weeks of evangelism. The outreach was as fulfilling as ever, but for some reason it was getting harder and harder to be away from Alan. I was so thankful for the three full months of vacation and ministry we now looked forward to.

Holding his hand like I'd never let it go, I looked into his contented face and smiled. My only regret in timing our departure so closely was that I'd only had a few minutes to see Samuel, who was now married and living in Honolulu. His big news was that his wife, Carol, was now expecting our first grandchild. Alan had spent several days with them, so now I eagerly pumped him for more details about Carol's pregnancy, Samuel's catering job, and their work with a church youth group.

"It's hard to believe our skinny, hyperactive son is now a mature and peaceful man!" I remarked. "And to think he'll be a father in the New Year!"

"Yes, and he even looks tall next to me," Alan added. "He's only five-foot-nine, but he passes me by a full two inches!"

We both chuckled and continued talking through the flight meal. Later, we moved our seats into a reclining position and I locked my arm in Alan's, groping for words to express the strange feeling I'd been having.

"You know, Darl, it seems that we've been away from each other more than ever," I began. "I guess I always assumed that when the children were gone, we'd be together more, traveling in ministry together. I had to move into a single cabin for the trip to Mexico, and I even told Deyon I might as well be a widow! Of course I enjoyed the outreach, but we could hardly get any mail and I felt so cut off from you."

Alan stroked my hand reassuringly. "I really missed you too, Luv," he said earnestly. "It was certainly a long while this time, but maybe…" His voice trailed off as he searched for words. "Maybe God's doing something new. Maybe it's your turn now."

I looked into his thoughtful face. "What does that mean?"

"Well…all our lives together, you've been beside me, kind of serving my ministry. I know you've done other things too, but I believe God wants you to develop your own ministry now. You have a lot to give. I don't even know why exactly, but I've sensed this for a while. It's your turn now!"

I was puzzled. "But I never really looked for a ministry of my own. You know I've always enjoyed supporting you. And remember, years ago God gave us the verse that He would unite us in one heart and one way!" (Jeremiah 32:39)

Alan nodded his understanding, but he had a far away look in his eye that made me a bit uneasy.

Soon he was getting drowsy, so I snuggled over to let him lean his head on my shoulder. I could never sleep on planes anyway, so as he drifted off, I pondered his words. Whatever did he mean by that?

For the last four years I had been writing more, and had even attended a writing seminar to develop my skills. I had sporadically worked at writing the story of our life together, but the book was far from complete. And even if Alan's words were somehow related to my writing, that still shouldn't keep us apart.

"Lord," I prayed silently, "I don't know why I've felt so uneasy away from Alan this time. I'm not complaining, but I somehow don't feel settled about the future. You know I only want to glorify You, and although I don't usually like change, I trust You to lead me in the best path."

Even with all the separations over the last year, God had given us some special times too. I remembered joyfully how he had made it possible for us to attend a three-month Leadership Training School (LTS) in Kona earlier this year. The staff there had given us a wonderful surprise celebration for our 25th wedding anniversary, complete with a gift of an engraved silver plate. We also received many verbal affirmations that night for our 14 years of service in YWAM.

For me, the most meaningful affirmation was my high grade on the LTS course exams, such a healing after all the poor marks I'd had in my earlier school days.

Now as Alan slept peacefully beside me in his airline seat, my mind raced with other events of the last year. Probably the most significant for the Mercy Ships was the completion of the sprinkler system on the Anastasis, after 19 months and great expense.

Then there was Samuel and Carol's wedding as well as a big evangelistic outreach in New York, Alan's preaching tours in South Africa and Jamaica, and a trip on the Anastasis I'd taken to California to raise support for the ship's upcoming outreach to Mexico.

It was easy to understand why we were both tired. But why was it bothering me so much to be apart? Was I belatedly experiencing the "Empty Nest Syndrome?" Surely not! I had greatly enjoyed motherhood, but I was happy with our children's healthy independence. So what was it?

I continued to pray and ponder into the night as Alan slept peacefully on. At last, morning dawned out the airplane windows, and Alan awoke with a start. We gobbled a quick breakfast and it seemed like only moments until the captain was announcing our descent to Auckland International Airport.

As soon as the airliner poked through the thick barrier of clouds, I could see the familiar signature of New Zealand's North Island, verdant fields dotted with grazing cattle and the blue waters of Manakau Harbor. Home? Not really. Long ago the world had become our home. But, for me, it was good to be back in the place of my birth and Alan loved New Zealand as the place of his spiritual birthplace. It had now been four years since our last visit here on the Anastasis.

At the flight captain's invitation, we set our watches at New Zealand time, 8 a.m. on December 17, 1987. It was the start of six weeks of the greatest rest Alan and I could ever remember as we spent time not only with each other but with our families. Alan's brother and his wife, Ronald and Janet, had converted the basement of their Auckland home into a small, but comfortable apartment for us to stay in, and I delighted to have a kitchen again to cook Alan all his favorite New Zealand dishes. Having time to really slow down after years of joyful but hard labor was a real refreshment.

It was especially a joy to see Alan's mother again, who had worried so for Alan during the trial and had grown more gray and frail in our absence. As she hugged him again for the first time, she shook with joy and thanked God over and over for bringing Alan back to her. It was a comfort to know she was so well cared for by Ron and Janet and other family members who lived nearby.

Over the six weeks in Auckland, Alan and I helped with the Sunday night services at our local church, but other than that and one short conference, the whole time was a true vacation. Of highest priority was spending time with both our families, and our photograph album began filling up: photos of a happy Christmas day spent with my mother; several at the home of my older sister, Yvonne, and her family; and fun shots of a day at the beach with Alan's entire extended clan, including one of Alan's mother grinning from ear to ear as she sat on her beach chair surrounded by her family once again.

As I placed the photos in my album, I thanked God for the good memories. Being on the mission field had meant years of being apart, and I knew these photos would help keep me going in years ahead.

I was especially glad to see Alan able to relax, something he couldn't do in his younger days. He actually put on a healthy amount of weight, and I knew it was because he was eating properly and relaxing. Over the last year, his chest pains had returned, and he was diagnosed with angina. He habitually took his medication and I knew the relaxation must be good for his heart.

One day at the beach, Alan pinched the tanned flesh above his waist.

"See my roll," he joked.

"That's no more than a filled hole!" I teased, and we both laughed heartily, something we did more often now that we were at ease.

Looking at his darkly tanned face, I couldn't help thinking how strong and healthy he looked. No wonder so many people said he looked younger than his 54 years. Now, after 26 years of marriage, I thanked God for the comfortable companionship we were now enjoying. It was as if we had come to a new level in our relationship, and I knew it was a product of the friendship we shared with God and the years of healing He had accomplished within us.

One evening a week later, Alan and I sat watching a movie on television and again, I marveled at how calm he was, with one leg flopped over the arm of the chair.

"It's so good to see you relaxing, Darl," I commented. "When we first met, you couldn't sit still for five minutes!"

We both chuckled, but as we looked at each other in lighthearted pleasure, a foreign thought flitted through my mind.

"Why this long, relaxing holiday?" I wondered. "Has God got something so hard up ahead that we needed this for preparation?" Quickly I pushed the thought away.

By early February, we were both becoming restless and happily anticipated the three weeks of concentrated ministry scheduled for three different YWAM Discipleship Training Schools (DTS) across New Zealand. We were rested and ready for action!

Our first trip was a drive from Auckland up north to Pahi, where we would spend the week teaching at a DTS geared specifically for Pacific Islanders. As we settled into the YWAM guest house, standing on the banks of an inlet from the ocean, I remembered our days of ministry in the Cook Islands. How good it was to be ministering together to Pacific Islanders again.

That week, more than 20 young students with a hunger for

God listened to Alan teach about God's character and father heart, while I taught new worship songs and shared testimonies of my own fight with inferiority and rejection. Afternoons were spent counseling individual students together.

After the Thursday session, while we walked arm and arm back to our guest room, I noticed Alan looked a little pale.

"Darl, are you all right?"

"I'm really tired. I just wish it was our holiday again," he joked, using a favorite Liverpool quip that supposedly quoted welfare receivers when they got a job. I grinned and poked him in the ribs.

"You've never lost that Liverpool humor!" I teased, shaking my head.

"And you love every minute of it!" he shot back at me.

Taking a deep breath of the sea air as we walked along, I turned to look at the blue sky.

"I love this," I said contentedly. "There's nothing on earth I'd rather be doing! Working together, seeing people set free from bondage, coming to know what God is really like – it's so fulfilling."

"Absolutely," Alan agreed. "But I have to admit, I really do get more tired these days."

"So you're getting old!" I teased, and he looked at me with mock amazement.

"That's rubbish!" he responded. "You know everyone says how young I look!"

But coming to our room, Alan headed straight for the bed and soon fell asleep. Alan's latest angina test in November had proved all right, but he really did seem to be tiring more easily. An Auckland physician had recently suggested Alan add jogging to his old three-times-a-week exercise routine, and he was fulfilling that faithfully along with his prescribed medication.

Watching his athletic form in a deep sleep on the bed, I quietly crept about the room and settled in a chair to read.

"He'll be fine. He'll probably outlive me," I thought.

After the final day of class the next day, we packed up the car with plans to stop for an hour or so at the home of our old friends,

Bob and Olive Stutt. The former owners of the YWAM property, Bob and Olive were now in their late 60s, but it was obvious their age had not deterred them from zealously serving the Lord.

Once sitting down in their comfortable living room, we listened as they caught us up on all that happened since our last visit four years ago. Then the room grew quiet as Bob began to describe the series of three heart attacks he recently had.

"I believe I actually died during one of the attacks," Bob recounted.

Alan's eyes widened. "Did you see the Lord, Bob?" he asked in fascination.

Sure enough, Bob began to describe his encounter with Jesus just a few months before. All at once an undefinable sliver of foreboding ran through me, but I quickly got caught up in Bob's vivid description of his encounter with the Lord.

Our next stop was three days back with Ron and Janet in Auckland. With other speaking engagements ahead in Wellington and Christchurch, we became increasingly aware of how little time we had left with our family. We determined to make the most of our days with Ronald and his family, and to spend some time with Alan's mother in her home. We planned to come back through Auckland after our two weeks of ministry, but we knew we'd be rushed then. Our plans called for us to fly on to Hong Kong to minister at the YWAM center there and to visit Joy and Rob and their newly adopted Chinese son, Yik Wah. Then it would be on to Kona, our new home.

The night before we were to fly to Wellington, I could tell Ronald was struggling with us leaving again so soon. Because he left for work so early each morning, he had told us to be sure to say goodbye to him that night.

"Alan, I've got an idea," I suggested. "Why don't we creep upstairs with my auto harp and sing to Ronald the old song, 'Now Is The Hour For Us To Say Goodbye'? Maybe that will shake him out of his gloom about us leaving!"

He laughed. "Good idea. I mean, we're only going away for two weeks, and he makes such a big deal out of it."

We were both snickering as we crept quietly up the stairs to where Ronald and Janet and their daughter were watching the TV news in their sitting room. Seeing the door ajar, we loudly began singing over the television noise, blending our voices in harmony with exaggerated opera style. By the time it was over, Alan and I burst into the room and the five of us doubled up with laughter. A dramatic goodbye, to say the least!

The next day, we were off to Wellington for another fruitful week of ministry. Finishing late Friday morning, we then flew on to Christchurch to spend the weekend resting and preparing for the coming week. After settling into our guest room, we took a walk through the rose gardens surrounding YWAM's stately English-style buildings that had once been a rest home for the elderly.

Alan opened his week of teaching with his usual vigor. He loved challenging the discipleship students to give their all for God, and the students were riveted by his stories of God's faithfulness. That first night, he was asked to address the staff at a special meeting to close the 40 days of prayer and fasting YWAM was observing worldwide. We gathered with the 20 or so staff in the spacious meeting room as the worship time began.

From my seat at the back, I noticed Alan seemed a bit restless, not unusual before a meeting. I could tell he was praying for those in the room. As he at last moved to the pulpit and began expounding on the life of the prophet Elijah, I sensed a special presence of the Lord emanating from him. The atmosphere in the room was electric.

"We desperately need the double portion of the spirit of Elijah," he said, spreading out his arms for emphasis. His face was beaded with perspiration as he continued with all the intensity of his being.

"We need, as never before, powerful young men and women to take up the mantle from some of us older ones." He sprang out from behind the pulpit. "Now, just as Elijah prayed for Elisha before he was taken up, I'm coming around to pray for some of you as the Lord leads."

I got up to join Alan in praying for several people, including Murray Alcock, the fine young leader of the base. What a sense of destiny was in that room! God had great plans for the lives of these dedicated people, and Alan preached with more power than I'd ever seen.

That week, Alan continued to preach powerfully to the discipleship students as well, challenging them to live radically for God, ready to lay their lives down to the point of prison or death if it were God's will. We thanked God to see the unusually motivated group respond with all their hearts, already desiring to serve the Lord in missions.

While many Christians in New Zealand had prayed earnestly for us during the Athens trial, apparently many had never heard the outcome; so on Wednesday afternoon, Alan and I agreed to be guests on New Zealand's only Christian radio station, Radio Rhema. The talk show hostess, former YWAMer June Coxhead, zeroed in on events of the trial, and Alan recounted the story in detail.

"Now the church is going out in evangelism, and there's a great boldness as they share Christ freely," he said.

"Was it hard spending 18 months thinking you would have to face prison?" June asked.

"My mind was absolutely filled with the ministry of leading YWAM's smaller ship, the Good Samaritan. But at the time, I brought my tracts for a prison ministry and planned to write a book," Alan said. "When the apostle Paul was in prison, he must have thought, 'I might as well write to a few churches,' and we got most of our New Testament!"

We chuckled together before June continued. That was Alan, not one to waste any opportunity! Memories of the trial were now flooding my mind and I had to gather my wits quickly when June began asking me questions at the end of the interview. Inside, I felt an excitement brewing. What did God did have up ahead?

Once outside the station, we decided to cap the fulfilling day with a visit to the famous Christchurch City Square. Parking the

YWAM van, we strolled around the square admiring the Gothic-style cathedral. Stopping at a little food stand, we bought some chicken and french fries and sat down on a bench to eat.

"Alan, let's give our leftover food to the pigeons."

Alan agreed, and before long we'd made some friends among the flock of birds living on the square.

"Don't feed that fat one!" Alan ordered, playfully slapping my hand as he pointed to a greedy bird. Making a game of it, he grabbed my french fry and gave it to a scrawny bird.

"You're nuts!" I said, but played along, feeding the skinny ones only. When the food ran out, we laughed out loud.

"Here we are acting like a couple of kids!" I said.

"You're never too old for fun," Alan countered as our laughter died down.

The game over, we wended our way slowly along the Avon River until dusk crept on the scene. We drank in the beauty of the graceful willow trees delicately draping the gentle river, while ducks began curling their heads under for yet another night of sleep.

As we walked back to the van together, a little toy lamb caught my eye in one of the many specialty sheepskin stores lining the street.

"Look!" I said pulling Alan to the store window. "Yik Wah would love that!"

Ever since we'd learned of Yik Wah, our first grandchild by adoption, as well as Samuel and Carol's little girl born just two weeks ago, we'd become very toy conscious. We were anxiously awaiting a photo of newborn, Amber Leilani.

"Come on, Grandma," Alan said, tucking his arm in mine. "We'll get some toys later. Let's get back to the base. There's a full day tomorrow and I'm really tired."

A little reluctantly, I accompanied Alan back to the van. Surely there would be time to come back and get the toy later.

Maybe tomorrow.

26

A Warrior Runs Home

On Thursday morning, March 3, 1988, the buzzing of the alarm clock pierced my consciousness rudely at 6 a.m. All my life I hated that first noise of the morning! Stretching out my arms to shake myself awake, I looked over to the empty side of the bed. As usual Alan was up first, and I assumed he was out jogging in the tree-lined park around the corner.

Throwing my legs over the side of the bed, I followed my usual ritual of a shower and cup of tea to help me wake up before settling into a chair to read my Bible and pray. Alan would be back soon, so I left the electric kettle plugged in for his morning cup of tea.

Soon I was lost in my daily psalm, but as I was reading I gradually realized Alan was later than usual.

"That's strange," I thought. "He's never late." Looking at my watch, I could see it was already 7:15 a.m. Alan usually left as early as 5:45 a.m. Where could he be?

Deciding to go to the park to make sure he was all right, I pulled on my walking shoes. A walk would do me good anyway. Heading out the door, I began moving at a brisk pace as nagging thoughts filled my mind.

Why hadn't I suggested Alan carry identification in case anything ever happened to him? What if Alan collapsed from his angina problem? No one would know where he lived. Of course, I told myself, he'd probably just gone to another park a few blocks farther away and decided to stay for his prayer time. But I knew how he hated to be sweaty, so I couldn't imagine him doing that.

Arriving at Elmwood Park, I looked both ways. "This is dumb," I told myself. The early morning sun was a comfort on my face as I looked at the children walking to school along the path, but no joggers were in sight. I checked behind a hedge row just in case, but no one was there. At last, I started back.

"He'll probably be there when I get back," I told myself. Jogging quickly along the road back, I bolted up the stairs two at a time, half expecting to see Alan's face as I entered the guest bedroom. But, the room was empty.

A quiet dread came over me. I was not inclined to panic, but deep down I knew I must face my fears. Alan must be in the hospital after a heart attack!

Walking quickly to the kitchen, I saw our hostess during our stay was preparing the 8 o'clock breakfast we requested. Checking my watch, I saw it was now 10 minutes before eight.

"Marge, have you seen Alan?" I asked.

"Can't you find him?" she asked, her tender blue eyes taking on a deep concern.

"No, he went out jogging and never came back. He has angina, you know, and I'm afraid he might have had a problem with his heart." I felt my voice quivering, but I took a deep breath and went on. "I've already searched Elmwood Park, but maybe he jogged somewhere else."

Another staff worker named Margaret overheard the conversation and joined us. "I'll take you around the streets in the van," she said, grabbing my arm. "Come on!"

Soon we were scanning every possible place, but all we saw were people hurrying to school or work.

I looked at Margaret. "Surely, if he collapsed in the street, someone would have taken him to the hospital by now."

Arriving back at the YWAM center, we found Alan was still missing. The 10 or so staff members gathered around me in compassion and support as I shared my fears.

"Could I call the hospital for you?" a man named Roger offered.

"Yes, thank you!" I said gratefully. "I don't even know the hospitals here, so that would help."

I sat down on the sofa, my emotions numb, to wait for the results of the call. People were talking, trying to keep me occupied, but all I could think about was what might have happened. Sitting on the edge of my seat, I watched Roger across the room as he began dialing another number.

After a moment, Roger put the phone down, his face drained white. Coming toward me, he awkwardly put his shaking arm on my shoulder.

"He's dead, isn't he?" I heard my voice say. Was it really mine?

"Well," Roger began shakily, "there is a man there with Alan's description…The police are coming to talk to you."

All at once, I felt every part of me being sucked into a dark tunnel. It was Alan, I knew it! But just as suddenly, what felt like a solid slab of marble slid underneath me, upholding me. It was Jesus, supporting me supernaturally. I was steadied by my faith in the God of all the Earth, who does all things well.

Then, amazingly, a new thought struck me and I raised my hands to God. "Oh, Lord, thank you for the wonderful, wonderful holiday you gave us together!"

Yes, I felt overwhelmed, but as the tears began to flow, I was yet buoyed up by God's love. How infinitely kind God was! He knew all along, and allowed us to have that precious time together.

As I continued to weep, suddenly I thought of our children: Joy…Samuel…Stephen. And what about the grandchildren Alan was soon to visit? Now, he'd never see them!

I wept harder, hurting for Joy and Samuel. What a wonderful grandfather he would have made. I knew it was not Alan, but we who would suffer. Alan was now in the presence of God. Even thoughts of his grandchildren would be overtaken by being near his glorious Savior.

As I grappled with the reality of it all, I was at the same time thankful for the dear YWAMers there beside me, who were also stunned by the news. Some I hardly knew, yet the feeling of love and care in that room was so strong. As we waited, Marge quietly replaced numerous cups of tea which had gone cold, untouched.

Soon two police officers arrived and were led into another room. Marge led me in after them, and as they began asking questions to verify Alan's identification, I numbly answered. How I wished it were all a mistake! But deep inside, I knew it wasn't. Now I had to face what was ahead.

"I'm so sorry to ask you all these questions, Mrs. Williams," the young sandy-haired officer said. I was thankful for his caring attitude. "Uh, but we do need someone to come down to the hospital and identify his body."

Just then the young leader of the YWAM center, Murray Alcock, swung into the room, interrupting the police officer.

"Fay, I'm so sorry! I've just heard. What a shock to us all!" He put his arms around me in a comforting hug. After a moment, he stopped and looked at me in concern.

"Fay, I heard what he said. Why don't you stay here, and I'll go with the officers? When I come back, I'll help you call your children and relatives."

I met his compassionate blue eyes. That very afternoon Alan and I were to meet with Murray and his wife, Jo, to pray for their future plans.

"No, Murray," I sighed deeply, steadying myself. "I need to go. I need to see him."

"I understand. Marge and I will go with you."

Soon the three of us were driving to the hospital. Walking into the small hospital chapel, my heart lunged as I saw the familiar form lying on the gurney. It was Alan's!

All I could do was stare with blurred eyes at the body I'd loved for 27 years. There lay the father of our children. There lay the one who had been so used by God. As I gazed at him, intense pain filled my heart. But at the same time, the stark fact faced me that this was but Alan's handsome shell. His spirit was gone!

Walking up to him, I ran my fingers through his fine brown hair. Could it be really true? For a moment, it was almost as if I could hear him laughing in that Liverpool lilt: "Na, na! Told you I'd see the Lord before you!" And as I heard it, I even smiled through my pain.

Then Murray led the three of us in a prayer before he and Marge went out to leave me alone with Alan in the chapel. As I gazed at the body of my husband, I tried to absorb all the fine details of the face I would no longer have with me. I couldn't help thinking that the coldness of death was so foreign to Alan Williams, a man whose life exuded fire and passion.

Over and over, I fondled Alan's hair, and at last, mingled with hot tears, I managed a kiss on that cold brow. Inside I knew the real Alan was away enjoying a hero's welcome into the arms of God. Even in my loss I strangely rejoiced for him. Yet, at the same moment, I winced as I faced the realization I had now become a widow. Such an ugly word!

"Lord," I said simply through my tears, "do you have anything to say to me?"

Without a pause, I heard that familiar voice resounding clearly in my heart: "Keep running with the torch!"

Until now, Alan and I had been holding that torch together, running side by side with the light of the Gospel. But now the torch was left in my hands. And what had Alan said? "It's your turn now!" I knew I had no choice, and not even a desire, to do anything else. As I tucked the words away in my heart, I knew that although now alone, I would keep on running to my last breath.

After 20 minutes alone with Alan, I knew it was time to go. After a long, tender gaze, I left the chapel to rejoin Marge and Murray for the 10-minute ride back to the base and the wretched task that lay before me.

How would I tell our children of their father's death? Even with all the supportive people around me, I knew I could never face these next hours without that solid rock beneath me.

Murray and his wife Jo graciously closed all the business at the YWAM base to give me full attention as I made those dreaded phone calls, all prefaced by, "I'm afraid I have some very bad news." But each time I said it, inside I thought, yes, it's bad news for us, but not for Alan! Now in the presence of God, he was experiencing the greatest joy of his life. How could we weep for him?

As I called Joy and then Samuel, my heart ached to think their dad would never see their children. In a different way, I hurt for Stephen. He adored his father, but as yet had no wife or close relative where he lived in London to stand by him through this loss.

When it came time to tell Alan's mother, I pushed aside my own grief for the moment. How would she react? And how would his brother Ronald take the news? Tears formed in my eyes again as I remembered the joke we had played on Ronald and Janet just a week and a half ago, singing our goodbye song. How could we have known that would be the last time they saw each other on earth?

Somehow the task was just too hard for me then, so I finally asked Ronald's wife, Janet, to tell her husband the news. Likewise, I asked Alan's even-tempered brother, Keith, to break the news to his mother in person.

Meanwhile, the stunned Discipleship Training School students began a morning of prayer for our family. Later I received a handcrafted card signed by each of them, revealing not only the depth of their concern, but the depth of challenge they had received from Alan's life. Only the day before, he had dared them to give their lives away for God, imploring them to take up the mantle passed on by those who went before. Now he was gone, but his solid testimony stood. Who would take up the Gospel torch and run in his place?

All that day, helping hands were there for me, and I treasured my YWAM family immensely. When at last I wandered into my bedroom like a lost child, I was exhausted. It was late, but I didn't expect to sleep.

Opening the closet to undress for bed, I stared at Alan's clothes, hanging neatly in a row. I could hardly bear it as pain again seared through my heart. Sitting on the edge of the bed, I opened his briefcase and fingered his worn Bible and books, all in perfect order, naturally. The events of this day didn't seem possible. How I wished it were all a bad dream!

Then, still in shock, I did a very human thing. I slipped into Alan's pajamas. Sitting up in bed and staring into space until sleep finally came, I was somehow comforted by the familiar feel of those old pajamas. I guess it was a strange way to try to say goodbye.

The next day, I was so thankful to learn Alan's brother, Ronald, was flying to Christchurch to be with me. Only the power of prayer could have given him strength to do that! Meeting him at the airport, we fell into each other's arms weeping. After a few moments, I looked into his tearful blue eyes.

"Ronald, you realize what you did, don't you? God led you to prepare that apartment for us so Alan and I could have a wonderful time together. Just like when Mary in the Bible anointed Jesus for burial."

Still stunned, Ronald stared back at me with tears streaming down his face, but I knew he was greatly comforted by the thought.

The next day, Ronald and I flew back together to his home in Auckland. Coming through the door, we hugged Janet and the kids, all crying together but taking comfort in being together again. All too soon it was time for me to face the task of entering the bedroom Alan and I had so recently shared on that delightful holiday together.

Walking into the room, I was overwhelmed by the sight of the familiar bed and furniture as memories of those precious vacation days flooded my being. Alan's memory was all over the room. But he wasn't here anymore, not now, not ever.

All at once a dark feeling came over me, and an insidious, mocking voice began to whisper in my ear: "Just like Naomi, you went away full and came back empty!"

Here they were, the words of scripture. But this certainly wasn't God's voice, nor even my own.

"Oh, no Satan!" I said aloud with authority. "I came to God so empty, and He has made me full!"

"The delight of your eye has been taken away in a stroke!" mocked the voice again, another familiar scripture in Ezekiel 24:16.

"Yes, that's true," I cried aloud again, "but it was allowed by my God who is just in all His ways, and kind in all His doings!" (Psalm 145:17)

At once, the voice left me as suddenly as it came, and even in my pain, I felt a peace fill my heart. Deep inside I knew I had won a private battle that would see me through the time ahead.

Because Alan and I had planned to move to Kona, I had all our important papers with us. As I began funeral arrangements, I pulled out the yellowing piece of paper Alan had prepared for me years ago when his life was in danger in Argentina: "Steps to Take" in the event of his death. Scanning the list, I laughed and cried at the same time as I read the words, "Contact Christian undertaker and see if he'll undertake for you." It was a precious memory as I set about arranging for his body to be flown to Auckland and followed the written instructions for cremation and "KIDS: "Keep It Dignified and Simple." Even in the event of death, Alan never lost his sense of humor or ability to be organized.

The sad news shot around the world in no time, thanks to the YWAM communication system. From every continent, phone calls, telexes, flowers and even poems began to pour in, as if from one large, loving family all deeply touched by Alan Williams.

Then, one by one, our children began to arrive from London, Hong Kong and Honolulu. To my surprise, Samuel brought Carol and their newborn, Amber Leilani, and how God used the little darling to soften the pain during that time as I often held her in my arms.

The Tuesday morning of the funeral, March 8, I awoke early to the sound of heavy winds and rain outside. As the storm grew more intense throughout the morning, we learned a full-scale cyclone was raging throughout Auckland. Still, by early afternoon, I was thankful to see that despite the conditions, the church was packed to full capacity for the service.

Taking my seat at the front next to Joy and the rest of the family, I was touched to see that so many had come from different parts of New Zealand. What a strength they were to me! Representing YWAM Kona was our dear friend, Dr. Bruce Thompson, who years ago had promised to look after me and the family when Alan faced possible death in Argentina.

But missing from the familiar faces was my dear friend, Deyon Stephens, whose flight had been delayed by the cyclone. At least, I comforted myself, she would be here later to pray with me and share her wisdom for what I was facing now.

As the piano began the opening music, I was still numb, but determined to speak out what God had given me. Our friend, David Garratt, had agreed to lead the worship, and as he moved to the front of the church, I was surprised to see my daughter, Joy, rise to assist him in several songs of praise to God.

Afterward, Pastor Don Dunn gave welcoming remarks and invited those in the congregation to speak. One by one, friends from around the world expressed how much Alan meant to them and the impact he had made on their lives.

"Alan was a man of God in action, a man of spirit and passion," said Murray Alcock, echoing the tributes that many had already expressed. "He loved God with a passion, and God loved him with a passion too.

"Alan was out running when he died, and one of our students had a vision of Alan running through the park," Murray said. "As he ran, his body fell, but his spirit kept on running. That is so much like Alan Williams, a man who ran with God with all his heart, and God took him running."

Then Dr. Bruce Thompson read a moving letter on behalf of Loren and Darlene Cunningham, who sent regrets they couldn't attend, but would be leading another memorial service back in Kona:

"In announcing Alan's home-going, one of our leaders said we have lost one of our heroes in YWAM," Bruce read from the letter. "But today I would say we haven't lost a hero; he's been promoted. He's now enjoying his coronation in the presence of the King of Kings..."

Few eyes were dry as Bruce recounted events of Alan's life, his early pioneering days back in Kona as well as the trip to Argentina where Alan believed he would be martyred.

"Intercessor, pioneer, prophet," Bruce said with a catch in his throat. "A man with the zeal of the Lord of hosts. He loved a challenge and looked for it. He laughed with deep joy in the Lord, and his laugh was infectious."

Next Ronald read a poem he and his wife had written, and Alan's brother Keith and sister Gwen also recounted what Alan had meant in their lives. Alan's mother followed them to the podium, speaking haltingly in her thick Liverpool accent.

"You may think I didn't want Alan to go, but God called him and we're so proud." Her tearful eyes were now shining. "He was one of the most monkey-ish rascals when he was little, but oh, lordy, lordy, what a beautiful man he turned out to be with God at his side!"

I was now smiling through my tears as Samuel rose and began to relate his gratitude for all Alan had invested in his life. I thought how much his chiseled cheekbones and strong jawline were like Alan's.

"When I left home I realized how much my parents loved me and all that they've gone through to be who they are," he said. "I know that my brother and sister could stand up here with me and say that they were the best parents we could have ever had. My father was the most realistic example of Jesus I could have had, and his death has challenged me to be more like God. I hope I'm what he wanted me to be."

Then it was my turn. With a peculiar grace and strength, I

arose and walked to the podium.

"Many people talk a lot, but they don't live what they claim to be," I began deliberately. "The greatest tribute I can give to Alan is that what he preached from the pulpit he lived at home." I sighed deeply, and began again.

"To have died at 54 seems so young, but Alan lived a fuller life than some men live in 70 years," I said, speaking stronger as I went on. "Now I'd like to challenge you all with the sacred trust he's left us.

"Alan spent his life running with the torch of the Gospel. If he were here today, I believe he would now challenge you to also take up that torch he left behind, the torch of spreading the light of the Gospel throughout the world.

"Alan fought a good fight, he finished his race, he kept the faith; and now there is in store for him the crown of righteousness, which God the judge will award him." (II Timothy 4:7)

Then at my signal, the sanctuary was filled with the strains of a song called *Runner* by Twila Paris:

> Courier valiant, bearing the flame,
> Messenger noble, sent in His name,
> Faster and harder, run through the night,
> Desperate relay, carry the light, carry the light!
>
> Runner, when the road is long, feel like giving in,
> But you're hanging on, oh, runner, when the race is won,
> You will run into His arms...

Listening to the words, I remembered all the times we felt like giving up: in Rarotonga, on the ship, times when Alan felt so alone and his ministry had ended. But through it all, we hadn't given up.

And now, Alan's race was over. Alan Williams – husband, father, friend, teacher, prophet, intercessor, and God's Great Warrior – had run into His arms.

Epilogue

So many questions about my future remained after Alan's death. One morning while alone in Ronald's house, I sat on a chair beside my bed and began to pray aloud.

"What now, Lord? Am I still to go to Kona, alone?" I waited for a moment and deep inside, I knew it had always been His will for me. Then the realization hit me. It was I — not Alan — who had received the promise back in 1978 about living in Kona again some day.

"But what do you want me to do there, Lord?" I asked. "You know I've mostly served Alan's ministry all these years." Suddenly a deep loneliness engulfed me, and I began to weep. "Lord, I feel so insecure! Where will I fit?"

All at once Alan's words came back to my mind. "It's your turn now. It's your turn now!"

Then the book I'd been writing on and off came to mind.

"Lord, is this the time to finish the book I started?" I asked. "Please show me clearly."

Suddenly the shrill ring of the telephone interrupted my prayers. Picking up the receiver, I heard the voice of Janice Rogers, the leader of the Writer's Seminar I'd attended in 1987.

"Fay, I hate to bother you at a time like this, but Loren Cunningham asked me to invite you to the writer's school I'm leading in Kona next month. I know you've been working on a book, and the school could be just what you need to put it all together."

I could hardly believe my ears! I cried as I told her I'd just been praying about the book and my next step. This was the answer.

The book you now hold in your hands is the fruit of that directive from God. It was a far longer and more difficult project than I could have ever imagined, but God's grace saw me through, just as it had for Alan and me all those years.

Besides working on the book part-time, I've found my last few years filled with fruitful service. While living in Kona, I used my growing writing skills to help pioneer the quarterly On Line newspaper at the University of the Nations (U of N), formerly Pacific and Asia Christian University. I have also served on the staff of U of N's School of Worship and School of Intercession, Worship and Spiritual Warfare. I have traveled to Switzerland, Singapore and Tonga to work with these schools and taken ministry trips back to Greece, Hong Kong, Jamaica, the Cook Islands, Fiji, Tonga, Western Samoa and Tahiti. Through it all, God has been faithful to supply all my needs and lead me into a ministry in my own right, just as Alan said.

Joy and Rob are now back in Rob's nation of Canada where he is pursuing further education at Regent University after 13 years in Hong Kong, where he and Joy pioneered the Cantonese School of Biblical studies, (SBS). They are raising their two adopted Chinese sons, Yik Wah and Yik Man.

Samuel and Carol and their growing daughter, Amber and Brittany Alani still live in Honolulu, where Samuel works in construction and is involved in church youth work.

Stephen and his wife Laura, who was formerly a preschool teacher on the Anastasis are currently in Virginia where Stephen is working at the international news desk of the 700 Club, and is pursuing his B. A. in communications at Regent University.

In 1992, YWAM opened its first Discipleship Training School in Greece, and Kostas Kotopoulos, to whom Alan gave the Greek Bible, has completed his YWAM training and is serving as an outreach leader for evangelism teams from the Anastasis.

The Mercy Ships ministry continues to thrive. Crews on the M/V Anastasis and M/V Good Samaritan have given medical and dental treatment to tens of thousands of patients in Africa, Eastern Europe, South America and the Caribbean Basin. They have also constructed clinics, schools and churches and shared the Gospel in hundreds of cities and villages.

Mercy Ships now have four ships. The most recent ship is

the *Caribbean Mercy* which works out of Florida. The Good Samaritan is now renamed the *Pacific Mercy* as it serves the Pacific Islands from New Zealand.

The Pacific Ruby was dedicated to Alan's memory. That ship was used in 1991 to carry a YWAM team to the only geopolitical country in which the mission had not yet ministered – tiny Pitcairn Island in the South Pacific.

Our pioneering efforts in the Cook Islands so long ago have also produced lasting fruit, especially from Alan's prayer and fasting for the students of the pastors' college. We learned some years ago that the college's present leader received Christ as an 11-year-old boy through Alan's preaching. YWAM now has a thriving ministry there.

People still stop me to say what an impact Alan made on their lives, and I know exactly what they mean. To me, Alan was not just a husband or the father of our children, but one who always provoked me to a dedicated, disciplined lifestyle.

As God challenged me upon Alan's death, I've committed myself to keep running with the torch of the Gospel. How about you? Remember, God takes the weak things of this world to confound the wise, a truth I've seen over and over in my own life. God can use even the weakest of vessels!

For those who have not yet joined the Christian life, I encourage you, it's never too late to enter at the starting gate, Jesus Christ Himself. For those already in the race, I urge you not to give up. Jesus and all of us need you!

Fay Williams, 1995

> *"Runner, when the road is long, feel like giving in,*
> *But you're hanging on. Oh Runner, when the race is won*
> *You will run into His arms…"*

> *From* Runner *by Twila Paris*

Youth With A Mission

Youth With A Mission is an international, interdenominational Christian mission reaching out to the world with the Gospel of Jesus Christ through evangelism, training and mercy ministries. YWAM has 7,000 full-time staff and annually trains approximately 25,000 short-term workers to minister in over 390 operating locations in 100 countries.

University of the Nations has as its primary aim the equipping of men and women to be communicators of the Gospel to all people of all nations in response to Christ's Great Commission found in Matthew 28:18-20. U of N has 150 training locations worldwide, and an international staff and student body. The original campus is located in Kona, Hawaii.

For more information on short-term missions opportunities or training with YWAM's University of the Nations, write to: Youth With A Mission, Registrar's Office, 75-5851 Kuakini Hwy., Kailua-Kona, HI 96740. Telephone: (808) 326-7228.

Mercy Ships, the maritime missions arm of YWAM, ministers to needy people in developing nations around the world. Through the "two hands of the Gospel" approach, the ships' crew offer practical help, free of charge, through disaster relief and medical aid, while sharing the Good News of Jesus Christ.

For more information, contact Mercy Ships, PO Box 2020, Lindale, Texas 75771-2020. Telephone: 1-800-772-SHIP.